ENABLE
Developing Instructional Language Skills

by Beth Witt

Foreword by
Marion Blank, Ph.D.

Communication Skill Builders

3830 E. Bellevue/P.O. Box 42050
Tucson, Arizona 85733
(602) 323-7500

Duplicating

You may prefer to copy the designated reproducible materials by using stencils or spirit masters. It is not necessary to tear pages out of this book. Make a single photocopy of the desired page. Use that photocopy to make a stencil or spirit master on a thermal copier.

© 1989 by

**Communication
Skill Builders, Inc.**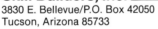
3830 E. Bellevue/P.O. Box 42050
Tucson, Arizona 85733
(602) 323-7500

ISBN 0-88450-308-9   Catalog No. 7476

10 9 8 7 6 5 4 3 2 1
Printed in the United States of America

Dedication

No woman with a husband, family, career, *and* creative bent *ever* successfully achieves her goals without a lot of support from her husband. Despite the fact that I have lived a life with lots of "hills and valleys," I have been *so* lucky to have the partner that I do, "beside me all the way!" This program is lovingly dedicated to my "super-enabler" of a husband, Larry Witt.

Note of Appreciation

Another special area of my life has been having the good fortune to always work with such a kind, tactful, and talented editor. Ricky Bourque, thanks for being *my* very special editor and friend!

About the Author

Beth Witt is presently an Educational Assessment Teacher for the Caddo Parish (Shreveport, Louisiana) Pupil Appraisal Team, a position she has held since 1983. As such, she specializes in Early Childhood programs, providing consultation, in-service workshops, and diagnostic evaluations for children from birth to six years of age. She has worked as a teacher of mentally retarded and of noncategorical preschool handicapped children for Bossier Parish (Louisiana) schools and for Caddo-Bossier Association for Retarded Citizens' Goldman School. She has worked as an Educational Consultant at Ruston State School in Simsboro, Louisiana.

Mrs. Witt is the codeveloper of the TOTAL program, a language-organized developmental package. She later authored *TOTAL Lesson Plans* and *TOTAL Summertime Activities*. She is a contributing author for *Parent Articles* published by Communication Skill Builders.

Mrs. Witt has presented workshops for school districts across the country; and for the Council for Exceptional Children national conventions, the national Head Start convention, Louisiana Association of Children Under Six conventions, both the Texas and Louisiana Early Childhood conventions, and the Texas Educational Diagnostician Convention.

Mrs. Witt is a member of the Communication Skill Builders Author Advisory Board. She has served as president of both her local CEC chapter and the Louisiana CEC Division of Mental Retardation. She is Louisiana CEC Federation Newsletter Editor, vice-president of Northwest State School Parents Group, and a board of directors member of Child Care Services of Northwest Louisiana. She is a Volunteer Educational Consultant for the Lighthouse Preschool for disadvantaged youngsters.

Contents

Foreword by Marion Blank, Ph.D. vii

INTRODUCTION

Overview 3

    What Is Listening Comprehension? 4

    The Two Developmental Levels of *ENABLE* 5

    Assessment 6

    Considerations for Evaluating Weaknesses 8
        Sensory 8
        Social-Emotional and/or Cognitive 8
        Memory 9
        Language/Basic Concept Development 9

    Individual Development 10

    Developmental Sequences for Listening Comprehension 11

    Functional Fund of Information 14

    Appropriateness of Responses 14

    What Is Question-Answer Competence? 15

    Programming for Question-Answer Competence 17

    Normal Acquisition of Question Forms 18

    Language Impaired Preschoolers and Question Forms 19
        Yes/No Questions 19
        What is he/she doing? Questions 20
        Where Questions 20
        Why Questions 21
        How and *When* Questions 23

    Importance of Question-Answer Competence 24
        Daily Group Checklist 24

    Response-Shaping Examples 26
        Associative Responses 26
        Inappropriate Response 26

    Pragmatic Suggestions in Use of *ENABLE* 27

ENABLE Assessment Materials
    Language Development in Early Childhood Classrooms 31

    Attending to Words and Sentences 36

    Memory and Memory Strategies 37

Directive Response Checklist 38

Question-Answer Competence Checklist 40

Question-Answer Competence Daily Group Checklist 42

References 43

Additional Resources 45

Level I
ENABLE I

Self 49
Family 57
Pets and Domestic Animals 65
Home 71
Furniture 79
Utensils 85
Simple Tools and Machines 91
Clothing 97
Self-Care 103
Transportation 109
Shopping 117
Community Helpers 125
Foods 131
Playtime 137
Nature 143

Level II
ENABLE II

Self 151
Family 157
Animals 165
Home 171
Furniture 179
Utensils 185
Simple Tools and Machines 191
Clothing 199
School 207
Health and Safety 215
Community People and Places 223
Foods 231
Playtime 237
Nature 243
Seasons 249
Holidays 257
Weather 265
Friends 271
Ball Games 277
Music 283

Foreword

A kindergartner, returning home after her first reading readiness test, described the experience to her mother. "We had to match letters today, like a big *A* with a little *a* and a Big *B* with a little *b*." She stopped and spontaneously amended her description, *"No, that would have been too easy. The letters were all mixed up. Like first there was an S, then a C, and then a P."*

Although she was not technically "listening," the child was nevertheless displaying the power of the listening comprehension concept that is central to Beth Witt's current work. The process of *active listening* is not bound to a sensory modality. It occurs, for example, in the visual mode when we are reading a book. The concept therefore is not so much a reflection of a modality as it is of the irrepressible human urge to scan the environment so as to find meaningful patterns by which to comprehend the world. The kindergartner, with no demands on her to do so, was exhibiting this predisposition. The intentional randomization that the tester introduced was seen not as a set of distractions but rather as part of a meaningful pattern.

That same randomization could have been overwhelming for a child in difficulty. Instead of seeing it as a clever move on the part of the test designer, the child would be prone to see it as a confusing disruption of the usual alphabet sequence. The consequences of this difference are profound. It leads children in difficulty to experience the variability of the normal world not as a source of interest and excitement, but as a generator of confusion and anxiety. Nowhere is this confusion more evident than in the world of language. Our verbal system, with its endless counterpoint of syntactic, semantic, phonological, paralinguistic, and pragmatic rules, represents almost the essence of unmanageable variability.

The core of effective intervention is to offer the children some order to this overwhelming system so that they may begin to extract the central patterns and rules that they have not independently grasped. Although our knowledge of how to proceed in this complicated area is far from complete, we do know some of the vital parameters. It is essential to have many, many repetitions so that the children have the time on task they need to discern the rules. At the same time, the teaching must involve motivating activities that will capture their attention and thereby make the effort worthwhile. The activities should also be varied so the children "see" that the rules hold over a variety of situations.

Beth Witt has attended to all of these factors in developing her program. While her comments focus on the goal of "instructional language," the acquisition of the material she is teaching is of far greater consequence. It will help young children not only in the school setting, but in understanding and relating to the vital role that listening comprehension plays in their everyday lives.

Marion Blank, Ph.D.

Director of Developmental Neuropsychology Service
Children's Hearing Institute
New York City

INTRODUCTION

Overview

Listening with comprehension—a "mystic" blend of auditory and visual attention, interest and desire to interact and respond, and evolving language and cognitive organization—is probably the most important "school-enabling" skill. This ability is surely as basic and necessary in substance—if not in degree—to children with severe levels of mental and language handicaps as it is to normal children and children with milder levels of those handicaps. Normal and mildly handicapped children have to learn to focus their attention on more and more selective and abstract aspects of narratives and discussions, to develop an effective working memory *and* to organize reasoned and appropriate responses, so that someday they can meet the instructional demands of the "elementary mainstream." The more limited children have to learn to attach meaning to sounds and gestures made by others, while learning to make appropriate and consistent responses to these, in order to control their behavior enough to attend and develop adaptive and functional skills.

And early childhood—the period between birth and six years of age—is the *critical* period for development of listening comprehension!

Two other most important school-enabling skills that develop during this early time are perceptual-motor and social-emotional abilities. The three are irrevocably tied together in competently functioning youngsters. Fundamentally, adequate attending skills, impulse control, and participatory/ cooperative behavior—basic elements of social-emotional skills—*must* be present for children to learn to combine listening with comprehending; and the children who consistently comprehend and respond with success establish strong self-concepts, motivation to learn, and confidence in learning—higher-level social-emotional skills. Motorically, adequate perceptions or integrated sensory impressions (the result of appropriate attending) are necessary for youngsters both to formulate comprehension of abstract concepts *and* to make correct gross- and fine-motor responses to directions, thus blending listening comprehension and perceptual-motor development.

Youngsters who enter kindergarten or first grade with weak or underdeveloped proficiency in listening comprehension are immediately and continually "at risk" for limited academic success and school failure. They have difficulty or are always "a step behind" in following directions and answering questions. They remember little from stories or discussions. There is a strong correlation between ineffective listening comprehension and the later development of inadequate reading comprehension (Dechant 1970; Stanovich 1982). Eventually, teachers expect and demand less of such youngsters, and the circle of failure is inevitably closed.

Groups that appear particularly apt to be weak in this important communication skill include:

1. Socioeconomically delayed (disadvantaged) youngsters

2. Mildly impaired preschoolers ready to reenter the mainstream after a period in early childhood-special education classrooms

3. Youngsters with slight to mild degrees of delay in:

    a. Sensory areas (vision and/or hearing)

    b. Language development (vocabulary, pragmatics)

    c. Specific learning skills (memory, perception, association, and organization)

    d. Behavioral areas (attention deficits, impulse control weaknesses, and interactive problems).

Frequently, weak listening comprehension alone will not be identified in the early childhood period or will not qualify those children for a special preschool placement or language therapy. Thus they begin primary programming with a serious strike against them.

Because ineffective listening comprehension is so prevalent as a limiting educational factor for elementary children, *ENABLE* was developed. *ENABLE* aims to provide early childhood teachers and caretakers of typical and atypical children with the structure and activities for systematic development of effective listening comprehension.

What is Listening Comprehension?

Normal babies and toddlers gradually and increasingly gain "information" from listening to people talk to them. In older preschoolers, a skill called *active listening* develops in which youngsters become cognitively aware that they *do not understand* specific words or concepts. At such a point, the normal preschooler develops strategies for coping with the breakdown. The more secure youngsters may ask, "What does *before* mean?" or "How you *get* between?" or "What's a kazoo?" Less verbal children or those with poor memory or attentional skills may constantly ask "What?" in hopes of receiving repetition, explanation, or more time to process the problem through to a response. The less confident children and those who lack the vocabulary for requesting help will constantly take a visual approach and watch their neighbors to see how to respond. The latter children become "step-behind" and inadequate comprehenders. Without systematic assistance to develop competent listening comprehension, these children learn less and less in elementary schools.

To help one develop a skill, we must begin with a good working definition of that skill. Primarily, basic listening comprehension includes two important skills: the ability to process and respond appropriately to directives of increasing difficulty and complexity through gross- and fine-motor performances; and the ability to comprehend the demands of given question forms and respond appropriately with accurate information (a verbal performance called question-answer competence). Basic listening comprehension is a coming together of adequate receptive and expressive language, gross- and fine-motor, social-adaptive, and cognitive skills. To progress from *basic* listening comprehension to *enabling* listening comprehension, youngsters must move through expanding levels of (1) memory skills, necessary for retrieval, organization, and output of specific aspects of information heard in *previous* narratives or discussions, and (2) comprehension and use of abstract concepts, or development of an "instructional language" vocabulary (Boehm 1986; Bracken 1984). The ability to "chunk together" a strand of thought from an ongoing discussion or narrative and hold it in working memory to reason about, mentally organize together with presently held information, and later answer relevant questions, should have developed by late early childhood.

The Two Developmental Levels of *ENABLE*

ENABLE consists of activities on two levels. The first level—ENABLE I— is appropriate for children with chronological, language, and/or cognitive ages of one to three years. The second level—ENABLE II—is appropriate for children with chronological, language, and/or cognitive ages of three to six years.

ENABLE I typically may be used in day-care centers or "nursery" schools for toddlers to early preschool, or in programs for three-year-old disadvantaged children, or in preschool handicapped programs, or in programs for older moderately handicapped children who need to develop functional, basic language skills. (See pages 31-35, Types of Language Development in Early Childhood Classrooms.) ENABLE I also may be used for children in four-year-old preschools who lack development of specific early concepts or have rather weak memories. Children should be successful with the majority of activities in ENABLE I before participating in ENABLE II activities.

ENABLE II is intended to be used in preschools through second grade for normal and disadvantaged children and special education programs for mildly impaired children (last year of preschool handicapped, early learning disabled, mild mentally handicapped, and language handicapped).

Material includes an organizational and informational overview, assessment material, and two levels of unit-organized activities and narratives for the development of listening comprehension. ENABLE I, for younger or more limited youngsters, presents activities for development of basic directive responses and typical question-responses expected of children from one to three years. At the same time, this systematic unit approach "chunks" information so that repetition and redundant experiences with these activities and narratives help young children to develop a "functional fund of information" about important environmental categories. The units organizing the activities, discussions, and narratives of ENABLE I are: self, family, pets and domestic animals, home, furniture, utensils, simple tools and machines, clothing, self-care, transportation, shopping, community helpers, foods, playtime, and nature. Visual materials to aid use of each unit include a list of suggested manipulatives, flannel board illustrations of objects and places, and pictures of people and animals which can be cut out and used as stick- or finger-puppets or standing figures.

ENABLE II (for children three to six) also is organized around a unit approach. Twenty somewhat higher-level units extend children's informational horizons. ENABLE II includes compound and complex directives about each unit (the directives usually organized in a game-like format) and narratives of increasing length and complexity followed by relevant reasoning and inferential questions. Art includes a few additional puppet figures and flannel board pictures. Two of the three stories in each unit are illustrated. One story without pictures is always included; children in the five- to seven-year range should begin to be able to mentally carry forward and hold the main narrative elements *without* visual aids to their memory. ENABLE II units are: self, family, animals, home, furniture, utensils, simple tools and machines, clothing, school, health and safety, community people and places, foods, playtime, nature, seasons, holidays, weather, friends, ball games, and music.

Also emphasized throughout the two levels of *ENABLE* (although much more so in ENABLE II) is the development of "instructional language" concepts. Current tests used to suggest the concepts receiving attention are *Boehm Test of Basic Concepts—Revised, Preschool and Kindergarten Versions* (Boehm 1986), *Bracken Basic Concept Scale* (Bracken 1984), and *Brigance Diagnostic Inventory of Early Development* (Brigance 1978).

ENABLE is designed to be used easily by teachers, paraprofessionals, parents, and caretakers.

Assessment

Effective use of a product with children is largely dependent on knowing which areas need addressing and where to begin. Listening comprehension is a skill which encompasses a number of subskills. To adequately determine the specific cause of weakness in a young child's comprehension, the following areas should be considered:

1. *Vision and hearing skills.* These sensory abilities are often screened (and sometimes given medical attention) as part of a diagnostic evaluation. However, because a number of visual weaknesses (amblyopia, farsightedness) first occur or are first noticed near age three, and because many children suffer intermittent hearing loss (which can significantly interfere with language and listening development) due to fluid build-up from recurrent colds and ear infections, teachers and parents should consistently monitor these abilities during the early childhood period. Medical evaluation should be sought when a sensory problem is suspected.

2. ***Attention skills.*** (See page 36, Attending to Words and Sentences.) This is the emerging ability of young children to focus auditorily or visually on exploring objects in order to learn; the interaction of persons and/or the attributes of persons in a communicative fashion; and/or the attributes and details of objects and pictures. A variety of sensory, cognitive/neurological, language, and social-emotional weaknesses can inhibit the adequate development of attentional skills in young children. Strengthening attention usually requires both classroom structure and a behavior-shaping approach.

3. ***Impulse control.*** This is the ability to *maintain* attention productively in order to learn, without being regularly drawn by sights, sounds, or activity in the immediate environment. Generally, impulsive children lack inner organization, and helping them develop organization and control will be imperative for them to be able to learn to listen productively. Again, physical structure and behavior-modification techniques will be necessary.

4. ***Emotional well-being.*** Young children must exhibit the interest and desire (social-emotional constructs), as well as the ability (cognitive construct), to respond to and interact with peers and adults, for comprehension skills to extend and progress. Programming to children individually, through considering their level of competence in every area and moving them forward from that point, is the prime consideration in strengthening the emotional well-being of children. This eliminates the factor of frustration.

5. ***Memory.*** This is the emerging ability to remember and later integrate heard and seen information. Young children move forward through an increasing complexity of memory levels—from short-term memory, through working memory, to storage, where information is integrated with existing information and can be called up much later.

   Children with memory deficits will require that teachers both use specific strategies in stretching their memory potential and teach these strategies to the children themselves as soon as they are cognitively ready. (See page 37, Memory and Memory Strategies.)

6. ***Adequate communication development.*** This is the increasing ability to attach meaning to sounds, words, and sentences, along with the motivation to use such understanding to respond to and communicate with others. An assessment of language development, for listening comprehension uses, should focus on vocabulary, auditory memory, pragmatics, and question-answer competence.

Considerations for Evaluating Weaknesses

An informal assessment of these areas can be conducted in an early childhood classroom, through observation structured by attempts to answer the following questions:

Sensory

Is vision adequate between ten and twenty feet from teacher?

Are perceptions being made about "parts" or specific aspects of pictures?

Are hearing and attention improved with louder or deeper voices?

Is there evidence of auditory misperception? (For example, the child points to tongue when asked to show thumb.)

Is the child obviously able to hear a single voice or message over conflicting sounds?

If the answer to any of these questions indicates a deficit, a medical evaluation of the weak sensory area should be recommended to the parents.

Social-Emotional and/or Cognitive

Is attention best one-to-one, in a small group, or in a large group?

Is attention best when moving objects or looking at pictures?

Do sights, sounds, or activity distract?

Does lack of structure in environment inhibit the youngster's ability to maintain adequate attentional levels?

Is there evidence of abnormal degree of shyness or withdrawn behavior (no participation), aggressiveness, resistiveness, or lack of interest?

Is maintenance of topic an interfering factor in comprehension?
a. Does the child get completely off topic usually?
b. Are responses bizarre, possibly indicative of emotional disturbance?

Information gained from answering these questions can be used in structuring the classroom environment and the individual child's interactions so as to maintain and extend adequate attending levels and decrease impulsive or negative behavior. Consultation from a school psychologist (if available) can aid in judging if weak attention is due to poor cognitive or social-emotional development or both. Poor cognitive development will require much repetition and a slowed, simplified rate of teaching, while poor social-emotional development will require more emphasis on reduced frustration level and positive social interaction.

Memory

Is short-term auditory or visual memory weak?

Is physical assistance or visual cuing necessary to elicit responses?

Through which strategy is working memory best?
a. Rehearsal—repeating core words of directive repetitively
b. Rhythmic presentation (singing, verse, "rapping")
c. "Chunking"—learning digits or material in "clumps" rather than one at a time and touching different finger with each clump
d. Associating—putting relevant information together (shoes—socks—foot)

Is more time needed for processing (10 to 15 seconds)?

Is occasional echolalia functional (that is, does it help processing and retrieval)?

Is information from presentation of sequenced information (narrative or discussion) remembered best when pictures are used?

Answers to these questions can guide the teacher in assisting youngsters to make the most of their memory, to extend it when possible, and to compensate with a multisensory memory approach when necessary.

Language/Basic Concept Development

Is response-shaping or demonstration needed to elicit appropriate answers?

Are the demands of given question forms understood? Where is the child in the sequence of emerging question-answer competence?

Is echolalia inhibiting (empty repetition with no evidence of processing or communicative intent) or used in a communicative fashion?

Can the youngster predict or infer?

Does the youngster have limited comprehension of concepts?
a. Can quantitative, positional, and other concepts be identified in pictures?
b. Can the child respond to concepts embedded in directions?

Do background perceptions or culture interfere with the youngster's ability to comprehend at presently demanded levels?

This information can be used to help direct and question children at their present level of competence, gradually extending their abilities forward. Some of the questions can be answered using the assessment material in *ENABLE*. (See pages 38-39, Directive Response Checklist; and pages 40-41, Question-Answer Competence Checklist.) Others can be answered with the assistance of speech-language pathologists. Some can be answered with increased familiarity with *ENABLE*, as all materials are leveled according to stated age expectations.

Individual Development

Any assessment of listening comprehension should always include a consideration of where a youngster is in a given sequence. To assist teachers in assessing the major areas of listening comprehension, the following sequences are presented for responding correctly to directions, answering questions appropriately and accurately, and participating in and benefiting from discussions and narratives. A guide for development of a functional fund of information also is included. Specific short assessment tools for evaluating directive response and question-answer competence, with scoring criteria and required testing materials, are included in Directive Response Checklist (pages 38–39) and Question-Answer Competence Checklist (pages 40–41). If evaluation of instructional language concepts is necessary, use of the previously mentioned *Boehm* and *Bracken* tests and the General Knowledge subtest of the *Brigance Diagnostic Inventory of Early Development* is recommended.

Developmental Sequences for Listening Comprehension

Age Range Expectancy   **Skills**

A. Responding correctly to directions

6-12 months

1. Routine-oriented directives. Very simple directives heard over and over in familiar environments (home, school) and usually visually cued through gestures and "body language":

   a. Whole body responses: *Come. Sit. Stop. No.*

   b. Object movement: *Let's go. Do this. Give. Bring.*

12-24 months

2. Simple one-step directives. Expansion of routine commands by adding new labels as objects:

   a. Choice of one item: *Bring me cup.*

   b. Choice of two familiar objects: *Give me shoe.*

   c. Choice of three familiar objects: *Give me crayon.*

2-6 years

3. Compound directives:

   a. Two-step directives:

   (1) Directives connected in some way: *Go to table, bring me spoon.*

   (2) Nonrelated directives: *Touch your stomach; turn around.*

3-6 years

   b. Three- to five-step directives. Focus on extending memory, vocabulary, and ability to respond in sequence.

2½-5 years

4. Complex directives. Simple and compound directions with embedded concepts (position, quantity, quality). One or two sentences may require a number of steps in retrieving, processing, and organizing: *Stand on the big red square behind the box and close your eyes.*

3-5 years

5. Conditional directives. May be very difficult because of youngsters' tendency to imitate visually rather than verbally respond and because of the need to understand and process condition: *If I _____ , then you _____ ; When I _____ , you _____ ; If I raise my hand, you close your mouth.*

4-6 years

6. Simple worksheet directives carrying information over from previous discussions: *Now that we understand what difference is, put a circle around the different one on each line.*

Age Range Expectancy	Skills

B. Answering questions appropriately and accurately

1-2 years

1. Answering basic labeling questions about present, visual information: *What is this/that?;* child responds *Cup. Who is this?;* child responds *Mama* (limited number of persons significant to child).

2-3 years

2. Answering questions requiring some manipulation of information (about present and visual objects or persons):

   a. Affirmation/negation (Yes/No): *Is this a ball?; Do you want a cookie?*

   b. Actions: *What is he/she doing?*

   c. Discrimination: *Which one cuts?* (pointing answer)

   d. Early locations: *Where's Daddy?; Chair; Outside* (child may not provide preposition + object)

3-4 years

3. Answering questions requiring the ability to associate information and comprehend early, basic concepts (present, visual information):

   a. Position: *Where is your coat?;* child responds *In my locker.*

   b. Function: *What do you do with scissors?;* child responds *Cut with them.*

   c. Situation: *What do you do when you're hungry?;* child responds *Eat.*

   d. Attribute: *Which one is red/big?*

3½-4½ years

4. Answering questions that require reasoning judgments (present, visual information):

   a. Cause: *Why do we need coats?;* child responds *To put on and keep warm.*

   b. Manner: *How do you run?;* child responds *We run fast!*

4½-6 years

5. Answering questions that require ability to sequence or comprehend early time concepts (with or without visual aids):

   a. Ordering/method: *How do you draw a person?;* child responds *First, you draw a head, then eyes and mouth, and then you draw arms and legs.*

   b. Cause: *How do we get seeds to grow?*

   c. Time concepts: *When do we eat breakfast?;* child responds *In the morning.*

4½-6 years

6. Answering questions that require the ability to make predictive judgments: *What will happen if he falls?; How can he get there in time?*

Age Range Expectancy	Skills

C. *Participating in and benefiting from discussions and narratives*

    1. Discussions, using objects and pictures:

1-2 years
      a. Labeling. Children can handle objects and point to pictures and name: *Cup.*

2-3 years
      b. Describing. Children can look at pictures and provide short, descriptive phrases that combine objects and actions, objects and locations, or objects and attributes: *Hold cup; Her red cup.*

3-4 years
      c. Discussing. Children can pull from a functional fund of information which they have developed to provide several short sentences about a multiimage or situational picture: *Those ladies drinkin' coffee. Mama drinks hot coffee. I like coffee with milk.*

4-5 years
      d. Defining. Children can organize information, provide categories, and make judgments and inferences. *Coffee is a hot drink. People like to drink it in the morning. You can put sugar and milk in it.*

    2. Demonstrating comprehension after narratives:

2-3 years
      a. After hearing two to four sentences and viewing simple pictures, children can answer basic labeling or discriminatory questions: *Who/what is this? What doing? Where is _____ ?*

3-4 years
      b. After hearing four to six sentences and viewing somewhat more complex pictures, children can answer associative/conceptual questions: *Where? What do with? Why?*

4-5 years
      c. After hearing six to eight sentences and probably viewing pictures, children can answer reasoning questions: *Why/how? What happened? When?*

5-7 years
      d. After hearing eight to twelve sentences, youngsters can answer sequenced, time, or inferential questions, *possibly* without benefit of pictures.

Functional Fund of Information

Use of a language unit approach (teaching core categories of words during specific time frames) can greatly facilitate development of the functional fund of information children must acquire to competently answer questions and follow directions.

A functional fund of information for youngsters in the early childhood period should include the following:

Age Range Expectancy	Skills	Examples
1-3 years	1. Labels (Home; Community Objects and People)	chair
	2. Actions	sitting
	3. Locations (place, part, space)	inside, seat, back
	a. Rooms of home	in family room
	b. Position	on the rug
	c. Community areas (stores, parks, natural areas)	in park
3-5 years	4. Attributes	
	a. Color	brown
	b. Shape	round
	c. Quantity	one
	d. Texture	hard, wooden
	e. Taste/smell	N/A (not specific attributes of furniture)
	f. Affective	comfortable
5-6 years	5. Categories and Organizational Terms	
	a. Home categories (food, clothing, etc.)	furniture
	b. Community categories (transportation, helpers, stores)	park benches
	c. Association Sameness/Difference	*Use with table* *Like couch,* not *like stove*

Appropriateness of Responses

In order to judge whether youngsters have adequate listening comprehension, attention must be given to their responses. Judgment of response to directives involves making a determination as to why a youngster makes an incorrect response or is unable to respond. Is this failure due to a weakness in attention or memory? This question can be answered by determining if the youngster can repeat all or the salient parts of the directive presented. Is the failure due to lack of comprehension of one or more concepts included in the directive? This question can be answered by requiring the child to move objects or body parts to simple, one-step directives using this/these concepts. If the child cannot do so, the concept is not understood. In that case, break down the directive to determine the cause of failure, so as to prevent future failure.

What is Question-Answer Competence?

Judgment of children's responses to questions requires an understanding of question-answer competence by the examiner. Martha Parnell and James Amerman (1983) were the first to provide a framework for determining the competence of children's responses to questions. From their research, they present two criteria: *functional appropriateness* and *functional accuracy*. To be judged *functionally appropriate*, a response must provide "the distinctive kind or category of information required by the particular question form." *Functional accuracy* is applied to responses that "provide factual, acceptable, logical, believable information." (p. 136) A response *cannot* be judged functionally accurate if it is not first functionally appropriate.

As an example, consider the responses to the following question:

Question	Response	Functionally Appropriate	Functionally Accurate
Why do we have dishes?	On the table.	-	-
Why do we have dishes?	Because we wash them.	+	-
Why do we have dishes?	Because we have to eat off them.	+	+

Clearly, the latter response both meets the demands of the *why* question *and* provides the requested information.

Parnell and Amerman's research also looked at effects on competence of subject age, stimulus type, and WH question form. Stimulus types included: Type I—an action, person, or object stimulus immediately available to the subject visually ("What's that?"); Type II—a picture stimulus in the subject's view ("What's he doing?"); and Type III—no visual referential source ("When do you brush your teeth?").

The research conducted in this area by Parnell, Amerman, Patterson, and Harding and reported in Parnell and Amerman (1983) concluded with this important finding:

> Recognition and delivery of the general category of information required by a WH form may substantially predate the ability to respond with fact, logic, credibility, etc. The data also suggest that children in the three to seven year range are notably less successful in determining the kind of information as well as less able to provide the specific information desired by the originator of the question when the question refers to objects, events, and persons *not represented in the immediate setting.* With increasing age it becomes easier for a child to provide both appropriate and accurate information in response to WH questions of different forms and in association with varied types of referential sources. (pp. 138-139)

Berlin, Blank, and Rose (1980) wrote of the effects on young handicapped children's ability to attend to language, answer questions, follow directions, and participate in classroom discourse activities. They provide a framework for closing the "perceptual-language distance" that often exists in early childhood and elementary classrooms. These authors organized a hierarchy of abilities through which a youngster must pass to close this *perceptual* (view of an experience) and *language* (words used to discuss the experience) distance:

1. Matching perception. The child has to apply language to what is seen in the world (identifying, naming, or imitating): *What is this? What do you see?*

2. Selective analysis of perception. The child must focus selectively on aspects of material and/or integrate separate components into a whole (describing, completing a sentence, selecting object by characteristics or attributes): *What is he doing? What is happening? Which are round? Is it green?*

3. Reordering perception. The child must restructure or reorder perceptions according to language constraints (excluding, following sequenced directions, assuming role of another): *How did he fix breakfast? Which is not furniture? Could you do that?*

4. Reasoning beyond perception. The child must go beyond perception to talk about logical relationships between objects and events (predicting, explaining, or finding a logical solution): *Why did the farmer take good care of the cows? How can we make her happy? What should we do next?*

Like the work by Parnell and Amerman, this framework by Blank and colleagues appears to point out that young children are *more* able to answer questions about information presently visible to them. Their assessment tool, based on the above hierarchy of skills, is *Preschool Language Assessment Instrument,* or PLAI (Blank, et al. 1978). This test, for youngsters between three and eight years, is considered by many professionals to be an excellent predictor of a preschool child's readiness to meet the instructional language demands of the elementary classroom.

Programming for Question-Answer Competence

Both normal and language-deficient children can benefit from systematic attention to development of question-answer competence. Such attention should provide structured, repetitive training, using the developmental emergence of questions as a guide, and proceeding forward using:

Concrete, immediate, familiar objects, and events

Simple, colorful pictures (pre-remote object, event)

Reading a few lines of a story, with answers to questions visible in a picture

Reading a short story, with no picture to "cue" the response

Discussion about past or future events in the youngster's life.

For *each child,* wise teachers will assess competence with specific question forms, need for visual referents, and need to be given response shaping. Once this information is available, each youngster can be questioned from 50% to 75% of the time, using questions with which the child is competent and therefore successful, and about 25% to 50% of the time with question types which require training and response shaping. Each youngster then will maintain confidence in attempting to reason through a response. Providing parents with this information will provide carryover at home.

Two techniques for insuring children's success and continued effort are:

1. Recognize immediately when a child is "in trouble" with a specific question, and back down to a simpler question about the same information. For example:

    Teacher: Why do we have telephones?
    Child: (no response, fidgeting)
    Teacher (cuing by pretending to put invisible receiver to ear):
                    What do we do with telephones?
    Child: Talk on 'em.
    Teacher: Yes! We talk on the telephone. *Why* do we have 'phones?
    Child: To talk on.

2. Accept a functionally appropriate answer and shape it into a functionally accurate answer. For example:

    Teacher: What do we do if our teeth are dirty?
    Child: Get a blue toothbrush.
    Teacher: What do you do with your toothbrush?
    Child: It's in my bathroom.
    Teacher: Your toothbrush is in your bathroom. Do you go in there
                    when your teeth are dirty?

Child: Yes.
Teacher (*providing the answer in a yes/no question*):
           Does your toothbrush help you clean your teeth?
Child: Yes.
Teacher (*providing a visual cue by gesturally pretending to brush teeth*):
           What do you do when your teeth are dirty?
Child: I brush my teeth with my toothbrush.
Teacher: Good boy!

Staying with children until they have competently answered a question, with or without shaping, is *very important*! When a child says "Uh-h-h" and hesitates, and the teacher moves to the next child with the question, the first child receives a message: "*I am unable to perform as desired.*" That message is damaging to self-concept. In the worst scenario, it can cause a youngster to cease making even an effort.

Normal Acquisition of Question Forms

A number of renowned linguists have conducted research and published findings on the normal acquisition of question forms in young children. Prominent among these were Brown (1973), Bloom and Lahey (1978), and Ervin-Tripp (1971). These linguists and others found that young children begin to give responses to yes/no and WH questions before they actively begin to use those question forms. Most normal children between eighteen months and two years can distinguish between a question requiring a yes/no response and one requiring a missing constituent. ("Is this a shoe?" "Yes." "What is this?" "Shoe.") The only WH questions used and answered consistently by children who have less than a mean length of utterance of 2.75 is "What's that?" (Brown 1973). Research by Ervin-Tripp (1970) indicated that *who, what,* and *where* questions are learned earlier than *why, how,* and *when* because these early questions make reference to people, objects, actions, and locations—language abilities that develop early (one to three years). Conversely, cause, manner, and time concepts (the answers to *why, how,* and *when* questions) are cognitively oriented language abilities that develop in the late preacademic stages, from three through five (Cole 1982). These earlier question forms require basic discrimination abilities (choosing and/or identifying), whereas the higher question forms require some reasoning and sequencing of internalized information. Such tasks require mental processing, organizing, manipulating, and outputting—much more complex mental and language functioning. A recent study by Parnell, Amerman, and Harding (1986), utilizing nineteen language-disordered children of three to seven years, found that: (1) questions asked with reference to nonobservable persons, actions, or objects were the most difficult; and (2) *why, when,* and *what happened* were the most difficult of nine WH forms of the study (*which, where, what be, what do, who, whose, what happened, why, when*).

Language Impaired Preschoolers and Question Forms

Language impaired children do *not* always develop more slowly but in the same way as their normal peers. Certain question forms may prove particularly difficult for them because of a specific disability or dysfunctioning in the cognitive, perceptual, conceptual, or linguistic areas (Parnell and Amerman 1983).

Yes/No Questions

Even normally developing children occasionally will appear to be having trouble with the proper response to simple questions requiring a yes/no response. Many children who have learned (and have been reinforced) to nod their head (yes) or shake it (no) do *not* actually know the difference between yes and no. These children, who are probably still in the functional one- or two-word utterance (primitive sentence) stage, use *no* to indicate absence, nonexistence, or rejection. They are unable to discriminate completely the difference between denial and affirmation (Bolles 1982) and often merely nod their head to all yes/no questions addressed to them ("Do you want juice?" "Are you a girl/boy?"). But normal children quickly pass through this "first language" (Brown 1973) and soon effectively answer such questions. Many language impaired children, delayed by cognitive, sensory integration, memory, processing difficulty, or perceptual delays or disorders, spend rather a long time in this functional language stage and need special structured and sequenced training to learn to answer yes/no questions. Other preschool handicapped children may be able to repeat or express themselves in three- or five-word sentences and answer who/what/which questions but be unable to answer yes/no questions. A possible explanation is that "What is this?" (pointing) involves a question that has a visible answer and is thus easier for the child to answer; by merely labeling the object pointed to, the child answers the question—and is likely to be strongly reinforced for doing so. However, "Is this a _____ ?" or "Do you want _____ ?" is *not* answered by labeling a visible object. Since the answer is not concrete or visible, special training involving rewarding the correct positive-negative response may be necessary to develop competence with a yes/no form.

Another problem can be failure to recognize a rising intonation to indicate that such a sentence is interrogative (Fay and Schuler 1980). This can result in children merely repeating the question uncomprehendingly. Many "slow processing" children may repeat the question but may be only structuring themselves to retrieve the correct information. Given a minute of quiet, they may properly affirm or deny. Young children with auditory memory problems sometimes have a tendency to repeat the last word or two of a question ("Do you have a nose?" "Nose.") and fail to comprehend the *type* of information required. Such children would need training in extending their auditory memory gradually. For example, "Have nose?" (pointing to child). "Yes" (child points to nose). Some young children, however, repeat the last word of a sentence when they have failed to hear or understand what was said. Training in answering yes/no questions can be facilitated for some children (particularly the cognitively impaired and autistic) by training them to answer specific question-answer *sets* and focusing first on *yes* questions, then *no* questions (Lovaas 1981). Training such severely impaired children to gesturally or verbally answer yes/no questions concerning their needs can be a most functional achievement.

What is he/she doing?

Research by Bellugi and Klima (1966) indicated that most normal children learn to answer *what . . . doing?* questions during what the linguists describe as Period I (Mean Length of Utterance = 1.75-2.25). During this period, WH words are used to ask for the objects, actions, and locations that the children are able to label.

What . . . doing? questions are usually comprehended after the children can well answer "What's this/that?" requiring a label for an object (Lund and Duchan 1983). Language handicapped children, "stuck" for an extended period in the functional utterance (primitive sentence) stage, can exhibit real difficulty comprehending action words. Objects are visible and tangible, and so easier to label for the language impaired child. Such children may need actual "moving through" an action and then labeling it to achieve comprehension.

> Teacher (*while jumping*): See jumping. Show me jumping. (*Teacher assists child to jump*) Tommy jumping! Tommy is . . . *jumping!*

> Child (*echoing*): Jumping.

Choosing a core vocabulary of functional action words, helping the children experience them kinesthetically and visibly, and using telegraphic language in communicating with these children can facilitate a child's acquisition of *What is he/she doing?* questions (Witt and Boose 1984). "Verbs should refer to actions or processes in which the children frequently engage or to those they want others to perform or to assist them in performing" (Cole 1982, p. 148). This statement should be considered in developing a list of action words functional to young handicapped children and in training them to answer early verb questions—a task a child *must* achieve to progress to higher question forms that require association, reasoning, and sequencing.

Where Questions

Usually between twelve and eighteen months, children develop the ability to recognize that a simple *where* question, usually presented with a good deal of game-like sing-song ("W-w-where's Daddy?"), requires them to look or move toward a certain place. This emerging awareness of location usually results in motoric responses, such as head-turning, walking and looking around, soon pointing, and—gradually—verbal use of a nonspecific location word, such as "Dar!" ("There") or "Heah!" Around age two, most youngsters will answer *where* questions with a label for a place (locative), such as "table" or "room," and pointing. By age three, most youngsters can provide five or six positional concept phrases to *where* questions, the most common possibly being up/down, in/out, on, and around (Boehm 1986; Brigance 1978). However, many socioeconomically or learning delayed youngsters continue on to age four without developing a positional concept vocabulary, and answer all *where* questions with pointing and nonspecific phrases, such as "Right heah" or "Over there."

Games to teach positional concepts and their use in responding to *where* questions are a most important aspect of nursery and preschool programs for typical and atypical children. Potentially learning disabled youngsters often show difficulty early in comprehension of and response to both directives and questions requiring them to functionally understand positional concepts. Such training should always pair the *where* question immediately after the directive response and proceed through:

Activities requiring children to *move their bodies* to positional directives: *Get in the circle.*

Activities requiring them to move *body parts* (or later *body sections:* top/bottom; still later left/right) to positional directives: *Put your hand in the circle; Where's _____ ? Put something on the top of your body in the circle.*

Activities requiring them to *move objects* to positional directives: *Put the car in the circle.*

And lastly, *recognition* of *position* in *pictures: Where is the car in the picture?*

Why Questions

The *why* question, with its cognitive requirements, is very possibly the most difficult for the young handicapped child to comprehend. *Why* questions require such information as function, situation, cause, reason, explanation, and even background information that asks a child to project into the past or future and sequence events. Examples of these are: "Why do we have beds?" "Why do we go to a doctor?" "Why do we cook food?" "Why did she do that?" "Why are you sad?"

Preschool handicapped children who are unable to answer *why* questions may include:

Those who have not yet internalized and conceptualized enough information about self and environment to reason and make judgments

Children who possess the information to provide the correct answer but are unable to comprehend the *why* form and respond appropriately to the question form

Children with processing difficulties who are unable to manipulate mentally and properly associate the correct object and agent to "output" the correct answer

Children with attention deficits and/or sensory integration difficulties who have failed to "look, listen, and feel" well enough to formulate basic concepts and/or cause-effect judgments about objects and people in their environment

Children with severe auditory memory problems who can remember and repeat no more than two or three nonassociated words.

Preparing a child to answer *why* questions involves backing down to a very basic language level and moving the child through a series of activities that involves such things as:

Functional matching. Matching objects or pictures of objects to associated action words (bed—sleeping, telephone—talking, spoon—eating, chair—sitting)

Verbalizing an adjective descriptor (hungry, sleepy, cold) and requiring a child to choose an associative picture that meets the needs from a choice of three to five pictures (eating food, sleeping in a bed, putting on a coat)

Playing "What to do when" games with set-up responses to role play. For example, teacher asks, "What do you do when (you cut your knee, the telephone rings, you do good work)?" The child chooses among a table with bandages, answering the phone, or getting a hug. Then the child "pretends" the answer.

Providing discussions that illustrate for the child the function of a body part. For example:

Teacher: Bobby wants to see. Does he use his eyes or ears? (*covering the child's eyes*) Can he see?

Bobby: No!

Teacher (*covering Bobby's ears*): Can he see?

Bobby: Yes!

Teacher: Why do we have eyes?

Bobby: To see!

Providing activities that demonstrate cause and effect, such as mixing dirt and water and making mud ("Why is the ground muddy?" "Because water got on it. That's what happens when it rains!"); planting seeds, watering them, and putting them in the sunshine ("Why did the plant grow?" "Because we gave it water and sunshine!").

If a handicapped child cannot answer a basic *why* question, sometimes backing up to a more basic question form will help the child connect the correct information to that question form. For example:

Teacher: Why do we have chairs?

Child: Dunno.

Teacher: What am I doing?

Child: Sitting chair.

Teacher: Are chairs for sitting?

Child: Yes.

Teacher: Why do we have chairs?

Child: Sit down.

Teacher: Right! Chairs are for sitting. That's *why* we have chairs. *Why* do we have chairs?

Child: For *sitting*!

Another important consideration in teaching a child competence with a new cognitively oriented question form (one that involves judgment beyond basic discrimination) is to *always teach a new question form in the context of old, familiar information* (Wiig and Semel 1980). Conversely, always teach a preschool handicapped child new information using familiar question forms!

How and When Questions

How and *when* are two other questions that can be difficult for preschool children to answer competently. *How* questions usually require an answer involving manner, method, or quantity-degree, as "How do you cut?" "How did he do that?" "How many (or how much, or other quantity words) is this?" Many children will answer the first two types of *how* (how-manner) questions by demonstrating or gesturing and saying, "Like this!" or "This way!" They are apt to answer *how-quantity* questions by gesturing (arms apart, hands out, "shaping" size, or holding up so many fingers) and saying, "This many!" or "This big." Parallel-talking a child through a procedure, and then repeating the procedure again one step at a time and questioning the child about each, can prepare a child to verbalize and demonstrate an answer to a *how-method* question. *How* questions requiring adverb answers may need moving through and experiencing kinesthetically and then verbalizing to truly comprehend the answer, as:

> Teacher: How do we run? (*teacher and child run across the room*)
> Run, run, run . . . fast! Did we run fast or slow?
>
> Child: Fast!

Having children answer a *how-manner* question is best managed by having them look, feel, taste, or smell the real object. For example, give children a fruit and have them sensorily explore it. How does an apple look, feel, taste, or smell? Round, red, slick, hard, crunchy, sweet, tart, . . . How does a shoe feel? Depending on the shoe, hard, soft, furry, slippery, smooth, . . . Any answer is acceptable.

How-quantity questions that require counting can be comprehended more quickly if the teacher moves the child through the procedure of responding, using parallel talk. For example:

> Teacher: How many blocks are here?
> *(Four blocks are on the table.)*
> *(Teacher puts one hand over the child's hand)*
> First we put our finger on one block at a time and move it here as we count. One . . . (*touching each block and sliding it over*) two . . . three . . . four blocks! The number where we stop is *how many*? How many blocks are here?
>
> Child: Four blocks.
>
> Teacher: Good girl! There are four blocks.

Asking *how-method* questions that require a sequenced response can prepare a child for the late developing *when* question. Both are time-based questions ("How do we get ready for school?" *First,* we get up. *Then,* we eat breakfast. *Then,* we dress . . .").

When questions will be *extremely difficult* for the preschool handicapped child, because comprehension of time usually does not develop in the normal child until age five. Many typical as well as atypical children have difficulty in comprehending this last dimensional concept, time. However, frequent statements that *correlate time* to *event* can *prepare* the child for later dealing with these questions. For example, "What time is it? It's work time (snack time, rest time)"; "When is supper? We work in the morning, we eat lunch at noon, we eat supper and go to bed at night."

Ellyn Lucas, in her 1980 work, *Semantic and Pragmatic Language Disorders,* points out the *pervasiveness* of spatiotemporal (space and time) dysfunction in language handicapped children. Children diagnosed as mentally retarded, learning disabled, language delayed, or emotionally disturbed are apt to exhibit dysfunction with spatiotemporal concepts. Preschool children who exhibit difficulty learning positional and quantitative concepts, in putting semantic relationships together, in making sentence relationships with appropriate space-time marking words (*next, before, etc.*), who have trouble talking in the past or future, and who have trouble answering *where, how,* and *when* questions, may have a spatiotemporal disorder. Such preschool handicapped children will need *carefully structured experiences* with emphasis on questions that match the child's perceptual abilities and language abilities.

Importance of Question-Answer Competence

Developing question-answer competence in the early childhood period is a complex but extremely pragmatic responsibility of professionals working with these children. Planning for giving children *repetitive practice* with questions at their level of perception and language competence, for assisting the child to answer accurately and appropriately, for coordinating efforts among professionals and caretakers, can result in (1) extension of both vocabulary and reasoning abilities; and (2) establishing a pattern of positive interactive success between adult and child that will increase the child's desire to learn and communicate.

Daily Group Checklist

See page 42 for a daily checklist, which can be used for monitoring each child's progress (within a group) with the question form on which programming for the youngster is presently being provided. Ideally, the teacher asks the question (after an activity, discussion, or narrative) while a paraprofessional scores the checklist. However, not all classrooms have aides, and this system will not always be possible.

Coding for responses is provided, as well as for type of assistance needed for a successful response (handling materials, looking at picture, being provided a visual cue, or "response shaping").

Generally, associative and inappropriate responses both require response shaping (see examples on page 26). Inappropriate responses are more difficult to shape and sometimes involve a willingness on the part of the questioner to accept less than "completely tuned-in" responses in shaping, as well as some role-playing.

"No response" usually suggests either that the child does not have the information or has difficulty interacting, participating, or making an effort to respond. Gradually intruding on such children, by requiring their responses first to be minimal gestures (pointing, nodding or shaking the head) and then gradually increasing the demands and reinforcing *every* response effort, will be *most* important. The teacher should make sure these children are presented with the information they may not have!

"Delayed response" children can benefit from being allowed some extra time for processing and sometimes being given a visual or verbal cue to help them in retrieving the information.

Echolalic responses must be judged as to their *function* before intervening. Slow processors sometimes repeat all or the last few words of a question before they can organize and output their response. Autistic or auditorily deficient children sometimes echo (in a modified manner) part of the question in an attempt to answer. ("Do you need to go to the bathroom?" "I go to the bathroom"—meaning "Yes"). Other autistic children meaninglessly echo questions, unable to answer. Resources for dealing effectively with types of echolalic responses include Fay and Schuler (1981), Lovaas (1981), and Prizant (1987).

Learning to modify and structure children's responses, using a systematic and repetitive approach, can be a most important responsibility of the teachers of disadvantaged, language, and learning handicapped children.

Response-Shaping Examples

Associative Responses

Teacher: Why do we need cars?

Child: Mama ha' one.

Teacher: What does she do with it?

Child: She start it up.

Teacher: She puts the key in and starts it. Then what does she do?

Child: She go work.

Teacher: Does Mama need a car to get to work?

Child: Yeah, she drive.

Teacher: Why do we need cars?

Child: Drive and go places.

Teacher: Good thinking!

Mom: Where do the forks go?

Child (*pointing to drawer of cabinet*): There.

Mom: What is this?

Child: Drawer.

Mom: Where do we *put* the forks?

Child: Drawer.

Mom (*laughing*): Under the drawer?

Child: No-o-o! In the drawer.

Mom: That's right!

Inappropriate Responses

Teacher: What should you do if you break something?

Child: I'm going to town tomorrow.

Teacher (*dramatically cuing*): Uh-oh! Crash! You broke the plate. What do you do?

Child: Broke plate downtown?

Teacher (*visually cuing*): Should we pick up the pieces of this broken plate?

Child: I pick up pieces downtown.

Teacher: Yes, we pick them up, and then do we put them in the garbage?

Child: Yes, in garbage.

Teacher: Are you sorry?

Child: I'm sorry?

Teacher: For what?

Child: I'm sorry for breaking plate. I clean up.

Pragmatic Suggestions in Use of *ENABLE*

ENABLE, a listening comprehension program, is designed to provide guidance for teachers and parents of normal and language and cognitively handicapped preschoolers and older handicapped youngsters. The progression from simple to complex, along with the age of expectancy (which may be either chronological or functional), provides the adult with an approximate level of expectancy for individual children. The introduction suggests how to cope with inadequate responses.

It is recommended that classroom use of *ENABLE* be used simultaneously with a language unit-based developmental curriculum, such as *TOTAL* (Witt and Boose 1984) and/or *A Planning Guide to the Preschool Curriculum* (Findlay, et al. 1976). In that way, the questions and directives may be fit easily into the language context and routine of the day. Parents who use *ENABLE* should attempt to provide the activities according to the unit their children are presently working on at school. Teachers may wish to make copies of questions and directives for a parent to provide the child at home. The questions and directives may be modified according to needs perceived by the adults, but the general level of competence and the need for experiences or visual input should always be considered.

When using the narratives of ENABLE II, questions initially should be asked after every three to five sentences, rather than at the end of the story. Gradually the questions can be asked after more material has been read. As the children hear similar types of questions after the stories of each unit, eventually they should begin to actively listen for the answers to those certain types of questions.

Many preschool children will be unable to answer all of the questions for the story that does not provide an accompanying picture as a visual help to their memory. Teachers may wish not to utilize those unillustrated narratives unless the children are in the five- to seven-year range (chronologically, cognitively, or linguistically) or have proven their readiness for them.

Children with moderate to severe cognitive or language deficits, who are at the routine-oriented responses and labeling questions level, should be provided experiences only in the units that are most environmentally meaningful to them; and (as set forth in *TOTAL*) they should spend up to two months receiving repetitive concrete training on each unit. Mildly impaired children should cover every unit and spend approximately a month in each. Normal children or children with only slight delays should spend two weeks with the activities of a given unit. Until youngsters are thoroughly competent at the ENABLE I level, activities at the ENABLE II level should *not* be provided to them. However, children within the same class *may* be questioned and directed at the higher level, therefore giving the lower-level children the opportunity to hear higher-level instructional language without having to be responsible for meeting its demands.

Preschool children with auditory memory deficits can begin to learn the strategies for extending their memory once they have developed to a cognitive range of four to five years. Before that time, the teacher or parent must help them by providing the appropriate strategy.

Repetitive experiences with the same *type* of directive or question through a variety of different language unit contexts can prove beneficial in building competence.

There are no right or wrong answers to the questions as long as they meet the criteria of functional appropriateness or accuracy. Children's background and culture will have much to do with how some questions are answered. In one family, the person who cooks or shaves may be entirely different from the one who does these in another family. The aim is to extend children's vocabulary of action words, attributes, and concepts through appropriately answering questions or following directives.

Another program that provides a hierarchy of questions based on a somewhat similar framework is *Manual of Exercises for Expressive Reasoning* (Zachman, et al. 1982). The aim of that program is to help youngsters "develop logical thinking skills and apply them to future experiences," therefore also developing "increased self-confidence."

It is hoped that repeated experiences with questions, directives, discussions, and narratives of *ENABLE* will not only improve competence in listening comprehension for preschoolers and older handicapped elementary children, but also extend their fund of information and their organizational and logical thinking skills. Such an outcome could ensure both confidence in trying to learn and a smoother course in so doing during later experiences in academic-level classrooms.

ENABLE
Assessment Materials

Types of Language Development in Early Childhood Classrooms

I. Basic Language of Daily Living (Functional Communication)
   Is usually taught in classrooms for handicapped children

   A. Develops:

      1. In normal children from birth to three years

      2. In mildly to moderately handicapped children from birth to six years

      3. In severely-profoundly handicapped children from two to fifteen years

   B. Generally includes:

      1. Comprehending enough auditorily or visually presented communicative signals to:
         a. Control behavior of self
         b. Respond positively and/or cooperatively (however briefly) to demands of others

      2. Developing labels (receptively and expressively) for as many objects as possible in the day-to-day environment

      3. Developing a functional awareness of the parts and possibilities of their bodies:
         a. Body parts
         b. Actions they can do or others do for them
         c. Basic degree of movement in space capabilities
            (1) Positions (*up/down, in/out, on/under*)
            (2) Quantities (*big/little, more, empty/full*)

      4. Learning names of significant others

      5. Learning "magic words" and basic requesting language:
         a. *Please, More, Thank you, Excuse me*
         b. *I want _____ , I need _____ , Help me*

      6. Learning functional responding language:
         a. Imitating visual demonstrations and auditory sounds
         b. Making appropriate motoric responses to common and/or routine-oriented demands (*go, get, give, show, bring, do*)
         c. Making appropriate and accurate verbal or manual responses to basic discriminatory questions about concrete, visual, present information (*Is this? Do you want/need? What/who is this? Where is _____ ? What . . . doing?*)

      7. Expressing needs and making comments pragmatically (in the right way at the right time)

      8. Learning to ask for information (question):
         a. Intonational questions (*Ha' cookie? Mommy go?*)
         b. Routine WH questions (*What dat? Where he go? What . . . doing?*)

C. Teaching considerations include:

1. Estimating individual degrees of auditory and/or visual memory (one to four words)

2. Using telegraphic language (one to four words—core words) when directing (*Jane, sit chair!*)

3. Possibly signing or "cuing" core words when directing may be necessary

4. Physically, verbally, or visually assisting youngster to respond, until such assistance is no longer necessary

5. Accepting verbal and gestural approximations, but gradually "shaping" into clearer message

6. Determining appropriate system of communication for each child via a multidisciplinary approach (teacher, speech-language pathologist, occupational therapist, parent):
   a. Motoric capabilities
   b. Oral-motor (verbal) capabilities
   c. Cognitive level
   d. Portability

7. Providing regular updates for parents, when children use alternative or augmentative communication system (low- or high-tech)

8. Monitoring appropriate time to accept "verbal only" communication

9. Extending verbal attending skills from attending while manipulating objects to attending when looking at pictures

10. Articulation and syntax should always be considered secondary to pragmatic use of language and extension of comprehension skills!

11. Avoiding correction; modeling corrected version, praising all efforts!

12. Language unit approach is imperative!

D. Teaching techniques include:

1. Listening to and participating in children's play (indicating interest in what they do)

2. Referencing—Calling child's attention to object or event (pointing, exaggeratedly moving self or objects)

3. Naming—Verbally and/or manually labeling objects environmentally important to child

4. Imitating—Repeating child's verbal attempts clearly

5. Demanding—Giving a direction, possibly accompanied by a visual cue or demonstration

6. Replying—Providing an appropriate verbal or nonverbal response to child's behavior (for example, child pulls mother to refrigerator; mother says, "You want to eat?")

7. Associating—When child handles an object curiously, adult provides functions or attributes (for example, child holds ball; adult says, "You can throw it" and demonstrates. Child picks up apple; adult says, "It's red. You eat it.")

8. Expanding—Repeating child's utterance with added information or correct syntax (for example, child asks, "Plane?" and adult says, "The plane can fly. Zoom-m-m.")

9. Parallel talk—Describing actions as they happen ("Little girls in pool. Swimming, swimming. Two girls are swimming.")

10. Questioning—Requesting basic information of children, at their level of competence. Provide response if necessary!

II. Social Language Competence (Effective/Affective Communication)
    Is taught in both normal and interventional early childhood programs

   A. Develops:

      1. In normal children from two to five years

      2. In mildly to moderately handicapped children from four to twelve years

      3. May or may not develop in severely handicapped children; if so, from eight to twenty years

   B. Generally includes:

      1. Developing functional fund of information about core words in child's expanding world:
         a. Functions
         b. Attributes (color, size, detail, shape)
         c. Categories

      2. Expanding expressive abilities:
         a. Describing (object-function, "knife cut"; object-attribute, "boy big")
         b. Discussing—Being able to participate in a discussion about an object or event; answering questions, making appropriate comments, handling and learning about materials
         c. Defining—Being able to provide succinct definitions of objects ("An apple is a fruit. You can eat it, cook it, and cut it. It is red and round. It tastes crunchy and sweet. It has a skin, pulp, stem, seeds, and grows on a tree.")

      3. Participating cooperatively in a conversation; understanding give and take, when to listen and when to speak

      4. Expressing feelings

      5. Developing appropriate articulation and syntax

      6. Learning and using tense, pluralization, negation, and possession

      7. Extending memory and attending skills from attending/remembering with visual aids, to attending to words only

C. Teaching techniques/considerations include:

1. Providing a structured developmental routine organized around a language unit approach

2. Language teaching should include:

   a. Encouragement of spontaneous expression by child

   b. Handling, playing, moving, and listening to stories about core words and categories

   c. Providing structured language group training, as well as naturalistic language expansion

   d. Ensuring a game and fun approach that encourages reason to communicate

III. The Language of Instruction (School-Enabling Language)
Is a focus of preschool and kindergarten programs for children who are socioeconomically delayed and mildly impaired, as well as normal children

A. Develops:

1. In normal children from four to eight years (preschool through second grade)

2. In mildly handicapped children from six to twelve years (and may remain a problem)

3. Seldom develops in severely handicapped children

B. Generally includes:

1. Developing both understanding and use of conceptual words (position, quantity, quality, relationship, condition, ordinal/sequential, sensory/affective, etc.); references: *Brigance Inventory of Early Development, General Knowledge Subtest; Boehm Test of Basic Concepts, Preschool and Kindergarten Versions; Bracken Basic Concept Scale*

2. Developing effective memory techniques:
   a. Short-term auditory memory
   b. "Working" memory (remembering with interference between problem and response):
      (1) Singing
      (2) Rehearsing
      (3) Chunking
      (4) Associating
   c. Recollection and recall (retrieval)

3. Learning to respond promptly and effectively to sequenced, compound, complex, and conditional directives

4. Learning to respond to instructional questions:
   a. Reasoning questions about visual information (why, how-manner, how-method, cause-effect)

      b. Reasoning questions involving manipulation of existing information (recognizing similarities and differences, excluding, event-telling, pretending or role-playing)

      c. Inferential questions (predicting, justifying decisions, determining causes or solutions, segmenting or organizing, explaining, telling a sequenced story)

  5. Learning to organize and order information

  6. Learning successfully to complete worksheets after a discussion or sequenced instruction

C. Teaching considerations include:

  1. Accurately assessing weak areas (concepts, auditory or visual memory, sequencing, attending, general listening comprehension)

  2. Providing appropriate practice for weak areas

  3. Considering possibility of hearing or visual difficulties (acuity, figure-ground, sound-field, distractibility levels) and addressing weak areas

  4. Teaching working memory strategies (rehearsal, chunking, associating)

  5. Beginning at level of competence in both motoric response to directions and appropriate answers to questions

  6. When teaching new question forms, use old information; when teaching new information, use old question forms.

  7. Developing listening comprehension a sentence or two at a time, and one complexity (of direction or question) at a time

  8. Ensuring that parents or caretakers understand child's present level of competence

  9. Staying with each child when questioning until success is achieved, not "hopping from child to child"

 10. Aiming for appropriate and accurate (on-target) responses; using shaping techniques when necessary

 11. Allowing at least ten to fifteen seconds for responses, before cuing response visually or backing down to a lower-level question

 12. Always providing acknowledgment of appropriate responses

Attending to Words and Sentences

First, children can listen to and attach meaning to words heard while handling or manipulating objects (sensorimotor stage: six months to two years).

That's your car. Driving your car. Zoom-zoom!

Putting teddy bear to bed. Night-night, bear.

Next, children can listen to words and sentences about very simple pictures, with a limited number of large, colorful objects on the page (15 months to 2½ years).

What happened after he caught the ball?

Next, children can listen to two to four lines about a simple story or participate in short conversations about objects and pictures (two to three years).

Gradually, children learn to maintain attention and remember pertinent facts about short stories and discussions and answer questions about the information presented (three to six years).

Memory and Memory Strategies*

Memory Types

1a. Short-Term Auditory Memory (STM-A)—Ability to repeat sequences of digits, syllables, and words

1b. Short-Term Visual Memory (STM-V)—Ability to remember what was just seen

2. Working Memory—Halfway between STM and Storage; ability to hold in memory long enough to respond correctly to simple-complex directives and answer simple-complex questions

3. Recollection—Ability to retrieve previously learned information from storage when given a choice of answers

4. Recall—Ability to retrieve and use previously learned information from storage with no "cuing" necessary

Memory Strategies Frequently Used by Teachers

1. Singing, rhyming, "rapping" (repetitious "sing-song" with rhythm and beat; for example, nursery rhymes, familiar tunes such as "Farmer in the Dell"), learning rote information by song ("Alphabet Song" and "One Little, Two Little Indians")

2. Rehearsal—Repeating core words of directive over and over, usually aloud. For example, adult says, "Go upstairs into the bathroom and bring me the blue towel off the top shelf," and child says (repetitively), "Upstairs bathroom, blue towel, top shelf."

3. Chunking—Touching finger while repeating "clumps" of digits or words desired to be learned. For example, learning telephone number: "328 (*touch thumb*), 49 (*touch index finger*), 45 (*touch middle finger*)."

4. Associating—Relating information learned to something already learned. For example, "*More* is like a *big* pile; *less* is like a *little* pile."

---

*Preschool children do not use memory strategies unless taught and encouraged.

References for memory and strategies include Case (1985), Baddeley (1985), and Elwinger and Morgan (1986).

Directive Response Checklist*

Name _____ Date _____

6-12 months	1. Routine-oriented directives:

    a. Whole body responses (2/3)   _____
       Come here.
       Sit down.
       Stop.

    b. Object movement (1/2)   _____
       Do this. (*Child imitates adult rocking baby, moving toy car, or putting block in cup.*)

       Give me this. (*Adult points to a single object—a block or a cup—in front of the child.*)

12-24 months   2. Simple one-step directives:

    a. Choice of one item (1/2)   _____
       Point to your shoes.
       Give me the cup.

    b. Choice of two items (1/2)   _____
       Show me the doll.
       Give me the spoon.

    c. Choice of three items (1/2)   _____
       Point to the ball.
       Bring me the block.

2-6 years   3. Compound directives (two to five steps):

2-3 years   a. Two-step directives:

      (1) Connected directives (1/2)   _____
         Go to the table and get the block.
         Look at your feet and touch your shoes.

      (2) Nonrelated directives (1/2)   _____
         Stand up and pat your stomach.
         Go to the door; pull your nose.

3-4 years   Three- to five-step directives

      (1) Three-step directives (1/2)   _____
         Turn around, sit down, and clap hands.
         Untie your shoes, take them off, and give them to me.

4-5 years   (2) Four-step directives (1/2)   _____
         Touch your hair, touch your nose, pat your stomach, and your toes.
         Pick up the crayon and draw a line. Draw another line and give me the crayon.

5-6 years   (3) Five-step directives (1/2)   _____
         Stand up, stamp your feet, clap your hands, jump, and sit down.
         Get the blocks. Stack them and build a train.
         Give me a block and put the others here (*pointing*).

2½-6 years   4. Complex directives (simple and compound directives with embedded concepts of position, quantity, negation, possession, quality, and degree)

2½-3½ years   a. Simple directives (1/2)   _____
Put the block on the table.
Get the spoon out of the cup.

3½-4½ years   b. Compound directives (2/4)   _____
Put the red block in the little cup.
Get the empty cup and turn it over.
Pick up the short pencil but not the long one.
Stack the red and blue blocks but not the yellow ones.

4½-6 years   c. Retrieving, processing, organizing (1/2)   _____
Manipulating objects: Put the yellow and blue blocks behind the big box.
Worksheet directives: Draw a circle and make it into a face.

(3-5 years)   5. Conditional directives (1/2)   _____
If I clap my hands, you jump.
Touch your ears when I open my mouth.

*Verbal directives may be visually cued.

Question-Answer Competence Checklist

This is not an assessment of vocabulary, but of ability to formulate responses to questions. The following familiar functional objects and pictures are used as cues.

Objects:

spoon	shoe	boy/girl dolls
cup	coat	box
ball	soap	five blocks or pennies
sock		

Pictures:

eating	dishes	key
drinking	house	refrigerator
sleeping	book	plane
talking	car	clock
bed	pots and pans	TV
chair	lights	police officer
phone	pencil	firefighter
cup	scissors	doctor
coat		

Question-Answer Competence Checklist

Name _____ Date _____

1-2 years	**1. Labeling**	
	What is this? (2/4)	_____
	Who is this? (1/3)	_____
2-3 years	**2. Yes/No**	
	Is this a _____ ? (4/8)	_____
	3. Action	
	What is he/she doing? (eating, drinking, sleeping, talking) (2/4)	_____
	4. Discrimination	
	Which is the (*label*)? (3/4)	_____
	Which one do we _____ with? (2/4)	_____
	5. Locations	
	Where is the _____ ? (object + preposition response) (in/out, on/under, beside) (2/5)	_____
3-5 years	**6. Reasoning**	
	Function (with objects or pictures)	
	What do you do with _____ ? (action phrase required)	
	Cause (with objects or pictures)	
	Why do we have _____ ?	
	(3 years) beds, chairs, phones, cups, coats, plates/bowls/dishes (3/6)	_____
	(4 years) houses, books, cars, pans/pots, lights, pencils, scissors (4/7)	_____
	(5 years) keys, refrigerator, clocks, planes, TV, police officer, fire fighter, doctor (5/8)	_____
	Situation	
	What do you do when _____ ? (no visual cue)	
	(3 years) you're hungry, you're thirsty, you're sleepy, you're cold, you have a cut (3/5)	_____
	(4 years) you're sick, you're dirty, you're in a dark room, you see a hurt person, your shoe is untied (3/5)	_____
	(5 years) you see a fire, you're outside and it rains, you're happy (or sad), you need to cross the street, somebody gives you a present, you want something (3/6)	_____
	7. How Manner/Method/Degree/Cause (no pictures needed)	
3-4 years	Manner (2/4)	_____
	How do: chips taste, pillows feel, dogs run, birds look?	
4-5 years	Method/Sequence/Ordering (requires sequenced account: first __ , then __ , last __) (2/3)	_____
	How do you: get ready for school? wash your hands? brush your teeth?	
4-5 years	Degree (amount to five; requires counting objects) (3/5)	_____
	How many is this? (blocks or pennies)	
4½-5 years	Cause (1/5)	_____
	How does the ground get muddy?	
	How does Daddy make the car go?	
5-6 years	**8. Time concepts (no pictures needed) (3/6)**	_____
	When do we: eat breakfast, go to bed, watch cartoons, wear coats, use umbrella?	
	When was the last time we ate supper?	

Code:
+ = Competence at this level (circle number correct)
/ = Emerging skills (at least one correct response)
— = Incompetence at this level

Date _____

Question–Answer Competence Daily Group Checklist

| Name | Question Type | Assistance Needed? | | Type of Assistance Needed | | | Response Code and Comments |
		Y	N	Visual Cuing	Response Shaping	Handling/ Experience	

Code: AA = Appropriate and accurate response
    A = Associative answer—Needs shaping
    I = Inappropriate response

NR = No response
DR = Delayed response
E = Echolalic response

References

Bellugi, U., and E. Klima. 1966. Syntactic regularities in the speech of children. In *Psycholinguistic Papers*, edited by J. Lyons and R. J. Wales. Edinburgh: Edinburgh University Press.

Berlin, L., M. Blank, and S. Rose. 1980. The language of instruction: The hidden complexities. *Topics of Language Disorders* I (December):17-58.

Bloom, L., and M. Lahey. 1978. *Language development and language disorders.* New York: John Wiley and Sons.

Boehm, A. E. 1986. *Boehm test of basic concepts—Revised (Preschool and kindergarten versions).* San Antonio, Tex.: The Psychological Corporation, Harcourt Brace Jovanovich, Inc.

Bolles, E. B. 1982. *So much to say.* New York: St. Martins Press.

Bracken, B. 1984. *Bracken basic concept scale.* Columbus, Ohio: Charles E. Merrill Publishing Co.

Brigance, Albert H. 1978. *Brigance diagnostic inventory of early development.* North Billerica, Mass.: Curriculum Associates, Inc.

Brown, R. 1973. *A first language: The early stages.* Cambridge, Mass.: Harvard University Press.

Cole, P. 1982. *Language disorders in preschool children.* Englewood Cliffs: Prentice-Hall, Inc.

Dechant, E. V. 1970. *Improving the teaching of reading.* Englewood Cliffs: Prentice-Hall, Inc.

Ervin-Tripp, S. 1970. Discourse agreement: How children answer questions. In *Cognition and the development of language,* edited by J. R. Hayes. New York: John Wiley and Sons.

_____. 1971. An overview of theories of grammatical development. In *The ontogenesis of grammar,* edited by D. Slobin. New York: Academic Press.

Fay, W., and A. L. Schuler. 1981. *Emerging language in autistic children.* Baltimore: University Park Press.

Findlay, Jane, Patricia Miller, Annie Pegram, Linda Richey, Anne Sanford, and Barbara Semrau. 1976. *A planning guide to the preschool curriculum.* Winston-Salem: Kaplan Press.

Lovaas, O. I. 1981. *Teaching developmentally disabled children: The ME book.* Baltimore: University Park Press.

Lucas, Ellyn. 1980. *Semantic and pragmatic language disorders.* Rockville: Aspen Publication Corporation.

Lund, N., and J. F. Duchan. 1983. *Assessing children's language in naturalistic contexts.* Englewood Cliffs: Prentice-Hall.

Parnell, M., and J. D. Amerman. 1983. Answers to WH questions: Research and applications. In *Pragmatic assessment and intervention issues in language,* edited by T. Gallagher and C. Prutting. San Diego: College-Hill Press, Inc.

Parnell, M., J. D. Amerman, S. Patterson, and M. A. Harding. 1982. *Answers to WH questions: A developmental study.* Unpublished manuscript.

Parnell, M., S. Patterson, and M. A. Harding. 1983. *Understanding of certain WH question forms by young children.* Paper presented at American Speech-Language-Hearing Association conference, Detroit.

Parnell, M., J. D. Amerman, and Roger D. Harting. 1986. Responses of language-disordered children to WH questions. *Language, Speech, and Hearing Services in Schools* (April):95-106.

Prizant, B. M. 1987. Clinical implications of echolalic behavior in autism. In *Language and treatment of autistic children,* edited by T. Layton. Springfield, Ill.: Charles Thomas, Publishers.

Sanford, Anne R., Julia McLean Williams, Jeanne Cunningham James, and Ann K. Overton. 1983. *A planning guide to the preschool curriculum.* Revised ed. Winston-Salem: Kaplan Press.

Stanovich, K. E. 1982. Individual differences in the cognitive processes of reading. II. Text-level processes. *Journal of Learning Disabilities* 15:9 (November):549-54.

Wiig, E. H., and E. M. Semel. 1980. *Language assessment and intervention for the learning disabled.* Columbus, Ohio: Charles E. Merrill Publishing Co.

Witt, B., and J. Boose. 1984. *TOTAL.* Tucson, Ariz.: Communication Skill Builders, Inc.

————. 1984a. *TOTAL curriculum guide.* Tucson, Ariz.: Communication Skill Builders, Inc.

Zachman, Linda, Carol Jorgensen, Mark Bennett, Rosemary Huisingh, and Mary Kay Snedden. 1982. *Manual of Exercises for Expressive Reasoning.* Moline, Ill.: LinguiSystems.

Additional Resources

Baddeley, A., et al. 1985. Components of Fluent Reading. *Journal of Memory and Language* 24:119-31.

Bangs, T. E. 1982. *Language and Learning Disorders of the Preacademic Child.* Englewood Cliffs: Prentice-Hall, Inc.

Blank, M. 1983. *Teaching Learning in the Preschool: A Dialogue Approach.* Cambridge, Mass.: Brookline Books.

Blank, Marian, Susan Rose, and Laura J. Berlin. 1978. *Preschool Language Assessment Instrument.* Orlando, Fla.: Grune and Stratton, Inc.

Carr, E. 1981. Sign Language. In *Teaching Developmentally Disabled Children: The ME Book,* edited by I. Lovaas. Baltimore: University Park Press.

Case, R. 1985. *Intellectual Development: Birth to Adulthood.* Orlando, Fla.: Academic Press, Inc., Harcourt Brace Jovanovich, Publishers.

Cazden, C. 1970. Children's Questions: Their Forms, Functions and Roles in Education. *Young Children* 25:202-20.

_____. 1972. *Child Language and Education.* New York: Rinehart and Winston.

Clarke, C. C. 1986. *An Investigation of Question-Response Verbal Interactions of a Hard-of-Hearing Child in a General Education Kindergarten Classroom.* Unpublished doctoral dissertation, University of Cincinnati.

Dore, J. 1977. Oh Them Sheriff: A Pragmatic Analysis of Children's Responses to Questions. In *Child Discourse,* edited by S. Ervin-Tripp and C. Mitchell-Dernan. New York: Academic Press.

Elwinger, E. S. 1983. Elementary Crutches. *Academic Therapy* (March): 457-67.

Elwinger, E. and A. Morgan. 1986. *Developmental Working Memory Test.* Manuscript in process.

Green, J., and C. Wallat (Eds.). 1981. *Ethnography and Language in Educational Settings.* Norwood, N.J.: Ablex.

Lasky, E. Z., and J. Katz. 1983. *Central Auditory Processing Disorders.* Baltimore: University Park Press.

Schuler, A. L., and B. M. Prizant. 1985. Echolalia in Autism. In *Communication Problems in Autism,* edited by E. Schopler and G. Mesibow. New York: Plenum Press.

Wilkinson, L. C. (Ed.). 1982. *Communicating in the Classroom.* New York: Academic Press.

Ying, E., and D. Brackett. 1984. Communication Evaluation: Academic and Social Considerations. *Seminars in Hearing* 5:367-383.

ENABLE I

Self

When working with children who are functionally one to two years, use a nonbreakable mirror (hand or full-length) and a doll with clearly defined body parts. With children whose language or cognitive ages are two to three years, use the ENABLE I puppet figures of the boy and girl. Colorful storybooks that feature *very simple* one- or two-object pictures of children in action also are helpful for this unit.

Physical assistance and, later, visual assistance may be needed to help a child consistently pair the correct response to the directive. This is especially important for children whose cognitive function is lower. Demonstration also may be helpful. Such assistance should be withdrawn as soon as possible.

Directives

1. Routine-oriented directives (12-18 months)
   Repetition is inherent in development of routine-oriented directives!

   a. These directives may be given using the child's body and a mirror, or a doll, as the response object.

Show me:	your (*or* baby's):	mouth.
Touch:		feet.
Pat:		tummy.
Look at/See:		nose.
Move:		eyes.
		hair.
		toes.

   b. Directives are given in an enthusiastic manner, possibly in sing-song. As the child responds (or is assisted to respond by caretaker), the adult describes the activity, as indicated.

Let's:	sit down.	"We're sitting!"
	stand up.	"We're standing!"
	make baby eat.	"Baby's eating!"
		"*You* can eat!"
	make baby sleep.	"Baby's sleeping!"
		"You *can* sleep!"
	go.	"We're going!"
Come here, please!		"You're coming here!"

   c. Storybook directives. As the child looks at a simple picturebook or storybook with the adult, directive is given, page by page.

   Show me/Point to: baby boy/girl   like you!

49

2. Simple one-step directives
   a. Body part actions (18-24 months)

Shake:	your:	head.
		hands.
Wiggle:	your:	fingers.
		nose.
		toes.
Close/open:	your:	eyes.
		hands.
		mouth.
Lift:	your:	foot/feet.
Pat:	your:	stomach (tummy).
		teeth.
Clap:	your:	hands.
Stick out:	your:	arms.
		thumb.
		tongue.
		chin.

   b. Whole body actions (18-24 months)

   Jump!
   Walk.
   Put baby down.
   Turn around.
   Run.
   Rock baby.
   Climb up stairs.
   Carry baby.

   c. Pragmatic directives—Actions given at home at appropriate times
      and places (18-30 months)

   In kitchen:
   Eat _____ .
   Drink _____ .
   Chew your food.
   Pick up _____ .
   Put down _____ .
   Wipe your face.
   Fill the glass.

   In bathroom:
   Open/Close the door.
   Go potty.
   Pull down pants.
   Sit down.
   Wipe bottom.
   Pull up pants.
   Flush potty.
   Wash your hands.
   Rub your hands.
   Wipe/Dry your hands.
   Wipe nose.
   Throw away _____ .

   In bedroom:
   Get up.
   Put on your (*clothing item*).
   Put away (*toys, clothing*).
   Take off your (*clothing item*).
   Lie down.
   Cover up.
   Be quiet.
   Go to sleep.

   In family room:
   Play with your toys.
   Look at your book.
   Watch TV.
   Move over.
   Listen to the music.
   Move your toys.

At school:

Come sit down.	Get in line.
Let's work.	Get a drink.
Be quiet, please.	Let's play.
Let's talk.	Walk here.
Stand here.	Stop now!
Let's eat.	Let's go outside/inside.
Let's sing.	

d. Storybook directives (18-30 months)

Point to:	sitting.	running.
Show me:	eating.	talking.
Touch:	washing.	playing.
	standing.	walking.
	drinking.	sleeping.
	drying.	climbing.
	boy/girl.	

Open the book.
Close the book.
Turn the page.

3. Two-step compound and complex directives with embedded concepts (2-3 years)

a. Body parts directives

Clap hands and stamp feet.
Wave hands and bend legs.
Open mouth and close eyes.
Nod head and wiggle eyebrows.
Rub stomach and pat back.
Tap elbows and touch knees.
Touch hair and pull ears.
Shake shoulders and touch fingernails.
Wiggle nose and wiggle toes.
Stick out tongue and tap teeth.
Shake head and lift arms.

b. Positional and quantitative directives
Italicized concepts can be emphasized and repeated in other directives than these. Use as a guide.

Put your head *down*. Hold your hands *up*.
Jump *one* time. Jump *another* time.
Run *across* the room to the *nearest* chair.
Tiptoe and touch the *tallest* person.
Carry a (basket/box) *full* of (books/balls).
Walk *backward on* the *longest* line.
Clap hands *many* times. Clap a *few* times.

Stamp your feet *loudly*. Stamp them *softly*.

Raise *both* arms *together*.

Throw the ball *far*, but drop the beanbag *near* you.

Pick *up* the *little* book. Put *down* the *big* book.

Go to the door and *stop*.

Put your hands *over* your head. Put your feet *under* the table.

Lay the paper *in* the box and take the pencil *out*.

Touch the *top* step. Sit *on* the *bottom* step.

Run *around* the circle. Jump *in* the *middle* of the circle.

Stretch *out both* legs.

Reach *across* the table.

Step *into* the box.

Sing *loudly*; sing *softly*.

c. Storybook directives—Body part functions

Turn the page, and find the boy/girl.

Touch the child's arm, and pat the child's face.

Touch the body part used to see.

Show me what the child hears with.

Show me what the child uses to throw a ball.

Point to what the child uses to talk and eat.

Point to what the child can blink.

Show me what the child uses to walk and run.

Put your finger on parts the child can bend or stretch.

Point to which body part the child uses to smell things.

Touch what the child uses to taste things.

Put your finger on what the child uses to play.

d. Storybook directives—Early attributes

Show me the *little* child. Show me the *big* person.

Touch the child with *red/yellow* hair.

Find the child with *more* food.

Look at the child with the *round* toy.

Point to the child with *blue/green* clothing.

e. Directives involving simple negatives
Use a doll.

Touch a body part that is *not* on the head.

Wiggle a body part that *cannot* walk/talk/see/hear.

Show me a body part that does *not* wear clothes.

Tap a part *not* on the bottom of the baby's body.

Point to a body part *not* on arms and legs.

Show me body parts *not* on the back of the baby.

Touch a body part that *cannot* open or close.

Touch a body part *without* hair.

Questions

1. Basic labeling questions (12-24 months)
   a. Body parts
      As the question is asked, adult points to child's body part.

      What's this/that?

Mouth.	Hair.	Legs.
Eyes.	Toes.	Stomach.
Nose.	Hands.	Fingers.
Feet.	Arms.	Ears.

   b. Personal data:

      What's your name? (or) Who are you?

2. Yes/No questions
   a. Questions about present, visual information (18-24 months)

Is this your:	mouth?	Is this:	(child's name)?
Is this baby's:	ears?		you?
Is this my:	legs?		baby?
	fingers?	Can you:	eat(ing)?
	eyes?	Is this:	sit(ting)?
	hair?		smile (smiling)?
	arms?		drink(ing)?
	nose?		walk(ing)?
	head?		hug(ging)?
	hands?		sleep(ing)?
	chin?		play(ing)?
	feet?		wash(ing)?
	stomach?		talk(ing)?
			jump(ing)?
			dry(ing)?

   b. Early negation questions (2-3 years)

      Can you fly? (No)
      Can you move? (Yes)
      Are you big? (No)
      Can you hold things? (Yes)

      Which body part(s) cannot:

bend?	smell?
turn?	hear?
wiggle?	sit?
see?	open?
blink?	taste?
catch?	walk?

   c. Extended personal data—Rote (2-3 years)

      Are you a boy?
      Are you a girl?
      How old are you?

3. What . . . do questions about visual actions (18-24 months)

What are you doing?	eat(ing)
What am I doing?	sit(ting)
What can you do?	jump(ing)
What can baby do?	drink(ing)
	stand(ing)
	play(ing)
	sleep(ing)
	walk(ing)
	wash(ing)
	talk(ing)
	run(ning)
	dry(ing)
	smile (smiling)
	cry(ing)

4. Early discrimination—Choice of two visual objects or pictures (2-3 years)

Which body part:

eats?	bends?	hears?
drinks?	sees?	blinks?
smells things?	tastes?	holds things?
walks?	opens/closes?	needs combing?
turns?		

5. Early location questions about visual information (2-3 years)

Where are you?	On the chair.
Where is baby?	Outside the house.
Where am I?	On the floor.
	Upstairs.
	Downstairs.
	Inside the (_____) room.
	At home.
	At school.

6. Early attribute/concept questions—Choice of two objects or pictures (2-3 years)

Which one is:		Which one has:	more?
Which body part is:	red?/yellow?	Which child has:	many?
	across?/around?		both?
	blue?/green?		another?
	far?/near?		one?
	big?/little?		
	tall?/short?		
	up?/down?		
	open?/closed?		
	on?/under?		
	empty?/full?		
	top?/bottom?		

Short Discussions and Narratives

Use a mirror, a doll, and puppet figures of the boy and girl.

Discussion and questions for 18- to 24-month-old children:
> We are looking in the mirror.
> We see our mouth and eyes.
> Open, eyes! Open, mouth!
>
> What do we see?
> What did we do?

Discussion and questions for 24- to 30-month-old children:
> You are a boy/girl/child.
> You can do many things.
> You can eat and drink.
> You can sit and stand.
>
> Who are you?
> Can you do many things?
> What can you do?

Discussion and questions for 30- to 36-month-old children:
> This is your face.
> You see with your eyes and hear with your ears.
> You talk and eat with your mouth.
>
> Is this your neck?
> Which part do you hear with?
> What two things can you do with your mouth?

Narrative and questions for 18- to 24-month-old children:
Use a doll and mirror to illustrate the story.
> Baby looks in the mirror.
> Baby sees her nose and hair.
>
> Who is this?
> What does she see?

Narrative and questions for 24- to 30-month-old children:
Use puppet figures of the boy and girl to illustrate the story.
> The boy can jump.
> The girl can run.
> They like to play!
>
> What can the boy do?
> Who can run?
> Do they like to play?

Narrative and questions for 30- to 36-month-old children:
Use a doll to illustrate the story.
> This baby can open and shut her eyes.
> She can walk and clap her hands.
> This is a *big* baby.
>
> What can the baby do with her eyes?
> Can she walk?
> Is this baby little?

Family

For this unit, provide flexible family dolls (Mama, Daddy, boy, girl, baby) and pictures and storybooks about the family. Use the ENABLE I puppet figures of Mama, Daddy, boy, girl, and baby. (Cutouts for four ethnic family groups are provided.)

Directives

1. Routine-oriented directives (12-18 months)

   a.
Show me:	your (*or* the):	Daddy.
Touch:		Mama.
Pat:		boy.
Look at:		girl.
Move:		baby.
Let's find:		

   b.
Let's make:	Mama	sit down.	"Mama is sitting!"
	Daddy	stand up.	"Daddy is standing!"
	boy	go to sleep.	"Boy is sleeping!"
	girl	eat.	"Girl is eating!"
	baby	drink.	"Baby is drinking!"
		come here.	"Baby is coming!"

   c. Family pictures or storybook directives After the child correctly identifies the family member, adult states the action in process ("Yes, that's Mama. She's reading.")

Show me:	Daddy.
Point to:	Mama.
Touch:	boy.
Look at:	girl.
See:	baby.

2. Simple one-step directives

   a. Object movement directives (18-24 months)

Pick up:	Mama.		Move:	Mama's	head.
Put down:	Daddy.		Shake:	Daddy's	arms.
Walk:	boy.		Twist:	boy's	hands.
Pat:	girl.		Turn:	girl's	legs.
Feed:	baby.		Lift:	baby's	hands.
Talk to:			Raise:		feet.
Run:			Wiggle:		hair.
Jump:			Bend:		
Turn:			Pat:		

57

b. Pragmatic directives—Actions given at home (24-30 months)

In kitchen:	Help Mama/Daddy:	clean off table.
		sweep floor.
		carry dishes.
		put dishes on table.
		put away (*utensil*).
		wipe table.

Give (*pronoun*) some more.
Chew your food slowly.
Wipe baby's face.

In bathroom: Lift/Put down the potty lid.
Wash your/baby's (*body part*).
Turn the faucet on/off.
Squeeze the toothpaste.

In bedroom: Get dressed.
Hang up the clothes.
Close the closet door.
Turn on the light.

In family room: Color in your coloring book.
Build something with the blocks.
Watch cartoons on TV.
"Read" your book.
Draw a picture.

c. Storybook directives (24-30 months)

Point to:	Mama	sitting.	reading.
Show me:	Daddy	eating.	running.
Find:	boy	washing.	talking.
Touch:	girl	cooking.	combing hair.
Tap:	baby	standing.	swinging.
		drinking.	climbing.
		drying.	playing.
		watching TV.	dressing.
		walking.	playing ball.
		sleeping.	hugging.
		working.	riding.

3. Two-step compound and complex directives (2-3 years)
   a. Object movement directives
   Use manipulative family dolls, doll furniture, utensils, and toy cars.

   Sit Mama and let her rock baby.

   Have the girl feed the baby and lay him in bed.

   Show me Mama cooking and the boy drinking.

   Show the children playing and the parents talking.

   Make Daddy hug the baby and Mama hug the boy and girl.

   Have the boy jump and the Daddy run.

   Make the baby crawl and the Mama walk.

   Turn the girl around and make the boy clap hands.

b. Positional and quantitative directives

Have Mama hold the baby *up*, then lay baby *down*.

Have the boy jump *one* time, then jump *another* time.

Make the baby crawl *across* to the *nearest* child.

Give the baby to the *tallest* person.

Make Daddy walk *backward on* the table.

Have the girl stamp her feet *many* times. Have the boy stamp a *few* times.

Put baby *near* to Mama and the boy *far* from Mama.

Make the boy run *around* the Daddy.

Put the baby *into* the bed and the girl *on* the chair.

Have the boy crawl *under* the table and the girl jump *over* the chair.

c. Storybook directives

Find the Mama and the Daddy.

Point to the boy and girl playing.

Touch the *littlest* family person.

Touch the *biggest* family member.

Find the boy *with the red shirt*.

Show me the girl *with blue clothes*.

Touch the Mama *cooking dinner*.

Touch the *back* of Mama.

Show me the Daddy's *shoulders*.

Point to the *arms* and *legs* of the boy and girl.

d. Directives involving simple negatives

Point to the child that is *not* a boy.

Show me the person who is *not* a man.

Point to the person who is *not* little.

Touch the person who *cannot* walk.

Show me the people who *cannot* drive.

Show me the child *without* long hair.

Touch the child *not* wearing a dress.

Touch the person *not* sitting down.

Show me people *not* wearing pants.

Show me the people who are *not* short.

Questions

1. Basic labeling questions
   a. Family members (12-24 months). As the question is asked, adult points to manipulatives, pictures, or puppet figures.

   Who is this/that?
   Mama.
   Daddy.
   Boy.
   Girl.
   Baby.

   b. Personal data (2-3 years)

Who is this?	Mama.
What is his/her/your name?	Daddy.
Is this a boy or girl?	Boy.
Which is a man?	Girl.
Which is a woman?	Baby.
	(*Child's name*)

2. Yes/No questions
   a. Questions about present, visual information (18-24 months)

   Is this: Mama?
             Daddy?
             boy?
             girl?
             baby?

Is:	Mama	eating?	climbing?
	Daddy	sitting?	talking?
	boy	hugging?	dressing?
	girl	smiling?	cooking?
	baby	drinking?	reading?
		walking?	riding?
		washing?	standing?
		crying?	running?
		sleeping?	swinging?
		playing?	working?
		drying?	pushing?
		talking?	turning?
		jumping?	going bye-bye?

   b. Early negation questions (2-3 years)

   Is boy/girl/baby big?
   Is Mama/Daddy little?

   Choice of adult or baby:
   Which person does *not* drive a car?
   Which person does *not* go to work?
   Which person *cannot* run?

   Choice of boy or Mama:
   Which person does *not* take care of baby?

3. What . . . do questions about visual answers (18-24 months)
   What is Mama/Daddy/girl/boy doing?

Eating.	Dressing.
Sitting.	Climbing.
Hugging.	Talking.
Smiling.	Riding.
Drinking.	Cooking.
Walking.	Reading.
Washing.	Swinging.
Crying.	Standing.
Sleeping.	Running.
Playing.	Pushing.
Drying.	Working.
Talking.	Turning.
Jumping.	Going bye-bye.

4. Early discrimination—Choice of two manipulative or pictured family members (2-3 years)
   Which one:

goes to work?	goes to school?
drives?	cooks?
wets pants?	cleans?
folds clothes?	washes dishes?
plays?	wears dresses?
shaves?	wears diapers?

5. Early location questions about visual answers (2-3 years)
   Use manipulative dolls and dollhouse.

   Where is (*family member*)?
      At home.
      At work.
      Outside.
      In (_____) room.
      At school.
      Downstairs.
      Upstairs.

   Where does (*family member*):
      cook/eat/wash dishes? (*In the kitchen.*)
      sleep? (*In the bed/bedroom.*)
      put away clothes/toys? (*In the closet.*)
      brush teeth/bathe/wash hands/potty? (*In the bathroom.*)
      watch TV/read/play/talk? (*In the living room/den.*)
      ride/drive? (*In car/On tricycle.*)

6. Early attribute/concept questions—Choice of two manipulative or pictured family members (2-3 years)

Which one *(family member/ person)* is:	big?/little? tall?/short? up?/down? far?/near? on?/under? in?/out?	
Which one has:	long hair?/short hair? a happy face?/a sad face? blue/red/yellow/green	pants? shirt? dress? shoes?

Short Discussions and Narratives

Use manipulatives or puppet figures.

Discussion and questions for 18- to 24-month-old children:
    Mama and Daddy love their little baby.
    They feed the baby. They clean the baby.
    They take good care of their baby.

    Do Mama and Daddy love the baby?
    What do they do for baby?

Discussion and questions for 24- to 30-month-old children:
    This little boy can run and jump.
    He likes to play ball.
    This little girl can ride a tricycle.
    She likes to look at books.

    What can the boy do?
    Does the girl like books?
    Who can ride a tricycle?

Discussion and questions for 30- to 36-month-old children:
    This is a family.
    Mama and Daddy are big.
    They do a lot of work.
    The little children like to play.
    But baby just likes to sleep a lot!

    Is this a family?
    Who is big?
    What do the children do?
    Which person sleeps a lot?

Narrative and questions for 18- to 24-month-old children:
    The Daddy and his little girl are playing ball.
    Mama and the baby are watching them play.

    Who is playing ball?
    What are Mama and baby doing?

Narrative and questions for 24- to 30-month-old children:
    The little boy and girl are playing with their blocks.
    The girl builds a train, and the boy builds a house.
    Uh-oh! The boy's house falls down!

    What are the children doing?
    Who builds a train?
    Which child's blocks fall down?

Narrative and questions for 30- to 36-month-old children:
    The children are watching TV.
    They see Mama, Daddy, and baby.
    The baby is crying and crying.
    Then Mama gives the baby a bottle.
    The children are happy that baby stopped crying!

    What are the children doing?
    What do they see?
    Who is crying?
    Did the bottle make the baby happy?

Pets and Domestic Animals

For this unit, provide realistic plastic models of domestic animals; a toy barn and animals; and pictures and storybooks about farms, farm animals, pets, and common animals and their babies. Use the ENABLE I puppet figures of dog, cat, horse, cow, and chicken.

Although directives and questions in this unit usually pertain to those animals only, parents and teachers should use them as a guide and extend them to include pig, duck, turkey, sheep, and other domestic animals.

Directives

1. Routine-oriented directives (12-18 months)
   a. Pat: dog/cat.
      Don't pull: dog's/cat's   hair/tail.
      See/Look at: chicken/cow/horse/cat/dog.

   b. Let's: feed dog/cat.
                       rub (*animal's*) back.
                       ride horse.
                       watch (*animal*).

   c. Storybook directives

      Show me: dog/cat/horse/cow/chicken.

      Point to: (*animal's*)   mouth.
      Touch: eyes.
                                     ears.
                                     tail.
                                     legs.
                                     back.
                                     nose.

2. Simple one-step directives (18-24 months)
   a. Make (*animal*) walk/run.   Make chicken sit on the nest.
      Make cat climb up the tree.   Find horse's mane/hooves.
      Make horse gallop.   Point to cow's horns.
      Put (*animal*) in the barn.   Point to chicken's beak/feathers.

   b. Pragmatic directives—Actions given at home
      Give (*animal name*) something to eat/drink.
      Put dog/cat outside.
      Let dog/cat in the house.

65

c. Storybook directives

Show me:	(*animal*)	eating.
Point to:		chewing.
		drinking.
		running.
		galloping.
		climbing.
		being milked.
		that moos/barks/clucks/meows/neighs.

3. Two-step compound and complex directives (2-3 years)

a. Associative directives

Show me the animal with feathers.

Point to the animal we can milk.

Touch the animal(s) that live(s) in the house.

Show me the animal(s) that live(s) in the barn.

Show me the animal that lays eggs.

Point to the animal we can ride.

Point to the animal(s) that has (have) fur.

Touch the animal(s) that eat(s) grass.

Show me the animal that chews bones.

b. Positional and quantitative directives

Put the cow *in* the barn. Take the cow *out*.

Pat the dog *one* time. Pat him *another* time.

Find the *biggest* animal. Touch the *little* animal.

Show me the animal with the *longest* neck.

Put the cat *on top* of the barn. Put the dog at the *bottom*.

Move the chicken *near* you. Move the cow *far*.

c. Storybook directives

Look at the animals with hooves.

Show me the animal running in the field.

Show me an animal with a saddle.

Show me what the dog wags.

Show me what the cat drinks.

Point to what the chicken sits on.

Point to the animal that likes to play with children.

Point to the horse pulling the wagon.

Point to the animal with claws.

Show me a:	dog with a puppy.
	cow and a calf.
	horse with her foal.
	cat and her kittens.
	chicken and baby chicks.

d. Directives involving simple negatives

Show me the animal *without* feathers.

Touch the animals that *don't* have hair.

Point to the animal that is *not* big.

Show me the animals that do *not* live in a house.

Point to the animals that are *not* little.

Show me the animals you *cannot* ride.

Questions

1. Basic labeling questions (12-24 months)
   As the question is asked, adult points to animal or animal part.

   What's this/that?
   (horse, cow, dog, cat, chicken)

   What is this?

Legs.	Tail.	Ears.
Back.	Mouth.	Beak.
Nose.	Hooves.	Mane.
Claws.	Udder.	Feathers.
Horns.	Neck.	Fur.
Head.		

2. Yes/No questions

   a. Questions about visual model or picture of animal (18-24 months)

Is this:	(*animal*)?	
Is this:	(*animal's*):	(*body part, as listed above*)?
Is this:	horse:	galloping?
		eating grass?/hay?
		pulling wagon?
		riding (*person*)?
	cow:	being milked?
		eating grass?/hay?
		feeding calf?
	chicken:	on nest?/laying eggs?
		eating corn?
	cat:	sleeping?
		playing with toy?
		eating?
		drinking milk?
	dog:	chasing a stick/ball?
		chewing a bone?
		playing with child?

   b. Early negation questions (2-3 years)

   Can (*animal*) talk?

   Do chickens have fun?

   Do cows jump?

   Do horses live in houses?

Which animal does *not* give milk? (choice of cat or cow)

Do dogs bark?

Which one does *not* have feathers? (choice of dog or chicken)

Do chickens have beaks?

3. What . . . do questions about visual actions (21-30 months)

What animal can:

run fast?	gallop?
scratch?	bite?
bark?	jump?
trot?	climb?
swim?	

4. Early discrimination—(2-3 years)
Choice of two objects or pictures

What animal:

barks?
meows?
neighs?
clucks?
moos?
gives us food?

What animal can:

give milk?
eat hay?
give eggs?
we cook for food?

What animal is:

a pet?
a farm animal?

5. Early location questions about visual answers (2-3 years)

Where is the (*animal*)?

In the barn.
In the house.
Under the chair.
On the nest.
On the floor.
Outside.
In the field.

6. Early attribute/concept questions—Choice of two objects or pictures (2-3 years)

Which one is:

big?/little?
far?/near?

Which one has more legs?

Short Discussions and Narratives

Use the animal puppets.

Discussion and questions for 18- to 24-month-old children:
   This is a cow and a horse.
   We can ride a horse.
   We can milk a cow.

   What animal is this?
   Can we ride a cow?

Discussion and questions for 24- to 30-month-old children:
   A dog and a cat are pets.
   They live in houses with families.
   The families take care of them.
   They feed them and play with them.

   What animals are pets?
   Where do they live?
   Who takes care of them?

Discussion and questions for 30- to 36-month-old children:
   Many animals live on farms.
   The farmer cares for them because they give food.
   Chickens lay eggs. We can eat the eggs and we eat chickens, too.
   Cows give us milk.

   What animals give us food?
   Does a chicken give milk?
   Which animals does a farmer care for?

Narrative and questions for 18- to 24-month-old children:
   The chicken is clucking on her nest.
   She is getting up.
   Oh, she laid an egg!

   What is this?
   What did the chicken do?

Narrative and questions for 24- to 30-month-old children:
   The girl is riding the horse.
   The horse gallops across the field.
   The girl is having a good time.
   They are going so-o fast!

   What is the girl doing?
   Is the horse walking?
   Are they going fast?

Narrative and questions for 30- to 36-month-old children:
   The cow has a baby calf.
   She is feeding her baby.
   The dog has babies, too—lots of them!
   See her feeding the little puppies.

   Is a calf a baby dog?
   Which animal has lots of babies?
   Are babies little?

Home

For this unit, use the *ENABLE* posters of the inside and outside of a house. You may want to provide a larger toy playhouse that opens to show a kitchen, bathroom, bedroom, and living room. Storybooks that feature pictures of homes, rooms, garages, porches, and yards also are helpful.

Directives

1. Routine-oriented directives (12-18 months)
   a. Home-situated directives

Let's go to the:	bedroom.
	bathroom.
	kitchen.
	living room.*
Let's go:	inside.
	outside.

   Den or family room may be taught in substitution for living room, as appropriate to individual child.

   b. Directives using playhouse or pictures

Show me:	the house/home.
Find:	porch.
Point to:	kitchen.
	wall.
	yard.
	bedroom.
	living room.
	door.
	garage.
	bathroom.
	floor.
	window.

2. Simple one-step directives (18-24 months)
   a. Pragmatic directives
   Child learns to move to correct place in response to action directive given.

In bathroom:	Go:	potty.	clean up.
		wash.	bathe.
		dry off.	brush teeth.

In kitchen:	Go:	sit down to eat.
		get a drink.
		get a snack.
		eat your (breakfast/lunch/dinner).
In bedroom:	Go:	get dressed.
		play with your toys.
		pick up your toys.
		get ready for bed.
		to bed.
		to sleep.
In living room:	Go:	watch TV.
		read your books.
		play with your toys.
		listen to the music.
		sit down and play.

Climb the stairs.
Play on the porch.
Shut/Open the door.
Play inside/outside.

b. Storybook directives

Show me:	house.
Point to:	porch.
Touch:	kitchen.
	hall.
	roof.
	yard.
	bedroom.
	living room.
	door.
	garage.
	bathroom.
	stairs.
	window.
Touch the room:	to sleep.
	to clean/wash.
	to play.
	to eat.
	to be together.
	to cook.
	to watch TV.

3. Two-step compound and complex directives (2-3 years)
   a. Directives given at home

In bathroom:	Wet the washcloth *in* the sink.
	Close the door and turn the light *on*.
	Dry your hands *on* the towel and hang it up.
	Open the door and turn the light *off*.
	Put the toothpaste *on* the brush.
	Put the *top* back *on* the toothpaste.
	Put the towel *on* the *nearest* rack.
	Rinse your hands a *few* times.

	Put *all* your clothes *in* the hamper.
	Wash *both* hands.
	Take your clothes *off*.
	Put them *on*.
	Wash *all* your body; don't *miss* any part!
In kitchen:	*Open/Close* the refrigerator.
	Sit *at* the table.
	Put your hands *on* your lap.
	Take *another* bite.
	Take your arms *off* the table.
	Drink *all* your milk.
	Put your hands *under* the table.
	Sit *across* from (*person's name*).
	Get a drink *out* of the refrigerator.
In bedroom:	Turn the bedcovers *down*.
	Hang your clothes *up*.
	Put your toys *in* the box/*on* the shelf.
	Put your clothes *in* the drawer.
	Put *both* shoes *under* the bed.
	Look *out* the window.
In living room:	Sit *on* the couch and: listen to the music.
	watch TV.
	read your book.
	Walk to the *middle* of the room.
	Run to the *side* of the room.
	Find the *missing* puzzle piece.
	Sit on *another* chair.
	Pick up *all* the toys.
	Go *in* the door.
Outside:	Play *on* the porch/*in* the garage.
	Walk *up/down* the stairs.

b. Room part functions

Use playhouse and family toys or puppet figures.

Put the boy in the room for sleeping.

Sit the Mama in the room for eating.

Walk the Daddy in the room for cleaning up.

Have the girl sit down in the room for talking together.

Put the baby on the floor of the living room.

Make Mama look outside.

Show me the chimney on top of the house.

Show me the parts you can open and close. (*windows, doors*)

Show me the place to park the car. (*garage*)

Point to the part for going up and down. (*stairs*)

c. Storybook directives—Early attributes

Show me the *littlest* (or smallest) room. (*bathroom*)

Point to the *biggest* room. (*living room*)

Show me the room that has *more* food.

Point to the room that is *blue/green/yellow*.

Show me the *top* part of the house.
Show me the *bottom* part of the house.

d. Directives involving simple negatives

Point to something hot you do *not* touch.
Show me a part of the house *not* for running.
Show me the room *not* for sleeping/eating/washing/playing.
Point to the room *without* chairs. (*bathroom*)
Show me a part of a room you *cannot* reach or touch.
Find a part of the house that is *not* on the inside.
Find a part of the house *without* furniture.
Find a wall *without* doors.

Questions

1. Basic labeling questions (12-24 months)
   Use actual rooms of home or playhouse.

What is this?	House/home.	Yard.	Doors.
	Furniture.	Closet.	Garage.
	Porch.	Windows.	Stairs.
	Chimney.	Roof.	Walls.
	Floors.	Hall.	

   What room is this?   Bedroom.
   Kitchen.
   Bathroom.
   Living room.

2. Yes/No Questions

   a. Questions about present, visual information (18-24 months)

   Is this: your/a: house/home?
   yard?
   door?
   furniture?
   garage?
   porch?
   window?
   stairs?
   roof?
   wall?
   floor?
   hall?
   bedroom?
   kitchen?
   closet?
   chimney?
   bathroom?
   living room?

Can you: eat   here?
          sit   in this room/place?
          dry
          drink
          climb
          cook
          sleep
          play
          talk
          wash
          look in/out
          go in/out

b. Early negation questions—With playhouse or pictured house present (2-3 years)

Where can't you sleep?

Where don't you eat?

What can't you walk on?

Where can't you take a bath?

Is the chimney on the roof?

Are windows on the floor?

Do kitchens have stoves?

Do bathrooms have beds?

3. What . . . do questions (21-32 months)
Adult points to playhouse room or pictured room.

What can you do here?

Kitchen: Eat.
                Cook.
                Keep food.
                Drink.
                Wash dishes.
Bathroom: Take a bath.
                Wash hands.
                Go potty.
                Brush teeth.
                Dry.
                Change clothes.
                Get dressed.
Living room: Watch TV.
                Listen to music.
                Sit on couch/chair.
                Play with toys.
                Talk on telephone.
                Read books.
                Hug Mama/Daddy.
                Rock.

Bedroom:	Go to bed.
	Put clothes/toys away.
	Sleep.
	Get dressed.
	Get up.
	Change clothes.
	Take a nap.
Door or window:	Open/Close.
	Go/look in.
	Go/look out.
Stairs:	Climb up/down.
Garage:	Park car.
	Get tricycle.
Closet:	Hang clothes.
	Put shoes.

4. Early discrimination—Choice of two visual rooms or parts of home (2-3 years)

Which room do you use to:

eat?	comb hair?
talk?	dry?
keep food?	brush teeth?
drink?	sleep?
wash?	dress?
keep clothes?	put blankets/covers?

Which part of the house do you:
open?/close?
put the car?
climb?
hang pictures?

5. Early location—With playhouse or pictured house visible (2-3 years)

Where is/are:

the garage?	the TV?
the porch?	the door?
the roof?	the bathtub?
the beds?	the walls?
the couch?	the windows?
the stairs?	the light switch?
the door knob?	the refrigerator?

6. Early attribute/concept questions—Choice of two pictured rooms or parts of a house (2-3 years)

Which part(s) is/are:
inside?
outside?
on the house top? (*roof, chimney*)
on the bottom of the house? (*floor*)
on the walls? (*walls, windows*)

Which part goes up and down?
Which room is:
    upstairs?
    downstairs?
    little?
    big?
Which room has:
    more food?
    another window?
    many chairs?
    a closet?
    one door?

Short Discussions and Narratives

Use playhouse or pictured house and family puppets.

Discussion and questions for 18- to 24-month-old children:
    A home is a house.
    A home is where we live.

    What is a home?
    Do we live in a house?

Discussion and questions for 24- to 30-month-old children:
    This house has many rooms.
    We cook and eat in a kitchen.
    We sleep and dress in a bedroom.
    We clean up and "go potty"* in the bathroom.

    What can we do in a bathroom?
    Can we sleep in a kitchen?
    Which room can we eat in?

    *Any term for toileting may be substituted for "go potty." Use of the term
    familiar to the child is preferable, unless wishing to teach a new term.*

Discussion and questions for 30- to 36-month-old children:
    See the parts of the house!
    The roof is on the top and keeps the rain out.
    The doors are for going in and out.
    We have windows to see outside.
    Stairs are to get upstairs and downstairs.

    What does a roof do?
    Which part can we use to go in and out?
    What do we use to see outside?

Narrative and questions for 18- to 24-month-old children:
    See the family at home!
    They are sitting in the living room.

    Who is this? (*family or family member's name*)
    What is this? (*home, house, living room*)

Narrative and questions for 24- to 30-month-old children:
What a busy house!
Mama cooks in the kitchen.
Daddy dresses in the bedroom.
The children play in the living room.

Is this a house?
Who is in the kitchen?
What is Daddy doing?
Where are the children?

Narrative and questions for 30- to 36-month-old children:
Mama opens the door and goes in the house.
She takes Baby upstairs and into the bathroom.
Mama washes and dries Baby.
She lays him on the rug on the floor to dress him.

What does Mama open?
Where is the bathroom?
Where does Mama dress Baby?
Was the rug on the ceiling?

Furniture

Actual furniture in a house or school, miniature playhouse furniture, and pictures and storybooks featuring furniture are useful in the activities for this unit.

Use the ENABLE I flannel board pictures of these furniture items:

1. bed
2. chest of drawers
3. table, chairs
4. refrigerator
5. stove
6. couch
7. TV (or television)
8. telephone
9. bathtub
10. potty (toilet)

Other typical furniture should be included for higher-functioning children.

Directives

1. Routine-oriented directives (12-18 months)

   a. Lie down on the bed.
   Get your clothes from the drawer.
   Put your clothes in the drawer.
   Sit on the couch.
   Look at/Listen to the TV.
   Talk on the phone.
   Sit at the table.
   Sit on the chair.
   Open/Close the refrigerator.
   Don't touch the stove.
   Go to/Sit on the potty.
   Get in/Get out of the bathtub.

   b. Let's: go to bed.
   put our clothes away.
   sit down.
   watch TV.
   go potty.
   take a bath.

   c. Show me: bed.
   Point to: refrigerator.
   telephone.
   stove.
   potty.
   chest of drawers.
   table.
   couch.
   bathtub.
   chair.
   TV.

2. Simple one-step directives (18-24 months)
   a. Pragmatic directives—Actions given at home
   Make the bed.
   Put the pillow on the couch.
   Pull the covers up/down.
   Turn on/Turn off the TV.
   Open/Close the drawers.
   Pick up/put down the telephone.
   Go eat at the table.
   Flush the potty.
   Set the table.
   Take a bath in the bathtub.
   Clean off the table.
   Put the pan/pot on the stove.

   b. Storybook directives

Show me:	the furniture for sleeping.
Point to:	the furniture to keep clothes.
Find:	the furniture to eat on.
Touch:	the furniture to sit on.
	the furniture to keep food.
	the furniture to cook food.
	the furniture for sitting together.
	the furniture to watch cartoons.
	the furniture for pottying.
	the furniture for washing/bathing.

3. Two-step compound and complex directives (2-3 years)
   a. Conceptual and sequenced directives
   Go to the bedroom and sit on the bed.
   Turn down the covers and get in bed.
   Open the drawer and get your clothes.
   Pull your chair up to the table.
   Open the refrigerator and get the (*food name*).
   Watch Mama/Daddy cook on the stove.
   Sit on the couch and watch TV.
   Lie on the couch and look at your books.
   Answer/Pick up the telephone and say "Hello."
   Go to the bathroom and use the toilet.
   Get in the tub and turn on/off the water.
   Crawl across the bed to the nearest chair.
   Put the telephone on the table.
   Sit near me on the couch.
   Stay far away from the hot stove.

Put your shoes under the bed.

Put the (*clothing name*) in the top/bottom drawer.

Put the dish in the middle of the table.

Put the soap on the tub.

b. Storybook directives

Point to:	the quilt on the bed.
Show me:	the child in the bed.
Find:	the (*dish name*) on the table.
	the person in the chair.
	the magazine on the couch.
	the picture on the refrigerator.
	the food in the refrigerator.
	the pot/pan on the stove.
	the picture on the TV screen.
	the potty in the bathroom.
	the bathtub full of water.

c. Positional and quantitative directives

Point to:	the back/legs of the bed.
Show me:	the bedcover.
Find:	the top of the chest.
	the handles on the drawers.
	the top of the table.
	the legs of the table.
	the door of the refrigerator.
	the shelf in the refrigerator.
	the top of the stove.
	the inside of the stove.
	the seat of the chair/couch.
	the back/legs/arms of the chair/couch.
	the controls on the TV.
	the TV screen.
	the handle/seat of the potty.
	the faucet/side of the bathtub.
	the telephone receiver/dial/base.

d. Directives involving simple negatives

Show me bedroom furniture you do *not* use for playing.

Find a piece of furniture *without* a drawer.

Touch furniture *without* a door.

Show me something that does *not* get hot.

Point to kitchen furniture where you do *not* eat.

Find bedroom furniture *not* for holding clothes.

Touch bathroom furniture *not* for washing.

Show me living room furniture *not* for sitting.

Questions

1. Basic labeling questions (12-24 months)
   As the question is asked, adult points to actual or toy furniture.

   What is this/that?

Bed.	Potty (toilet).	Bathtub.
Refrigerator.	Stove.	Chairs.
Telephone.	Table.	TV.
Chest.	Couch.	

2. Yes/No questions

   a. Questions about visible furniture (18-24 months)

   Is this a (*furniture name*):

leg?	shelf?	handle?
back?	back?	door?
top?	inside?	control?

   Is this for:

eating?	listening?
sitting?	talking?
keeping food?	watching?/looking?
drinking?	going potty (toileting)?
cooking food?	washing/bathing?
sleeping?	

   b. Early negation questions (2-3 years)

   Can you take a bath in a bed?

   Do you put food in a chest of drawers?

   Would you stand on a table?

   Are chairs for sitting?

   Do you jump over a couch?

   Do you cook in a refrigerator?

   Can you talk on the TV?

   Do you put trash on a stove?

   Are beds for taking naps?

   Can you watch cartoons on a telephone?

   Would you take a bath in a tub?

3. What . . . do questions about visible furniture (21-30 months)

   What can you do with (*furniture name*)?

Eat.	Sit together.
Sit.	Cook.
Put away/take out/clothes.	Talk.
Drink.	Take a bath.
Wash.	Take a nap.
Put away/Take out/Keep food.	Potty/toilet.
Sleep.	Watch cartoons.
Dry.	

4. Early discrimination—Choice of two visual pieces of furniture (2-3 years)

Which furniture can you use to:

sleep on?	store milk and eggs?
get under covers?	cook breakfast?
keep your clothes in?	heat soup?
put dishes on?	read a book with Mom?
eat on?	talk to Grandma?
do work on?	put tissue in?
sit on?	get clean?
keep food fresh?	

5. Early location questions about furniture pictured in rooms or in flannel board house (2-3 years)

Where is the:

bed, chest of drawers? (*In the bedroom.*)
table, chairs, refrigerator, stove (*In the kitchen.*)
couch, chair, TV, telephone? (*In the living room.*)
potty, bathtub? (*In the bathroom.*)

6. Early attribute/concept questions—Choice of two pictured furniture items (2-3 years)

Which one is:
big?/little?
blue?/yellow?/green?/red?
together? (*table and chairs*)
full? (*bathtub*)
tall? (*refrigerator*)
open?/closed? (*chest of drawers*)
on?/off? (*TV*)

Short Discussions and Narratives

Use playhouse and furniture or flannel board house and pictured furniture along with family puppets.

Discussion and questions for 18- to 24-month-old-children:
Couches and chairs are for sitting.
A couch is a big, long chair.

What is for sitting?
Is a couch little?

Discussion and questions for 24- to 30-month-old children:
We have beds and chests of drawers in bedrooms.
We can sleep in a bed and keep warm at night under the covers.
We can keep our clothes in the chest of drawers.

Where are our beds?
Do we sleep under a bed?
Which furniture has drawers?

Discussion and questions for 30- to 36-month-old children:
   All our meals are cooked in the kitchen.
   Mama gets the food out of the refrigerator and cooks it on the stove.
   She puts it on the table, and we sit there and eat it.

   Does Mama cook in the bathroom?
   Where is the food cooked?
   Which place do we eat?

Narrative and questions for 18- to 24-month-old children:
   Mama and Daddy are sitting on the couch.
   Mama is watching TV, and Daddy is talking on the telephone.

   Are they sitting in a chair?
   What is Mama doing?

Narrative and questions for 24- to 30-month-old children:
   The boy takes his pajamas out of the drawer.
   He puts them on and gets in the bed.
   Mama tucks the covers around him and kisses him goodnight.
   The boy is so-o sleepy!

   Are the boy's pajamas under the bed?
   Where is the boy?
   Who tucks his covers around him?
   Is the boy going to sleep?

Narrative and questions for 30- to 36-month-old children:
   Mama is cooking lunch on the stove.
   Baby is sitting in her high chair waiting. She is hungry.
   Mama brings soup to the table and begins to feed Baby.
   See her smile!

   What is Mama doing?
   Is Baby hungry?
   What will Baby eat?
   Where is Baby sitting?

Utensils

For the activities in this unit, use these ENABLE I flannel board pictures:

11. placemat	16. spoon
12. plate	17. napkin
13. glass	18. stove
14. fork	19. pot
15. knife	20. pan

Actual and toy utensils also are helpful and fun.

Provide pictures and storybooks about utensils. A sorting tray for silverware, toy storage cabinet for dishes, and toy table for setting are useful materials for this unit.

Directives

1. Routine-oriented directives (12-18 months)

   a. Use your spoon/fork.
      Bring your cup/glass here.
      Take a drink.
      Get your bowl/plate.

   b. Show me the: plate.
      Point to the: glass.
      Get the: spoon.
                       bowl.
                       knife.
                       pot.
                       cup.
                       fork.
                       pan.

2. Simple one-step directives (18-24 months)
   Pragmatic directives—Actions given at home

      Keep/Put your plate on the table.

      Eat with your spoon/fork.

      Let's spread butter (jelly, peanut butter) with your knife.

      Pick up your glass/cup.

Put your glass/cup down.

Pour cereal in the bowl.

Pour milk in the glass.

Get Mama the pot/pan.

Let Mama cut your meat.

3. Two-step compound and complex directives (2-3 years)

a. Associative directives

Show me:	what we eat on.
Point to:	what we cut with.
Find:	what Mama cooks bacon in.
Bring me:	the dish to eat soup.
	what we eat meat with.
	what we drink from.
	what we eat cereal with.
	the dish to drink coffee.
	what Mama cooks soup in.
Show me:	eating.
	cooking.
	heating/warming.
	drinking.
	pouring.
	freezing.
	cutting.
	spreading.

b. Positional and quantitative directives

Get your glass and take it to the table.

Take the cereal and pour it in the bowl.

Drink the milk out of the full glass.

Stir the chocolate/sugar in your cup.

Put the knife/fork/spoon beside the plate.

Put the spoon in the bowl.

Put the fork on the plate.

Bring the empty plate/bowl to the sink.

Put the pot/pan in the dishwasher.

Stack the plates/bowls together.

Sort the utensils/silverware.

Match the (*utensil name*).

Put all the knives/forks/spoons together.

Carry the pots and pans to the nearest shelf.

Give me all the dishes.

Put the glass near the plate.

Put the bowl in the middle of the table.

Give me both the fork and spoon.

c. Storybook directives

Point to: the baby with a cup.
Show me: the man cutting with a knife.
Find: the boy without a plate.
              the girl eating with a fork.
              the empty bowl.
              the Mama/Daddy cooking with a pot/pan.
              the spoon in the bowl.
              the handle of the pot/pan.
              all the dishes.
              one of the bowls.
              the forks and spoons in the tray.
              the plates and bowls on the shelf.

d. Directives involving simple negatives

Point to a utensil that will *not* break.

Show me a utensil that will *not* cut.

Show me utensils you would *not* use to cook.

Show me a dish that does *not* hold soup or cereal.

Find a utensil *not* for eating meat.

Show me utensils *not* for drinking

Find utensils *without* handles.

Find utensils *without* lids.

Questions

1. Basic labeling questions (12-24 months)
   As the question is asked, adult points to actual or toy utensil.

   What is this/that?

Plate.	Bowl.	Cup.
Glass.	Knife.	Fork.
Spoon.	Pot.	Pan.

2. Yes/No questions

   a. Questions about visible utensils (18-24 months)

      Is this a (*utensil name*)?

      Is this for:

eating?	heating food?
cooking?	cutting?
drinking?	holding food?

   b. Early negation questions (2-3 years)

Can you eat soup on a plate?	Is a pot for eating cereal?
Do you drink coffee in a cup?	Is a pan for cutting meat?
Can you cut meat with a spoon?	Can you find dishes on a shelf?
Can you eat meat in a glass?	Do you eat peas with a knife?

3. What . . . do questions about visible utensils (21-30 months)

What do/can you do with (*utensil name*)?

Eat.	Cut.
Cook.	Heat food.
Wash.	Set table.
Drink.	Hold food.

4. Early discrimination—Choice of two visible utensils (2-3 years)

Which one do we need/use to:

eat soup?	cook soup?
eat cereal?	eat meat?
cook meat?	hold ice cream?
set the table?	eat peas?
cut meat?	spread jelly?

5. Early location questions about toy utensils or pictured utensils (2-3 years)

Where is the (*utensil name*)?

On the table.	In the cup.
By the plate.	On the shelf.
In the drawer.	Under the bowl.
In the bowl.	Beside the plate/bowl.
On the stove.	

6. Early attribute/concept questions—Choice of two pictured utensils (2-3 years)

Which one is:
biggest?/littlest (smallest)?
blue?/yellow?/red?/green?
in the drawer?
on the shelf?
on the stove?

Short Discussions and Narratives

Use actual, toy, or pictured utensils and family puppets.

Discussion and questions for 18- to 24-month-old children:
Forks and spoons help us eat food.
Knives are to cut up food.

What do we do with knives?
Is a knife for cutting?

Discussion and questions for 24- to 30-month-old children:
We use pots and pans to cook food.
We can fry meat and cook eggs in a pan.
We can heat soup and cook vegetables in a pot.

Are pots and pans for cooking?
Which one do we use to fry meat?
What can we do with pots?

Discussion and questions for 30- to 36-month-old children:
Dishes hold our food for us to eat.
We put meat and vegetables on our plates and soup and cereal in our bowls.
We drink milk and juice out of glasses.
Mama and Daddy drink coffee from a cup.

Where do we put our meat?
Which dish holds cereal?
Do Mama and Daddy drink coffee from a glass?

Narrative and questions for 18- to 24-month-old children:
The boy is helping to set the table.
He gets the plates and the glasses.

Who is this? (boy)
What is he doing?

Narrative and questions for 24- to 30-month-old children:
Mama is teaching the boy to cut his meat.
She sticks the fork in the meat and holds it and then begins to cut with the knife.
"That looks hard!" says the boy.

What is Mama doing?
Where does she put the fork?
What does the boy say?

Narrative and questions for 30- to 36-month-old children:
The girl wants to make her own breakfast.
She pours cereal in the bowl.
She puts milk and sugar on top of it.
Then she pours a glass of orange juice.
What a good breakfast!

What is the girl doing?
What does she put in the bowl?
Which juice does she put in the glass?

Simple Tools and Machines

The activities in this unit are developed around the radio, record player, iron and ironing board, washer, dryer, hammer and nails, broom, shovel, rake, and ladder.

While actual tools or machines are most meaningful to youngsters, toys or pictures also are useful.

Use the ENABLE I flannel board scenes of:
21. kitchen/utility room, with washer, dryer, and iron and ironing board
22. school room, with radio and record player
23. yard and back porch, with a ladder, hammer and nails, broom, shovel, and rake

Directives

1. Routine-oriented directives (12-18 months)

   a. Listen to the radio/record player.
   Stay away from the iron.
   Give me your dirty clothes.
   Put away your clean clothes.
   Hammer the nail.
   Sweep the floor.
   Dig the dirt/sand.
   Rake the leaves.
   Climb the ladder.

   b. Show me the: radio.
      Point to the: washer.
      Bring me the: hammer.
                        shovel.
                        dryer.
                        nails.
                        rake.
                        iron.
                        broom.
                        ladder.
                        ironing board.
                        record player.

2. Simple one-step directives (18-24 months)

   a. Pragmatic directives—Actions given at home

      Turn on/Turn off the radio/record player.

      Pretend you're ironing, like Mama.

      Take the/your clothes to the washer.

      Get your clothes off the dryer.

      Hit the nail with the hammer.

      Sweep the floor with the broom.

      Help Daddy shovel the garden.

      Rake a pile of leaves.

      Step on the ladder.

   b. Associative directives—Using objects or pictures

Show me the:	radio/record player	at school.
Point to the:	washer, dryer	at home.
Find the:	iron/ironing board	in the utility room.
	hammer and nails	in the yard.
	broom	on the porch.
	shovel	
	rake	
	ladder	

Show me:	listening.
Point to:	washing clothes.
	sweeping.
	drying clothes.
	digging.
	folding clothes.
	building.
	ironing clothes.
	hammering.
	shoveling.
	raking.
	dancing.
	climbing.

3. Two-step compound and complex directives (2-3 years)

   a. Positional and quantitative directives

      Turn the volume up/down on the radio.

      Put a record on the record player and dance.

      Start the record player and listen to it.

      Turn on/off the radio.

      Put the iron on the ironing board.

      Put the dirty clothes in the washer and close it.

      Get the clothes out of the dryer and put them in the basket.

      Help Mama fold the clothes and put them on the dryer.

      Hold a nail on the board and hit it with the hammer.

      Sweep all of the kitchen floor with the broom.

      Shovel piles of sand to build a house/castle.

      Rake up piles of leaves and jump in the pile.

      Lean the ladder against the wall and run under it.

b. Find: the knob to turn the record player/radio on.
the cord and plug for the record player.
the antenna to the radio.
the folding legs of the ironing board.
the door to the washer/dryer.
the handle of the broom/shovel/rake.
the steps of the ladder.

c. Storybook directives

Point to: the child playing the record player.
Show me: the lady putting a record on the record player.
Find: the person listening to the radio.
ironing board with/without an iron/clothes.
washer/dryer full of clothes.
the empty washer/dryer.
the person building with hammer and nails.
Mama working in the garden.
family raking their yard.
man climbing the ladder.

d. Directives involving simple negatives

Find a kitchen machine *not* for washing.

Show me a kitchen machine you do *not* use with clothes.

Find a yard tool you *cannot* climb.

Show me a machine that makes *no* sound.

Touch a tool *not* for digging.

Show me the ones that are *not* machines.

Show me what plays music *without* records.

Questions

1. Basic labeling questions (12-24 months)
As question is asked, adult points to actual tool or machine.

What is this/that?

Radio.	Record player.	Rake.
Washer.	Shovel.	Nails.
Dryer.	Iron.	Ladder.
Broom.	Hammer.	Ironing board.

2. Yes/No questions

a. Yes/No questions about visible tools and machines (18-24 months)

Is this a (*tool or machine name*)?

Is this for:

listening?	ironing?	pressing?
hammering?	dancing?	sweeping?
cleaning floors?	hitting nails?	digging dirt/sand?
washing?	building?	climbing up and down?
drying?	raking leaves?	

　　b. Early negation questions (2-3 years)

　　　　Is a radio for watching?

　　　　Can you listen to music without a record on the record player?

　　　　Can you turn on a radio?

　　　　Do you press clothes and then plug in the iron?

　　　　Does a washer need shampoo?

　　　　Should you hammer screws?

　　　　Are nails and hammers for building?

　　　　Can you mop a floor with a broom?

　　　　Is a shovel for hoeing?

　　　　Do you put clothes in a dryer?

　　　　Can you sweep the floor with a rake?

　　　　Is a ladder short?

3. What . . . do questions about visible or pictured tools and machines (21-30 months)

　　　　What do/can you do with (*tool/machine*)?

Listen to music.	Iron clothes.
Build things.	Pull out nails.
Dance to music.	Climb.
Repair things.	Press clothes.
Dig dirt.	Sweep floors.
Listen to news.	Wash clothes.
Hammer nails.	Clean floors.
Rake yards.	Dry clothes.

4. Early discrimination—Choice of two visible tools or machines (2-3 years)

　　　　Which one do you find:

in a kitchen?	leaning on a wall?
in a living room?	in a yard?
in a bedroom?	on a porch?
in a utility room?	at a school?

　　　　Which one do we need to:

listen to the news?	sweep up dirt?
dry our clothes?	iron/press our clothes?
put on a record?	put detergent in?
build a box?	repair things?
have a dance?	dig holes in a garden?
hang pictures on a wall?	rake a pile of leaves?
wash our clothes?	climb up on a roof?

5. Early location questions about actual or pictured tools and machines (2-3 years)

　　　　Where is the (*tool/machine*)?

On the shelf.	On the tool rack.
In the utility room.	In the kitchen.
On the table.	Leaning on the house.
In the tool box.	On the ironing board.
In the closet.	

6. Early attribute/concept questions—Choice of two pictured tools or machines (2-3 years)

Which one has:
        a round record?
        a big door?
        a little knob?
        a long handle?
        big legs?
Which one is:
        long?
        hot?
        short?

Short Discussions and Narratives

Use ENABLE I family puppets and unit pictures.

Discussion and questions for 18- to 24-month-old children:
        We can listen to music with radios and record players.
        We turn this knob and then we can dance!

        Is a radio for listening?
        What do we turn?

Discussion and questions for 24- to 30-month-old children:
        We like to have nice, clean clothes.
        We can wash dirty clothes in a washer.
        Then we dry them in a dryer.
        We can press the clothes with an iron, and then we're ready to wear them.

        Where do we put dirty clothes?
        What does a dryer do?
        Are irons for pressing?

Discussion and questions for 30- to 36-month-old children:
        We need tools to do yard work.
        We can dig up dirt with shovels and rake up leaves with rakes.
        You can build a ladder, using a hammer and nails.

        Are shovels for digging?
        What do you use to build things?
        Are tools for doing work?

Narrative and questions for 18- to 24-month-old children:
        Mama is getting the boy's clothes ready for him to wear.
        She puts them on the ironing board and presses the iron across them.

        Who has the boy's clothes?
        What is she doing?

Narrative and questions for 24- to 30-month-old children:

The children are having a birthday party.

Mama puts a record on the record player and turns it on.

The children are playing "Musical Chairs."

What are the children doing?

Where does Mama put the record?

What game do they play?

Narrative and questions for 30- to 36-month-old children:

The family is working in the yard.

Mama digs in the garden, and the girl rakes the cut grass.

Daddy climbs the ladder to the roof. He takes his hammer and nails to fix the roof.

What is the family doing?

What does Mama use in the garden?

Where is Daddy?

What does he need to fix the roof?

Clothing

Actual clothing items are particularly beneficial in this unit and should include shoes, socks, pants, shirt, dress, sweater, jacket, raincoat, gloves, mittens, and cap. Pictures and storybooks about these clothing items for boys and girls, as well as clothing items typically used by men and women, also are helpful.

Use the *ENABLE* large boy and girl figures and magnetic vinyl clothing items. For the girl there are shoes and socks, a dress, cardigan sweater, and raincoat. For the boy there are shoes and socks, pants, shirt, jacket, mittens, and winter cap. (Note: Additional magnetic vinyl clothing items are used in ENABLE II activities, as described on page 199.)

Directives

1. Routine-oriented directives (12-18 months)
   a. Get your: shoes.
      Bring me your: socks.
      Let's put on your: coat.
      Pull up your: pants.
      Push down your: (*clothing name*).

   b. Show me the: shoes.
      Point to your: dress.
                      gloves.
                      cap.
                      socks.
                      sweater.
                      pants.
                      coat.
                      shirt.
                      raincoat.

2. Simple one-step directives (18-24 months)
   a. Pragmatic directives—Actions given at home

      Put on/Take off (*clothing name*.)

      Pull up your socks.

      Pull off your shirt.

      Fold the clothes.

   b. Associative directives

      Show me: child dressing.
      Point to: boy with coat/gloves/cap.
                      buttoning.
                      zipping.
                      child folding clothes.
                      girl with sweater/raincoat.
                      snapping.
                      tying.
                      buckling.

   c. Clothing parts

      Show me: your (the):   buttons.
      Find: buckles.
                               pocket.
                               front.
                               back.
                               snaps.
                               laces.
                               hood.
                               zippers.
                               collar.
                               sleeves.

3. Two-step compound and complex directives (2-3 years)
   a. Associative directives

      Find: what we wear on our feet.
      Bring me: what we wear to keep dry.
                      what girls wear.
                      what we wear on our hands.
                      what we wear to keep warm.
                      a pair of shoes/socks.
                      what we wear on our head.

   b. Conceptual and sequenced directives

      Get your shoes and put them on.
      Put your socks over your toes and pull them up.
      Button/unbutton your coat and put on your cap/hood.
      Snap/unsnap your pants, and buckle/unbuckle your belt.
      Untie/undo your shoes, and take them off.
      Put your shirts in the drawer.
      Hang your coat in the closet.
      Put your shoes beside the bed.
      Put the sweater on over your coat.
      Zip/unzip your coat/pants up/down.
      Put your cap on your head and fasten it.
      Put your gloves in your pocket.
      Put your arms in both sleeves.

Wear your shirt and sweater together.

Show me the collar of the coat.

c. Storybook directives

Point to: the girl dressed for rain.

Show me: the buttons on the coat.

the boy with hands in his pockets.

the sleeves of the shirt.

the dress with a collar.

all the clothes.

the front of the dress.

another shirt.

the laces of the shoes.

the zipper on the coat.

d. Directives involving simple negatives

Show me clothing *not* for wearing on the head.

Point to clothing *without* buttons.

Touch clothing with *no* zippers.

Find clothing you *cannot* lace or tie.

Show me clothing you do *not* wear inside the house.

Show me clothing boys do *not* wear.

Point to clothing *without* snaps.

Find clothing with *no* pockets.

Questions

1. Basic labeling questions (12-24 months)
As the question is asked, adult points to the actual or pictured clothing item.

What is this/that?

Shoes.	Sweater.	Coat.
Dress.	Cap.	Shirt.
Gloves.	Pants.	Raincoat.
Socks.		

2. Yes/No questions

a. Yes/No questions about visible clothing (18-24 months)

Is this (*clothing name*)?

Is this for:

wearing?

keeping dry?

taking off?

putting on?

keeping warm?

b. Early negation questions (2-3 years)

Do we wear coats in hot weather?

Do we wear dresses with shoes?

Do we wear gloves on our heads?

Are dresses for girls to wear?

Do we wear shoes on our hands?

Do shoes have buttons?

Can raincoats keep you dry?

Do hats have zippers?

Do pants have collars?

Do shoes have pockets?

Can sweaters keep you warm?

3. What . . . do questions about visible clothing (21-30 months)

What can/do you do with (*clothing name*)?

Wear.	Take off.
Keep dry.	Button.
Zip.	Fasten.
Put on.	Keep warm.
Dress.	Buckle.
Snap.	Unfasten.

What are you (What is he/she) doing?

Dressing.	Drying.
Washing.	Folding.
Putting away.	Hanging.
Undressing.	

4. Early discrimination—Choice of two visible clothing items (2-3 years)

Which one do we need to:

go outside?	cover our head?
keep warm?	keep dry?
keep feet warm?	cover our hands?
cover our feet?	wear with pants?

Which (part) do we need to:

(un)button?	put legs in?
(un)lace?	(un)zip?
put arms in?	(un)buckle?
(un)snap?	put fingers in?
(un)tie?	put toys in? (*pocket*)

5. Early location questions about visible clothing items (2-3 years)

Where is the (*clothing name*)?	Which ones go together?
On our head.	Shoes and socks.
On our hands.	Coat and gloves.
On our feet.	Pants and shirt.
Over our dress/shirt.	
On the top of our body.	
On the bottom of our body.	

6. Early attribute/concept questions—Choice of two pictured clothing items (2-3 years)

> Which one is:
>> (un)buttoned?
>> (un)zipped?
>> (un)snapped?
>> (un)fastened?
>> (un)laced
>> big?/little?
>> blue?/yellow?/red?/green?/orange?/purple?
>
> Which one do we wear in pairs?
>> Socks/shoes/gloves.

Short Discussions and Narratives

Use dolls and clothing for this unit.

Discussion and questions for 18- to 24-month-old children:
> We put shoes and socks on our feet.
> They cover our feet and keep them warm.
>
> Are shoes and socks for hands?
> What do they keep warm?

Discussion and questions for 24- to 30-month-old children:
> Here are pants and a shirt.
> Boys and girls wear pants and shirts.
> Girls wear dresses sometimes, but boys do not wear dresses.
>
> What are these?
> Who wears pants and shirts?
> Who does not wear dresses?

Discussion and questions for 30- to 36-month-old children:
> Sometimes the weather is cold.
> That's when we wear warm clothing, like sweaters, coats, gloves, and caps.
> Sometimes it rains.
> Then we wear raincoats, and sometimes we put *umbrellas* over our heads.
>
> What do we wear to keep warm?
> Are raincoats for sunny weather?
> Where do we put umbrellas?

Narrative and questions for 18- to 24-month-old children:
> The little girl's Mama dressed her so-o pretty!
> See her blue dress, blue socks, and the blue bow in her hair!
>
> Is the little girl dressed pretty?
> What is she wearing?

Narrative and questions for 24- to 30-month-old children:
  The children have been playing outside.
  They got so dirty!
  They give Mama their dirty shirts and pants to wash.
  Then they take a bath!

  Where were the children playing?
  Are they still clean?
  What will Mama wash?
  What will the children do?

Narrative and questions for 30- to 36-month-old children:
  It snowed today! It is so cold!
  The boy and girl dress warmly to play outside.
  They put on sweaters, coats, gloves, caps, and even mufflers.
  Now they can go play in the snow!

  Is it warm today?
  Where do the children want to play?
  What do they put on to wear outside?

Self-Care

Actual self-care items that can be used in this unit include soap, washcloth, towel, tissue, toothbrush, toothpaste, hairbrush, comb, and bandage. Pictures and storybooks about self-care also are helpful.

Use these ENABLE I flannel board pictures:
24. bathroom sink, with soap, washcloth, towel, toothbrush, toothpaste
25. bathroom dresser, with comb, tissue, and box of bandages

Directives

1. Routine-oriented directives (12-18 months)

   a. Wash your hands/face.
      Brush/comb your hair.
      Dry your hands/face.
      Get a bandage.
      Brush your teeth.
      Blow your nose.

   b. Show me: the (your): soap.
      Point to: washcloth.
      Get: towel.
                          toothpaste.
                          toothbrush.
                          comb.
                          hairbrush.
                          bandage.
                          tissue.

2. Simple one-step directives (18-24 months)

   a. Pragmatic directives—Actions given at home

      Get your toothbrush and toothpaste.
      Put the toothpaste on the brush.
      Brush your teeth.
      Rinse your mouth.

Turn on the water.
Get the soap.
Lather your hands/face.
Scrub your face/hands.
Rinse your hands/face.
Get the towel.
Rub your hands/face dry.

b. Associative directives

Show me:	child (person):	washing.
Point to:		opening.
		lathering.
		taking top off.
		putting paste on brush.
		putting top on.
		scrubbing.
		rubbing.
		rinsing.
		drying.
		brushing.
		combing.
		bandaging.
		blowing.
		wiping.

Show me:	(*self-care item*)	on the sink.
Point to:		on the brush.
		in the water.
		on the dresser.
		on the shelf.
		in the box.
		on the rack.
		in the wrapper.

3. Two-step compound and complex directives (2-3 years)
   a. Associative directives

Find:	what we need to wash hands and face.
Bring me:	what we need to bathe ourselves.
Get:	what we need to dry ourselves.
	what we put on hurt places.
	what we use to blow/wipe noses.
	what we need to clean teeth.
	what we use to take care of hair.

   b. Conceptual and sequenced directives

Turn on the water and get your hands wet.

Rub your hands together to lather the soap.

Rinse the soap off your hands and dry them with a towel.

Hang the towel and washcloth over the rack.

Wring the water out of the washcloth.

Take the cap off the toothpaste and squeeze some on the toothbrush.

Put the cap on the toothpaste and put it on the shelf.
Brush your hair and then comb it.
Take the wrapper off the bandage and throw it away.
Tape the bandage on the hurt place.
Blow your nose and then wipe your face.
Throw the dirty tissue in the trash.

c. Storybook directives

Point to: the boy with a hurt knee.
the dirty child.
the clean child.
the child getting ready to brush teeth.
the child rinsing hands/teeth.
the girl wiping nose.
the Mama combing the child's hair.
the child who needs: a washcloth.
a towel.
a hairbrush.

d. Directives involving simple negatives

Show me something you do *not* use *without* water.
Find something *not* for wiping.
Touch something you do *not* use with teeth.
Find something you do *not* put on a hurt knee.
Point to something *not* for use with hair.
Show me something that we do *not* use to clean our nose.
Find something for cleaning that you do *not* squeeze.

Questions

1. Basic labeling questions (12-24 months)
   As the question is asked, adult points to actual self-care item.

   What is this/that?

Soap.	Toothbrush.
Tissue.	Comb.
Hairbrush.	Towel.
Washcloth.	Toothpaste.
	Bandage.

2. Yes/No questions

   a. Yes/No questions about visible self-care items (18-24 months)

   Is this (*self-care item*)?

   Is this for:

washing?	combing?
scrubbing?	cleaning?
brushing?	blowing?
drying?	bandaging?
wiping?	

b. Early negation questions (2-3 years)

Do we use soap on our hair?

Do we use shampoo on our face?

Do soap and washcloths get wet?

Do we dry with a tissue?

Do we blow noses with a towel?

Is toothpaste used with a toothbrush?

Can we brush teeth with a hairbrush?

Do we put bandages on teeth?

Do tissues help clean our nose?

3. What . . . do questions about visible self-care items (21-30 months)

What can/do you do with (*self-care item*)?

Wash.	Blow.	Comb.
Wipe.	Rub.	Clean.
Bathe.	Brush.	Bandage.
Scrub.	Dry.	

4. Early discrimination—Choice of two visible self-care items (2-3 years)

Which one do we need to:

take dirt off?	bathe?
clean our teeth?	keep our hair neat?
scrub face?	dry ourselves?
brush our teeth?	fix our cut/hurt places?

5. Early location questions about visible self-care items (2-3 years)

Where do we use (*self-care item*)?

In the bathroom.	In our room.
On our face.	On our nose/eyes.
At the sink.	On our teeth.
On our hands.	On our hair.
In the tub.	On a cut/hurt place.
On our body.	

What goes together?

Soap and washcloth.

Washcloth and towel.

Toothbrush and toothpaste.

Tissue and nose.

6. Early attribute/concept questions—Choice of two pictured self-care items (2-3 years)

Which one is:

wet?/dry?

dirty?/clean?

big?/little?

red?/blue?/green?/yellow?/orange?

long?/short?

open?/closed?

Short Discussions and Narratives

Use self-care items and family puppets.

Discussion and questions for 18- to 24-month-old children:
 Toothbrushes help us have clean teeth.
 We put toothpaste on them and brush, brush, brush our teeth.

 Are toothbrushes to keep teeth clean?
 What do we do with toothpaste?

Discussion and questions for 24- to 30-month-old children:
 We use a hairbrush and comb to make our hair look nice.
 We can get tangles out of our hair with the comb and then brush it.

 What gets tangles out of hair?
 Can we brush hair with a toothbrush?
 Where do we use combs?

Discussion and questions for 30- to 36-month-old children:
 Children get so dirty!
 When they want to clean their nose, they use a tissue.
 They have to wash with soap and water to get all the dirt off.
 Next they dry off with a big, thick towel—and then they're clean again!

 What do we use to clean noses?
 Can you get all the dirt off without soap?
 Are towels for washing or drying?

Narrative and questions for 18- to 24-month-old children:
 Poor little boy!
 He fell down and scraped his knee.
 But his Mama put a bandage on it and now he's OK!

 Is the boy's knee hurt?
 What did Mama do?

Narrative and questions for 24- to 30-month-old children:
 The little girl is learning to brush her teeth.
 She wets her toothbrush and puts toothpaste on it.
 Then she brushes her top and bottom teeth.
 Now she rinses her mouth.
 What clean teeth!

 What is she doing?
 Does she use toothpaste?
 Did she brush the top and bottom teeth?

Narrative and questions for 30- to 36-month-old children:
 The little girl is playing in the bathtub.
 She has washed herself, and now she is washing her baby doll.
 She rubs soap all over the doll, and then rinses it off with the washcloth.
 "Mama, Mama," she calls, "bring us a towel so we can get dry!"

 What is the girl doing?
 What does she use to wash the doll?
 Which does she ask Mama to bring—a towel or soap?

Transportation

Toy transportation items that are useful in working with this unit include a car, truck, plane, boat, train, and tricycle. A toy garage, riding vehicles, and pictures and storybooks about vehicles also are helpful.

Use the ENABLE I flannel board pictures of:
26. car
27. plane
28. truck
29. train
30. boat
31. tricycle

Directives

1. Routine-oriented directives (12-18 months)

   a. Drive your car/truck.
      Ride your tricycle.
      Fly your plane.
      Play with your (*vehicle name*).
      Make your (*vehicle name*) go.

   b. Show me: your (the):   car.
      Get: truck.
      Bring me: plane.
      Point to: train.
                                     boat.
                                     tricycle.

2. Simple one-step directives (18-24 months)

   a. Pragmatic directives—Actions given at home

      Get in the car/truck/plane/boat.

      Sail the boat.

      Get on your tricycle.

      Pedal your tricycle.

      Open/Shut the (*vehicle name*) door.

      Ride the (*vehicle name*).

b. Associative directives

Show me: Point to:	riding. landing. starting. stopping. sailing. opening. flying. pedaling. shutting. taking off. sailing. speeding. driving. sitting. turning. the plane in the sky. the train on the track. the boat on the water. the car/truck on the road. the tricycle on the sidewalk.

c. Vehicle parts

Find the: Touch the:	car: truck:	door. wheels. seats. keys. windows. horn. lights. steering wheel.
	plane:	wings. nose. tail. propellers.
	train:	engine. caboose.
	boat:	sail. motor.
	tricycle:	seat. wheels. pedals. handlebars.

d. Persons associated with vehicles

Put the pilot with the plane.

Put the engineer with the train.

Put the man/woman with the car.

Put the child with the tricycle.

Put the truck driver with the truck.

3. Two-step compound and complex directives (2-3 years)
   a. Associative directives

Bring me:	the vehicle that takes Daddy/Mama to work.
Get:	the vehicle that travels on a track.
	the vehicle that flies through the air/in the sky.
	the vehicle that little children ride.
	the vehicle with three wheels.
	the vehicle that travels on water.
	vehicles that start with a key. (*trucks, cars*)
	vehicles that wind pushes over water. (*sailboat*)
	the vehicle with several cars. (*train*)
	vehicles that move lots of people/passengers. (*plane/train*)
	vehicles that stop at red lights.
	vehicles that drive on highways.

   b. Conceptual and sequenced directives
   Get on your tricycle and ride it fast.
   Make the car move slowly.
   Drive the train around the track and over the hill.
   Fly the airplane across the room to the nearest table.
   Line up the vehicles that ride on highways.
   Put the boat in the water and move it to the other side.
   Ride the tricycle over the grass and into the garage.
   Put the "freight" in the truck until it is full.
   Find another boat without a motor.
   Fly the longest airplane to the middle of the table.
   Make the train go backward many times.
   Put the smallest cars outside the garage.
   Push both the trucks together.
   Pull all the train cars under the table.

   c. Storybook directives

Find:	the big truck on the road.
Show me:	the car stopped at the light.
	the plane with long wings.
	the engineer driving the train.
	the child getting on/off the tricycle.
	the blue/red cars and the yellow/green trucks.
	the little tricycle by the house.
	the keys in the car.
	a big and a little boat.
	the car with lights turned off.
	the family buying tickets for the plane/train.
	the red caboose of the train.
	all the vehicles.
	both planes in the sky.
	all the traffic on the highway.

d. Directives involving simple negatives
Show me a vehicle that does *not* fly.
Find a boat *without* sails.
Point to the vehicles that do *not* move on tracks.
Touch the vehicle *without* handlebars.
Point to the vehicles that do *not* need keys to start.
Show me a vehicle *without* a door.
Find vehicles that Daddy *cannot* drive.
Point to the vehicle children should *not* ride in the street.
Drive the vehicle that does *not* need a pilot.

Questions

1. Basic labeling questions (12-24 months)
As the question is asked, adult points to toy vehicle.

What is this/that?

Car.	Seats.	Motor.
Tricycle.	Keys.	Horn.
Truck.	Caboose.	Lights.
Boat.	Handlebars.	Engine.
Plane.	Wheels.	Pedals.
Train.	Windows.	Steering wheel.
Door.	Wings.	

2. Yes/No questions

a. Yes/No questions about visible vehicles (18-24 months)

Is this: (*vehicle name*)?

Can this vehicle:

fly?	sail?
pedal?	land?
take off?	stop?
drive?	carry people?
turn?	carry things?
start?	

Does this vehicle have:

doors?	caboose?
seats?	engine?
keys?	sails?
wheels?	horn?
windows?	pedals?
wings?	handlebars?
motor?	steering wheel?
lights?	

b. Early negation questions (2-3 years)

Can we fly planes in the water?
Do boats sail on highways?
Are trains driven by pilots?
Can children ride tricycles?
Are tricycles for riding in the street?
Do cars have wings?
Do planes have sails?
Do trucks need wheels?
Can planes fly slowly?

3. What . . . do questions about visible vehicles (21-30 months)
   What can a (*vehicle name*) do?

drive	turn
take off	move on water
carry things	fly
start	carry people
land	move on highways
move on a track	give children a ride
stop	

4. Early discrimination—Choice of two visible vehicles (2-3 years)
   Which one do we need to:
   take a trip?
   buy tickets to ride?
   fly far away?
   ride down the highway?
   drive to town?
   use handlebars to drive?
   ride around the neighborhood?
   use keys to drive?

   Which of these has a(an):

pilot?	horn?	rider?
sail?	engine?	wings?
keys?	driver?	windows?
seats?	doors?	wheels?
engineer?	lights?	handlebars?
motor?	caboose?	steering wheel?

   Which of these:
   has a horn you can toot?
   goes choo-choo?
   do children pedal?
   goes on a track?
   goes on water?

5. Early location questions about visible vehicles (2-3 years)

> Where is the vehicle?
>> On the road/street/highway.
>> In the middle of the lake/ocean/water.
>> Up in the sky.
>> Stopped at the light.
>> Down on the ground.
>> Flying high.
>> Over/Under the bridge.
>> On the track.
>> In the water.

> Which go together?
>> Trains and tracks.
>> Pilots and planes.
>> Cars and keys.
>> Engineers and trains.
>> Boats and water.
>> Cars and roads.

6. Early attribute/concept questions—Choice of two pictured vehicles (2-3 years)

> Which one is:
>> moving?/stopped?
>> red?/green?/blue?/yellow?
>> fast?/slow?
>> up?/down?
>> big?/little?
>> high?/low?

Short Discussions and Narratives

Use family puppets and transportation pictures.

Discussion and questions for 18- to 24-month-old children:
> Mamas and Daddys need cars to go to work and to town.
> Children like to ride tricycles.

> What goes to town?
> Can Daddys ride tricycles?

Discussion and questions for 24- to 30-month-old children:
> We can take trips on planes and trains.
> We can go far away and visit people.
> We just buy our tickets and get on them!

> Can we travel far on planes and trains?
> Where can we go?
> What do we do?

Discussion and questions for 30- to 36-month-old children:

There are big boats and little boats.

There are big trucks and little trucks.

Big boats and trucks can carry freight from one place to another.

We call big trucks "eighteen-wheelers" and big boats "ships."

Do little vehicles carry freight?

Where do they go?

What is a ship?

What is a big truck called?

Narrative and questions for 18- to 24-month-old children:

The family has a pretty, new car!

Honk! Honk! There they go for a ride!

Is the car new?

What is the family doing?

Narrative and questions for 24- to 30-month-old children:

Daddy and the little boy are putting trash in their truck.

They cleaned up their yard.

Now they will drive the trash to the dumping place.

What are they doing?

What did they do to the yard?

Where are they going?

Narrative and questions for 30- to 36-month-old children:

The little girl is riding her tricycle in her yard.

She looks up and sees a plane in the sky.

What fun it would be to fly on a plane!

She pretends her tricycle is a plane and she is flying it!

Where is the girl?

What does she see?

Does she like planes?

What does she pretend?

Shopping

For this unit, it will be helpful to provide a purse, play money, and a toy shopping cart. In the classroom, prepare play areas that resemble a grocery store, library, clothing store, restaurant, barbershop, and drugstore. Pictures and books about community shopping areas also are useful.

Use these ENABLE I flannel board pictures:
32. grocery store
33. library
34. the mall, featuring a clothing store and restaurant
35. a shopping center, featuring a barbershop and drugstore

Parents and teachers should utilize these exercises frequently during actual shopping trips, field trips, and community outings.

Directives

1. Routine-oriented directives (12-18 months)
    a. Let's go.
       Hold this.
       Get your purse.
       Be still.
       Push the shopping cart.
       Don't touch.

    b. Show me the: purse.
       Point to the: money.
       Find the: store.
                       books.
                       food.
                       clothes.
                       shopping cart.

2. Simple one-step directives (18-30 months)
    a. Pragmatic directives—Actions given in community settings

       Bring your purse.   Sit in the barber chair.

       Sit at the restaurant table.   Pick a book.

       Get the cart.   Find a box of cereal.

       Try on the clothes.   Find a can of soup.

       Go in the store.   Find the bandages.

       Let's get a haircut.

117

b. Location and person identification

Point to the:	grocery store.	librarian.
Show me the:	library.	clerk.
Find the:	clothing store.	barber.
	restaurant.	waitress.
	mall.	druggist.
	barbershop.	customer.
	grocer.	shopper.
	drugstore.	

c. Associative directives

Show me: shopping.
Point to: selling clothes.
ordering food.
reading.
buying food.
eating food.
checking out books.
paying money.
opening/closing purse.
pushing grocery carts.
buying (bandages, shampoo, medicine).
cutting/combing/washing hair.
filling/carrying grocery bags.

d. Object/Location relationships

Put the:	shopping cart	with the grocery store.
	meat	
	cereal	
	fruit	
	food cans	
	food packages	
	books	with the library.
	magazines	
	clothes	with the clothing store.
	shoes	
	food	with the restaurant.
	drink	
	dishes	
	utensils	
	menu	
	mirror	with the barbershop.
	scissors	
	comb	
	brush	
	medicine	with the drugstore.
	bandages	
	shampoo	
	soap	

3. Two-step compound and complex directives (2-3 years)
   a. Associative directives
      Put the food in the shopping cart and bring it here.
      Get your money out of the purse and give it to the clerk/waitress.
      Get the book off the shelf and bring it to the librarian.
      Try on the (*clothing item*) and show it to me.
      Find the menu and give it to me.
      Be still while the barber cuts your hair.
      Look on the shelf and find the bandages.
      Find the clothing store/restaurant in the mall.
      Show me the person who brings food to our table.
      Point to the person who cuts our hair.
      Find the person who helps us find books.
      Point to the person who sells us food/medicine.
      Show me the store that sells food/medicine/clothes.

   b. Conceptual and sequenced directives
      Open the door and go in the (*community location*).
      Chew your food slowly.
      Pick out the red cans on the shelf.
      Walk around the store and show me pants/shirts/dresses/shoes.
      Look on the shelves and find the children's books.
      Sit on the chair and look in the mirror.
      Pour the drink in the glass until it is full.
      Find the food without a package.
      Put all the food in the shopping cart.

   c. Storybook directives

Find:	the man selling groceries.
Show me:	the boy looking for books to read.
Point to:	the family shopping for clothes.
	the druggist helping the man find bandages.
	Mama and the girl eating at a restaurant.
	the baby getting a haircut.
	the stores in the mall.
	the big chair at the barbershop.
	the open door at the store.
	the store windows of clothes.
	the long shelves in the grocery store.
	the red and yellow cans of food.
	all the stores.
	the family entering/leaving the store.
	the place to find books.

d. Directives involving simple negatives

Show me a store that *doesn't* sell food.

Find places that do *not* have books.

Find the place you *cannot* have your hair cut.

Find something on wheels you would *not* use at a barbershop.

Find the person who does *not* sell food.

Find a place *without* chairs/shelves.

Find a place where you do *not* need money.

Questions

1. Basic labeling questions (18-24 months)

What is this/that?

Grocery store.	Barber shop.
Mall.	Purse.
Restaurant.	Money.
Library.	Shopping cart.
Clothing store.	

Who is this/that?

Grocer.	Barber.
Clerk.	Druggist.
Librarian.	Waiter/waitress.

2. Yes/No questions

a. Yes/No questions about pictured shopping locations, persons, and objects (18-24 months)

Is this a:

grocery store?	mall?	barber?
clothing store?	barbershop?	waiter/waitress?
drugstore?	money?	druggist?
library?	grocer?	customer?
restaurant?	clerk?	shopping cart?
purse?	librarian?	

Is this place for:

buying groceries?

borrowing books?

eating food?

going shopping at stores?

getting a haircut?

buying clothes?

buying medicine?

b. Early negation questions (2-3 years)

Can you get a haircut at a library?

Do you go to a restaurant for medicine?

Are grocery stores for buying clothes?

Can you check out books at the library?

Do druggists work at barbershops?

Do librarians sell clothes?

Do you buy cereal at the grocery store?

Do waitresses give haircuts?

3. What . . . do questions about pictured shopping locations and persons (2-3 years)

What do you get at (*shopping location*)?

Food.	Magazines.	Dresses.
Drinks.	French fries.	Pizza.
Medicine.	Shampoo.	Coats.
Bandages.	Pants.	Books.
Haircut.	Shirts.	Shoes.
Soap.		

What does a (*person*) do?

librarian: help find/lend books

barber: wash/cut/comb hair

waiter/waitress: take orders, bring/serve food

grocer: sell food

druggist: sell medicine and bandages

clerk: help find/sell clothes/groceries

4. Early discrimination questions—Choice of two shopping pictures (2-3 years)

Which place do we use to:

borrow books?	buy a purse?
buy lunch/supper?	buy toothpaste?
read magazines?	shop at a lot of stores?
buy new shoes?	listen to stories?
get a haircut?	

Which person works at a (*shopping location*)?

waiter/waitress: restaurant

barber: barbershop

librarian: library

druggist: drugstore

grocer/clerk: grocery store

clerk/salesperson: clothing store

5. Early location questions about pictured shopping locations (2-3 years)

Where does a (*person*) work?:   librarian *(library)*
waiter/waitress (*restaurant*)
grocer/clerk (*grocery store*)
clerk/salesperson (*clothing store*)
barber (*barbershop*)
druggist (*drugstore*)

Where can you find:
a snack to eat?
a storybook?
a good haircut?
cans of soup?
a box of tissues?
medicine?
many stores?

Short Discussions and Narratives

Use family puppets and shopping pictures.

Discussion and questions for 18- to 24-month-old children:
Grocery stores sell many foods.
We can buy milk, eggs, bread, and apples there.

Can you buy food at grocery stores?
What can you buy there?

Discussion and questions for 24- to 30-month-old children:
People often shop at drugstores and clothing stores.
At drugstores, you can buy bandages, medicine, tissue, and shampoo.
You can buy all your clothes at a clothing store.

Where do people often shop?
What can you buy at drugstores?
Can you buy hats at clothing stores?

Discussion and questions for 30- to 36-month-old children:
Going to town can be fun.
You can get a haircut at the barbershop and go to the library to borrow some storybooks.
Then you can stop at the mall and get a hamburger at a restaurant.

What can be fun?
Where do you get a haircut?
Can you borrow books at a restaurant?
Where could you get a hamburger?

Narrative and questions for 18- to 24-month-old children:
The little girl is helping her Daddy shop at the grocery store.
She picks out the soup and cereal.

What is the little girl doing?
Does she pick out the fruit?

Narrative and questions for 24- to 30-month-old children:
     The children are having so much fun at the mall!
     They got new shoes and a school bag at the clothing store.
     Now they are eating ice cream at a restaurant! Mm-mm good!

     Where are the children?
     Where did they get ice cream?

Narrative and questions for 30- to 36-month-old children:
     The children are at the library for storytime.
     The Story Lady is reading a story about a little boy getting his first haircut.
     The little boy was afraid at first, and he cried.
     At the end of the story, he saw how nice he looked, and he smiled.
     The children liked the story.

     Where are the children?
     What does the little boy in the story do?
     Did the children like the story?

Community Helpers

For this unit, provide flexible wooden or puppet toys of community helpers, and pictures and storybooks that feature the helpers in action.

Use the ENABLE I puppet figures of teacher, police officer, doctor, mail carrier, and firefighter.

Although the exercises in this unit are organized around only those five helpers, young children should be taught a functional fund of information about a variety of community helpers. Using the structure of this program as a guide, introduce extra helpers, including nurses, farmers, mechanics, dentists, carpenters, and painters.

Directives

1. Routine-oriented directives (12-24 months)

   Show me the: teacher.
   Point to the: police officer.
   Get the: doctor.
   firefighter.
   mail carrier.

2. Simple one-step directives (21-30 months)
   Associative directives

   Show me the (*community helper's*): book.
   Point to the: blackboard.
   scissors.
   chalk.
   crayons.
   paper.
   pencil.
   police car.
   uniform.
   cap.
   mail truck.
   stamps.
   letters.
   mailbag.
   packages.
   mailbox.

Show me the (*community helper's*): stethoscope.
thermometer.
medicine.
ambulance.

hose.
hat.
hydrant.
fire truck.

Show me the (*community helper*):
reading to the children.
helping the children cut/color

Point to the (*community helper*):
directing traffic.
selling stamps.
checking the child.
taking temperature.
spraying water on fire.
carrying mail.
in the school room.
at the hospital.
at the police station.
at the fire station.
at the post office.

3. Two-step compound and complex directives (2-3 years)
   a. Associative directives

   Find: what the teacher reads to the children.
   Get: what the teacher writes with on a blackboard.
   Point to: what a police officer drives.
              what a police officer wears.
              what a doctor uses to listen to your heart.
              what a doctor needs to take temperatures.
              what a firefighter drives.
              what holds the mail carrier's letters.
              where people put letters to be mailed.
              where doctors take care of sick people.
              where police officers work.
              where teachers help children learn.
              where fire trucks are kept.
              where people buy stamps and mail packages.
              what people put on letters.

   b. Conceptual and sequenced directives

   Look at the pictures and listen to the teacher read.
   Color and cut the picture the teacher gave you.
   Show the teacher your picture and tell her about it.
   Wait until the police officer tells you to cross the street.
   Open your mouth so the doctor can see your throat.

Close your mouth so the doctor can take your temperature.

Stay away from the fire until the firefighters put it out.

Give the letters to the mail carrier to be mailed.

c. Storybook directives

Point to the: teacher playing games with the children.
teacher helping the children learn to cut/color.
police officer finding the lost pet.
doctor putting a cast on a broken leg.
firefighter fastening the hose to the hydrant.
firefighter climbing a ladder to save a child.
mail carrier delivering letters to the lady.
mail carrier putting bags of mail in the mail truck.
two police officers in the police car.

d. Directives involving simple negatives

Touch a helper who has *no* uniform.

Show me a helper who does *not* teach school.

Point to a helper *not* in a vehicle.

Find a helper *without* a hose.

Touch a helper who does *not* carry mail.

Show me a helper who does *not* climb ladders.

Find a helper who does *not* use books.

Touch the helpers *without* hats.

Questions

1. Basic labeling questions (18-24 months)
   As the question is asked, adult points to toy or picture of helper.

   Who is this?
   Teacher.
   Firefighter.
   Police officer.
   Mail carrier.
   Doctor.

   What is this?

School.	Hospital.
Fire truck.	Mailbox.
Blackboard.	Stethoscope.
Hose.	Mailbag.
Police car.	Thermometer.
Hydrant	Post office.

2. Yes/No questions

   a. Yes/No questions about visible helpers (21-30 months)

      Is this a (*helper name*)?

      Can a (*helper name*):
- help children learn things?
- help people in an accident?
- direct traffic?
- fix broken arms?
- help children get well?
- put out fires?
- deliver mail?

   b. Early negation questions (2-3 years)

      Do teachers direct traffic?

      Can a doctor put a cast on a broken leg?

      Can firefighters teach children to read?

      Do doctors need fire hydrants?

      Can a police officer find a lost child?

      Can a mail carrier give you medicine?

      Does a police officer sell stamps?

      Does a teacher work at a school?

3. What . . . do questions about visible helpers (2-3 years)

      What does a (*helper name*) do?
- Teach children.
- Help children learn.
- Tell stories.
- Tell cars to stop and go.
- Find lost children.
- Put out big fires.
- Pick up mail.
- Deliver letters and magazines to people.

4. Early discrimination—Choice of two visible helpers (2-3 years)

      Which helper do we need to:
- show us how to paste pictures?
- help find our lost car?
- call because our house is on fire?
- go to see if we feel very sick?
- give the letter we wrote to?

5. Early location questions about visible helpers (2-3 years)

      Where can we find (*helper name*)?

At school.	At the post office.
At the fire station.	At a hospital.
In the classroom.	In a mail truck.
In a fire truck.	In an ambulance.
In a police car.	At a mailbox.
At a fire.	Near a fire hydrant.
At a police station.	

What goes together?

teacher:	school
	blackboard
	books
	crayons
doctor:	white jacket
	thermometer
	stethoscope
	medicine
firefighter:	hose
	fire truck
	hydrant
	fire hat and
	uniform
mail carrier:	mailbag
	magazines
	letters
	stamps
	mailbox

Short Discussions and Narratives

Use the community helper puppet figures.

Discussion and questions for 18- to 24-month-old children:
   Sometimes children get sick or hurt.
   A doctor helps them to get well.

   Can children hurt themselves?
   Who helps them get well?

Discussion and questions for 24- to 30-month-old children:
   Firefighters and police officers help people in trouble.
   If you had an accident, a police officer would help take care of you.
   If your house were on fire, a firefighter would put the fire out.

   Who helps people in trouble?
   Which person helps put out fire?
   Who would help you in an accident?

Discussion and questions for 30- to 36-month-old children:
   Sometimes we write letters to people far away, like our grandparents.
   We put a stamp on the letter and give it to the mail carrier.
   The mail carrier makes the letter get to the right person.

   What do we write to send to people?
   Who do we give it to?
   Does the mail carrier take our letter to the right person?

Narrative and questions for 18- to 24-month-old children:
   The children are at school.
   Their teacher tells them a story about a police officer!

   Are the children at home?
   Who is reading a story?

Narrative and questions for 24- to 30-month-old children:
 The family was driving home.
 There was too much traffic, and they had to stop on the highway!
 But a police officer helped the cars get moving again.
 Now Daddy smiles!

 Where was the family?
 Could they go?
 Who helped them go?

Narrative and questions for 30- to 36-month-old children:
 Oh, no! The little girl fell off the slide.
 She might have a broken leg.
 An ambulance takes her to the hospital.
 The doctor puts a cast on her leg, and now she is better!
 What a good doctor!

 Where did the girl fall?
 What did she do?
 Who helped her?
 What did he do?

Foods

Actual or play foods and pictures of food are helpful items to use with this unit. Using the actual food item will be more significant for the children.

The activities and exercises focus on two each of fruits (apples, bananas), vegetables (beans, carrots), and meats (hamburger, chicken). However, a variety of foods may be taught using this format.

Use these ENABLE I flannel board pictures:
36. apple
37. banana
38. beans
39. carrots
40. hamburger
41. chicken (drumstick)

Directives

1. Routine-oriented directives (12-18 months)

   a. Eat your food.
      Taste (*food name*).
      Chew your food well.
      Get the (*food name*).
      Take a bite of (*food name*).

   b. Show me: apple.
      Point to: banana.
      Find: beans.
                   carrots.
                   hamburger.
                   chicken.

2. Simple one-step directives (18-24 months)

   a. Find: the person: eating   apple.
      Touch: cooking   banana.
                            cutting   beans.
                            peeling   carrots.
                            chewing   hamburger.
                            buying   chicken.

Peel the apple/banana.
Take a bite of beans/carrots.
Chew the hamburger well.
Cut a piece of hamburger/chicken.
Cut the (*food name*).
Buy some (*food name*).

b. Show me the: apple skin.
   Point to the: applesauce.
   apple stem.
   apple slice.
   apple seed.
   banana skin/peel.
   can of beans.
   bean pod.
   hamburger sandwich.
   hamburger patty.
   chicken leg.

3. Two-step compound and complex directives (2-3 years)
   a. Attributes
      Find: the red (or green) fruit.
      Point to: the round fruit.
      the soft fruit.
      the crunchy fruit.
      the long fruit.
      the green beans.
      the yellow fruit.
      the red beans.
      the curved fruit.
      the brown beans.
      the salty vegetable.
      the sweet fruit.
      fried chicken.
      baked chicken.
      the orange vegetable.
      raw carrots.
      cooked carrots.

   b. Associative directives
      Touch: the fruit salad.
      Show me: the vegetable soup.
      the apple tree.
      the vegetable garden.
      the banana cluster.
      the meat market.

   c. Positional and quantitative directives
      Put the apples in the basket and get the bananas out.
      Peel one banana and cut up another one.
      Put the chicken and beans on your plate.
      Give the biggest hamburger to the biggest person.

Put mustard and mayonnaise on the hamburger.
Eat the vegetable nearest to you.
Put the vegetables together.
Move the chicken to the center of the table.
Get the longest banana and the little apples for the salad.

d. Storybook directives

Point to where apples grow.
Find the fruit that tastes good with ice cream.
Show me the Mama cooking carrots.
Point to the man opening a can of beans.
Find the children eating fruit salad.
Show me the family eating fried chicken.
Point to the children making hamburgers.

e. Directives involving simple negatives

Find the fruit that is *not* round.
Show me a fruit you eat *without* the skin.
Find a vegetable you cook *without* the shell.
Show me a vegetable that is *not* green.
Point to the meat *without* legs and wings.
Find a food you can eat *without* cooking.

Questions

1. Basic labeling questions (12-24 months)

What's this/that?

Fruit.	Vegetable.	Meat.
Apple.	Beans.	Hamburger.
Bananas.	Carrots.	Chicken.

2. Yes/No questions

a. Yes/No questions about visible food (18-24 months)

Is this: a/an   *(food name)*?
apple tree?
apple skin?
apple seed?
applesauce?
banana split?
banana peel?
can of beans?
carrot top?
hamburger patty?
hamburger sandwich?
chicken package?
chicken leg?

b. Early negation questions (2-3 years)

Can we eat raw chicken?

Do hamburgers taste sweet?

Is hamburger a meat?

Can we eat bean shells?

Are carrots yellow?

Do we eat banana peels?

Are apples round and red?

Are beans big?

3. What . . . do questions about visible actions (21-30 months)

What (*food name*) can we:

eat?	buy?	taste?
boil?	cut?	pick off tree?
bake?	peel?	put in salad?
chew?		

4. Early discrimination—Choice of two foods or pictures of foods (2-3 years)

What food is:

a fruit?	a meat?	in a pod?
salty?	sweet?	red?
a vegetable?	orange?	brown?
crunchy?	green?	yellow?

What food:

grows on trees?

comes from animals?

grows in the ground?

5. Early location questions about visual answers in pictures (2-3 years)

Where is the (*food name*)?

In the bucket.	At the store.
On the table.	On the plate.
On a tree.	In the can.
On the stove.	In the bun.
On the shelf.	In a bowl.
In the garden.	At the restaurant.
In the oven.	

6. Early attribute/concept questions—Choice of two foods or pictures of foods (2-3 years)

Which one is:

red?	round?	crunchy?
green?	salty?	smooth?
yellow?	sweet?	soft?
brown?	long?	rough?
orange?	curved?	

Short Discussions and Narratives

Use actual foods or unit pictures with family puppets.

Discussion and questions for 18- to 24-month-old children:
   This is a red apple and a yellow banana.
   You can peel and eat these fruits.
   They are so good!

   What fruits are these?
   Do you peel them?

Discussion and questions for 24- to 30-month-old children:
   Carrots and beans are vegetables that we eat.
   We can clean carrots and eat them raw or we can cook them.
   We need to cook beans.
   Sometimes we eat beans and carrots in salad.

   Which vegetables did we talk about?
   Can we eat carrots without cooking them?
   Do we cook beans?

Discussion and questions for 30- to 36-month-old children:
   Two good meats are hamburger and chicken.
   You can cook lots of things with hamburger, but most people like hamburger as a sandwich on a bun.
   And most people like their chicken fried!

   Is hamburger a meat?
   Which way do people like hamburger best?
   Is fried chicken good?

Narrative and questions for 18- to 24-month-old children:
   Mama is cutting up a chicken.
   She is going to bake it for supper.

   What is Mama doing?
   Is the chicken for supper?

Narrative and questions for 24- to 30-month-old children:
   The children are finishing a snack.
   Danny peeled the banana and ate the whole thing!
   Connie ate only part of the crunchy apple.

   What are they doing?
   Which fruit did Danny eat?
   Which child ate the whole fruit?

Narrative and questions for 30- to 36-month-old children:
   The family is at the grocery store.
   They want to buy some vegetables to make soup.
   Daddy picks out green beans, and Freddie picks out carrots.
   Mama buys tomatoes, onions, and potatoes.
   This soup will be good!

   Where is the family?
   What are they going to make?
   Did Daddy buy tomatoes?
   Who picked out the carrots?

Playtime

Gather and display pictures about a park, circus, and zoo, along with storybooks and manipulative toys relevant to these entertainment locations. Field trips to these places are significant and fun.

ENABLE I flannel board pictures for this unit include:
  - 42. park scene
  - 43. circus scene
  - 44. zoo scene

Directives

1. Routine-oriented directives (18-24 months)

   a. Location

Find the:	zoo.
Point to the:	circus.
	park.

   b. Objects and people

Show me the:	swing.
Find the:	slide.
	sandbox.
	picnic.
	swimming pool.
	lady.
	clown.
	trapeze.
	cage.
	lions.
	kangaroo.
	giraffe.
	elephant.

   c. Pragmatic directives—Actions

Get on the swing.	Climb the ladder.
Get in the water.	Look at the clowns.
Kick your feet.	Slide.
Dig the sand.	Look at the animals.
Eat your sandwich.	

2. Simple one-step directives (21-30 months)
   a. Associative directives

Find:	the park swing/slide.
Show me:	boy sliding.
	girl swinging.
	people at the picnic.
	people eating.
	baby digging.
	children swimming.
	diving.
	floating.
	the clown running.
	zoo animals.
	lady swinging.
	people laughing.
	circus cages.
	wild animals.

   b. Storybook directives

Point to:	the giraffe eating tree leaves.
Find:	the elephant eating peanuts.
	the kangaroo jumping.
	the animal that roars.
	the children eating popcorn.
	the pretty lady.
	the food basket.
	the funny clowns.
	the sandpail.

3. Two-step compound and complex directives (2-3 years)
   a. Associative directives

   Find the plaything with a moving seat.
   Find the plaything that goes up and down.
   Touch the place with funny people.
   Show me the pretty lady hanging on a trapeze.
   Point to the people with painted faces and silly clothes.
   Touch the animal with a big mane.
   Find the animal with a long neck.
   Point to the animal with a pouch.
   Point to the animal with a trunk.
   Touch the animals in the cage.
   Climb up the ladder and slide down the slide.
   Swing back and forth.
   Put the sand in the pail and dump it out.
   Hold on to the side of the swimmming pool.
   Find the people eating and drinking.
   Run like the clowns and jump.
   Swing high like the trapeze lady.

Find the animal with a big tail.

Point to the animal with big ears.

Show me the place to see lots of animals.

Find the place with a three-ring show.

Touch the place to run and play.

b. Directives involving simple negatives

Point to the place where you *cannot* play.

Show me the animal that is *not* short.

Find the park place you *cannot* climb.

Touch the place *without* animals.

Find the places *without* clowns.

Show me a park place *without* sand.

Touch a place with *no* trapezes.

Questions

1. Basic labeling questions (12-24 months)

What place is this?

Zoo.

Park.

Circus.

Who/what is this?

Elephant.	Picnic.	Cage.
Swing.	Giraffe.	Lion.
Sandbox.	Clown.	Circus lady.
Kangaroo.	Trapeze.	Swimming pool.
Slide.		

2. Yes/No questions

a. Yes/No questions about visible playtime pictures (18-24 months)

Is this:

zoo?

park?

circus?

Do you see:

elephant?	swimming	sliding?
swing?	pool?	eating?
sandbox?	clown?	walking?
circus lady?	cage?	climbing?
kangaroo?	lion?	laughing?
slide?	swinging?	running?
picnic table?	swimming?	digging?
trapeze?	jumping?	looking?
giraffe?		

b. Early negation questions (2-3 years)

Can elephants talk?

Do you go up and then go down on the slide?

Do clowns make us sad?

Can we swim in a sandbox?

Are swings for digging?

Is the circus inside a great big tent?

Do you have picnics in the swimming pool?

Are giraffes tall animals?

Is a trapeze down low?

3. What . . . do questions about visible playtime pictures (21-30 months)

What are the children doing at the park?

Swinging.	Swimming.	Digging.
Shoveling.	Sliding.	Sitting.
Climbing.	Eating.	Running.

What do clowns do?

Laugh.

Run.

Fall down.

Act silly.

What do you do at a circus?

Have a good time.

Eat popcorn/cotton candy.

Watch the show.

Laugh at clowns.

What do you do at a zoo?

See wild animals.

Learn about animals.

4. Early discrimination—Choice of two playtime pictures (2-3 years)

Which place can we:

eat food?	swim?
dig sand?	see wild animals?
climb things?	run?
see clowns?	slide?

Which animal can:

jump fast?

roar?

eat leaves from trees?

swing its trunk?

give people a ride?

shake its mane?

stretch a long neck?

carry a baby in its pouch?

5. Early location questions about visible playtime places (2-3 years)

Where can you see:

swings?	trapezes?	swimming pools?
clowns?	giraffes?	elephants?
kangaroos?	sand piles?	picnic tables?
slides?	lions?	animals in cages?

6. Early attribute/concept questions—Choice of two playtime pictures (2-3 years)

Which child is:
wet?/dry?
in the pool?
up high?/down low?
on a swing?

Which animal is:
tall?
fast?
big?

Which animal:
swings a trunk?
has a long neck?
jumps on two feet?
has big ears?

Short Discussions and Narratives

Use unit pictures and family puppets.

Discussion and questions for 18- to 24-month-old children:
Circuses are fun!
We can see clowns and trapeze ladies, and we can eat cotton candy!

Are circuses fun places?
What do we see there?

Discussion and questions for 24- to 30-month-old children:
Wild animals live in the zoo.
These are big animals that are not pets.
They live in cages, and we go to see them.

What lives in the zoo?
Are wild animals pets?
Where do they live?

Discussion and questions for 30- to 36-month-old children:
We go to the park to have a good time.
We can swing, climb and slide, dig in a sandpile, and have a picnic.
We can run and jump and make friends with other children!

Where do we go for a good time?
What can we do at the park?
What do we do with other children?

Narrative and questions for 18- to 24-month-old children:
    The children are watching the elephant.
    She puts water on her back with her trunk! She's all wet!

    What is this?
    What is she doing?

Narrative and questions for 24- to 30-month-old children:
    The circus clowns are being silly.
    One clown pushes the other clown.
    He rolls over and over.
    Oops! He pops his balloon!

    What does the clown do?
    Are there two clowns?
    Does the clown run?

Narrative and questions for 30- to 36-month-old children:
    The family is having a picnic at the park.
    Daddy is drinking a soda, and Mama is eating a hot dog.
    The children have finished eating, and they are playing.
    The little girl is swinging and the boy is playing in the sandbox.

    Where is the family?
    What are Mama and Daddy doing?
    Which child is swinging?
    Where is the boy playing?

Nature

For this unit, provide pictures and storybooks about nature, "the child's outdoors." Field trips and excursions into the outdoors will facilitate the use of this unit.

Use these ENABLE I flannel board pictures:
45. an outdoor scene, with grass, trees, flowers, and the sun
46. a lake scene, with fish swimming near the surface and a turtle on the shore
47. a night scene, with moon and stars

Directives

1. Routine-oriented directives (18-24 months)
   a. Location

Find the:	ground.
Point to the:	water.
	sky.

   b. Object

Touch the:	grass.
Show me the:	trees.
	sun.
	flowers.
	lake.
	turtle.
	fish.
	moon.
	stars.

   c. Pragmatic directives—Actions

   Touch the grass.

   Pick a flower.

   Look at the tree.

2. Simple one-step directives (21-30 months)
   a. Associative directives

Show me:	leaves.	plants.
Find:	trunk.	branches.
	petals.	roots.
	stem.	animals.

143

b. Storybook directives

Point to: green grass.
red flowers.
blue lake.
sun shining.
moon glowing.

3. Two-step compound and complex directives (2-3 years)
   a. Associative directives

   Find something with many branches and green leaves.
   Point to pretty plants that have stems and petals.
   Point to the green plant that covers the ground.
   Show me the plant with a tall trunk.
   Find the animals in the water.
   Touch the animal sitting by the water.
   Touch two things we see in the sky.
   Show me the lake and the ground.
   Find what shines bright in the daytime.
   Point to things we see in the night sky.
   Show me red and yellow flowers.
   Point to a bird in a tree.
   Find a bee on a flower.

   b. Directives involving simple negatives

   Show me the plant that is *not* short.
   Find the plant *without* leaves.
   Point to the things *not* on the ground.
   Find the things *not* in the sky.
   Show me something you do *not* see at night.
   Show me something that does *not* shine in the daytime.
   Find something that is *not* green.

Questions

1. Basic labeling questions (12-24 months)

   What place is this?
   What is this?

Sky.	Turtle.	Flowers.
Lake.	Trees.	Fish.
Grass.	Lake.	Stars.
Sun.	Moon.	Ground.

2. Yes/No questions

   a. Yes/No questions about visible nature pictures (18-24 months)

      Is this:
      Do you see:

sky?	flowers?	fish?
lake?	trees?	moon?
grass?	lake?	stars?
sun?	turtle?	ground?

   b. Early negation questions (2-3 years)

      Can plants move?

      Is the sun in the sky?

      Is the sky under us?

      Is grass green?

      Are animals green?

      Is the ground above us?

      Do fish live in water?

      Do animals have roots?

3. What . . . do questions about nature pictures (24-30 months)

What do plants do?	(*grow*)
What do fish do?	(*swim*)
What does the sun do?	(*shines, keeps us warm, makes sunlight, makes daylight*)
What can we do with grass?	(*mow it, sit on it*)
What can we do at the lake?	(*swim, go fishing, ride boats*)
What can we do with flowers?	(*watch them bloom, pick them*)

4. Early discrimination—Choice of two nature pictures (2-3 years)

   Which place:
   has clouds?
   do fish swim?
   does sun shine?
   do boats sail?
   do plants grow?

Which plant:
    has leaves?
    has stems?
    is many colors?
    covers the ground?

5. Early location questions about visible nature places (2-3 years)

Where can you see:

sun?	fish?	boats?
water?	flowers?	clouds?
trees?	stars?	grass?
moon?		

6. Early attribute/concept questions—Choice of two nature pictures (2-3 years)

Which plant:
    is big?
    is short?
    has big roots?
    is tall?
    is many colors?
    is green?
    has many leaves?

Which place:
    is up high?
    is wet?
    is dry?
    is under our feet?

Short Discussions and Narratives

Use unit pictures and family puppets.

Discussion and questions for 18- to 24-month-old children:
    Let's walk outdoors.
    We can see green grass, pretty flowers, and tall trees.

    Are we walking outdoors?
    What do we see?

Discussion and questions for 24- to 30-month-old children:
    The ground is made of dirt.
    Plants grow up from the ground.
    They have roots that hold them up.
    They need sunshine and water to grow.
    Flowers, grass, and trees are plants.

    Is the ground dirt?
    Where do plants grow?
    What makes plants grow?

Discussion and questions for 30- to 36-month-old children:

The sky is bright in the daytime.
The sun shines and gives us light.
We can see clouds.
But at nighttime, the sky is black and dark.
Only the moon and stars glow in the night sky.

What do we see in the day sky?
Is the sky dark at day time?
Where is the moon?

Narrative and questions for 18- to 24-month-old children:

The children are watering the flowers.
They like to see the flowers grow.

What are these?
Did they put water on the flowers?

Narrative and questions for 24- to 30-month-old children:

The family is riding a boat in the lake.
The children watch the fish swim in the water.
The little girl drags her arm in the water and gets it wet.
That feels good and cool!

Where is the family?
What do the children see?
What did the girl do?
Did it stay dry?

Narrative and questions for 30- to 36-month-old children:

Mama and Daddy are sitting under the tree.
They are watching the clouds in the sky.
The sky is blue and the sun is shining.
The flowers look so pretty in the sunshine!

What are Mama and Daddy doing?
Where are they sitting?
Can they see the sun?
What looks pretty in the sunshine?

ENABLE II

Self

In this unit, children are required to focus on the body parts, actions, attributes, and feelings of themselves and their classmates, siblings, and friends.

It will be helpful to provide individual pictures and storybooks that feature boys and girls in action. Younger children (three to four years) will continue to require visual or manipulative assistance to follow directions and answer questions, but older children (four to near six) should more and more be able to answer some reasoning questions without looking at material that cues the response.

For the first narrative (Hop, Skip, and Jump!), use the ENABLE I puppet figure of the boy. Use these ENABLE II flannel board pictures to illustrate the other two narratives for this unit:

48. What a Big Girl!
49. The Happy Boy

Directives

Compound and complex directives of two to five steps (3½-5 years)

1. Body parts game
   Four to ten children are seated in a circle. Children respond to teacher directives that focus on body parts, possessives, and actions typical for children in this age range.

   Hop fast beside the line.

   Boys, open your mouths and yell loudly.

   Girls, roll over on your stomachs and touch your heels.

   Open your mouth, tap your teeth, and stick out your tongue.

   Look at her, pat her head, and squeeze her ankle.

   Rub the body parts you use to hear and talk. (*ears and mouth*)

   Twist your head, wrists, and thumbs.

   Bend your arms, and straighten your legs.

   Stick out the body part used to help eat and talk. (*tongue*)

   Rub the body part used to turn your head. (*neck*)

   Touch your nose and take a deep breath.

   Swing your arms, sway from side to side, and dance.

   Look at his (*or possessive of boy's name*) face and touch the body part in the middle. (*nose*)

Pull the two body parts on the side of her (*or possessive of girl's name*) head. (*ears*)

Lift both of your knees and touch them to your chin.

Tap one of your fingers on both of her elbows.

Walk in a circle around his (*or name possessive*) body.

Close both your eyes, swing both arms, and raise your eyebrows.

Stand in front of a girl and put your hands on her shoulders.

(*Pointing*) You two girls run together across the room and stand still back to back.

Jump behind him (*or boy's name*) and cover his eyes with your hands.

Move the body part you see with and hold your legs still.

Touch your elbows to your knees, and lean your head on your arms.

Walk slowly to another boy (*or girl*) and sit down behind him (*or her*).

2. Conditional directives—Attributes and feelings
   Children sit in a group and respond one by one to conditional directives. If they respond incorrectly, they are "out" temporarily.

   If you are a boy, then smile and look happy.

   If you are a girl, then jump two (or three) times.

   If you have on pants, then put your hands on your waist.

   If you have on socks, then pull them up.

   If you have a friend, give him/her a hug.

   If you have a sister, raise your hand.

   If you have a brother, stamp your feet.

   When I look sad, smile at me.

   When I touch my shirt, you touch yours.

   If you have long hair, then shake it.

   If you have short hair, then rub it.

   Find a boy with blue/brown eyes.

   Touch a girl with black/brown/blond hair.

   When I look happy, clap your hands.

   Walk around the biggest person and touch his head if he smiles.

   Count all the boys without belts.

   All the girls, stand up.

   If you are not big, then stretch up tall.

   If you are not a girl, stand beside a boy.

   If you can move fast, jump across the room.

   If you know your colors, find something orange and something purple.

3. Object movement directives

These ball and beanbag games require recognition of sex and pronouns, object movement actions, position and quantity concepts, and attributes.

Roll the ball under his (*or a boy's*) legs.

Bounce the ball two times in front of you.

Kick the ball to another girl (or boy) with long (or short) hair.

Catch the ball thrown by a boy.

Roll the ball between two boys.

Pass the beanbag down the line behind your backs.

Move the beanbag up the line between your legs.

Throw the ball to the farthest corner of the room.

Bounce the ball to the girl with blond (or red) hair.

Kick the ball to the girl with blue eyes.

Throw the ball to the boy at the end of the line.

Bounce the ball once and roll it to someone wearing a dress.

Roll the ball slowly to someone not a boy.

4. Hide and seek

Have one child hide a doll according to positional or quantitative directions, then relate the same directions (changing "put" or "hide" to "find") to another child to find the object.

Put the doll on top of the table under something red.

Put the doll under a big box.

Put the doll beside the bed under a blanket.

Hide the doll under a pair of shoes.

Hide the doll in an empty box.

Hide the doll in the middle of the room under a coat.

Put the doll in a corner of the room behind a chair.

Hide the doll next to the wall below a table (or desk).

Put the doll under a chair that a boy is sitting in.

Put the doll under the table in a girl's lap.

Questions

1. Reasoning questions—Function (3-5 years) Use objects or pictures.

   a. Level 1 (3-4 years)

   What do you do with:

food?	chairs?	friends?
bowls?	eyes?	phones?
balls?	towels?	plates?
comb?	toys?	ears?
juice?	beds?	legs?
clothes?	cups?	mouth?
soap?		toothbrush?

b. Level 2 (4-5 years)

Why do we have:

houses?	hands?	fingers?
books?	keys?	tricycles?
cars?	TV?	lights?
noses?	teachers?	scissors?
tongues?	arms?	glue/paste?
teeth?	knees?	pencils/crayons?
	elbows?	

2. Reasoning questions—Situational/Adaptive (3-6 years) No visual aids

a. Level 1 (3-4½ years)

What do you do when:

you're hungry?	you're cold?	you cut your finger?
you're thirsty?	you're wet?	your nose is running?
you're sleepy?	you're dirty?	your shoe is untied?
you're tired?	you're sick?	it gets dark?

b. Level 2 (4½-6 years)

What would you do if:
Mama fell and hurt herself?
you saw a house on fire?
you were outside and it started raining?
you needed to cross the street?
you wanted more snack?
somebody gave you something nice?
you were sad?
you sneezed?
you were afraid?
you burped?
you were mad?
you put on someone else's coat?
you broke a bottle in a store?
you wanted to make Daddy happy?
you had your gloves on the wrong hands?

3. Reasoning questions—How (3-6 years)
Use materials, pictures, or experiences.

a. Level 1—Manner (3-4 years)

How do you: run?
line up?
chew food?
act in school?

b. Level 2—Method/Ordered sequence (4-5 years)
Child receives practice in providing at least three steps in an ordered account. (For example, "How do you get ready for school?" Child answers, "First you get up, then you eat breakfast, and then/last you get dressed.")

How do you: get ready for school?
wash your hands?
brush your teeth?
wipe your nose?

c. Level 3—Degree (4-6 years)
Child is required to count or compare.

How old are you? (*Child tells correct number of years and shows correct number of fingers.*)

How many eyes/ears/arms/legs do you have? (*Child touches each, says "two."*)

How many fingers are on one hand?

How many fingers/toes do you have?

d. Level 4—Cause (4½-5 years)
An ordered account is required.

How do you make friends happy?

4. Time-based questions (5-6 years)
With or without pictures

When do you:
get up?
wear coats?
go to bed?
use an umbrella?
eat lunch?

Narratives

Hop, Skip, and Jump!

"I can do many things!" the boy said to himself. "I can walk slowly and run fast. I can jump over a rope and hop on one foot. I can skip, too! I can throw and catch a ball. I can color a pretty picture and cut it out." The little boy smiled happily. "I'm growing up!" he said.

Who is the boy talking to?
How does he run?
What can he do with pictures?
Where can he jump?
Is he happy?

What a Big Girl!

Grandma was coming to visit the family.

The little girl was excited. "I'm going to show Grandma what a big girl I am now!" she told her Mama.

"What a good idea!" said Mama.

When Grandma came, the little girl showed her all the things she could do by herself. She could wash her face and brush her teeth. She could put all her clothes on by herself! She could set the table for dinner.

Grandma was very surprised. "I am so proud of you!" Grandma said as she gave her a big hug. "What a big girl!"

Who was coming to visit?
What could the little girl do by herself?
Why was Grandma proud?
How did she show that she was proud?

The Happy Boy

One day a little boy didn't have anything to do. He was bored and he was sad.

His mama wanted to make him happy. "If you'll help me fold these clothes and put them away, then we'll fix a picnic and go to the park!" she told her son.

The little boy jumped up, and smiled. He helped his mother finish her work. Then they made ham sandwiches. They packed a basket with the sandwiches, apples, peanut butter cookies, and soda.

The little boy had *such* a good time at the park! He played with other children on the swings and slides. He and Mama ate the good food, and they watched the leaves blow in the wind. They had a wonderful day!

Why was the boy sad?
What did his mama want to do?
How did the boy help his mama?
What happened at the park?
Do you think Mama made the boy happy?

Family

For this unit's activities, gather storybooks and pictures of families and family members. Laminated photographs of each child's mother, father, and siblings are most helpful.

Use the ENABLE I puppet figures of family members. These ENABLE II flannel board pictures illustrate two of the narratives:
50. The Messy Baby
51. My Parents

Directives

Compound and complex directives of two to five steps (2½-5 years)

1. Body parts game.
   Children sit in a circle. Pictures of Mama, Daddy, baby, boy, and girl are in the center. Teacher gives directives that focus on possessive pronouns, body parts, and actions.

   Find the picture of the girl and point to the top of her body.

   Pick up Daddy's picture and show me what he uses to hear. (*ears*)

   Show me the boy's and the baby's knees and ankles.

   Show me the body parts the family uses to stand up. (*legs, feet*)

   Show me what the children wiggle on their hands. (*fingers, thumbs*)

   Touch what the baby uses to crawl. (*arms, legs*)

   Point to the body parts Mama uses to smile. (*mouth, eyes*)

   Get the picture of Daddy and touch what covers his head. (*hair*)

   Move to the picture of Mama and point to something above her arms. (*shoulders*)

   Pick up the baby's picture and show me what she can open and shut. (*eyes, mouth*)

   Find the picture of the child like you and find his or her waist.

   Put the picture of Daddy and boy together and touch their necks.

   Get Mama's picture and show me what she uses to hold the baby. (*arms*)

   Get the girl's picture and show me what she uses to smell. (*nose*)

   Put Baby's picture on top of Daddy's and touch the Baby's elbows.

   Touch the body parts the children can bend on their arms. (*elbows, wrists*)

157

2. Conditional directives—Attributes and feelings
   Pictures of a variety of ethnic family members with a variety of emotions evident are necessary for this activity. Children sit in a circle, with pictures in the center.

   When I smile, find a Mama who is happy.

   When I frown, find a baby who is sad.

   When I show this picture, find another child like it. (*May match by sex or hair color.*)

   If you have long hair, find a picture of another long-haired person.

   When you find all the parents, put them together with the babies.

   If you have brown eyes, find all the children without blue eyes.

   If you have a baby in your family, find two baby pictures.

   If you have a brother, get all the pictures of boys.

   If you have a sister, find the pictures of girls with black hair.

   Get a picture of a Daddy without a smile.

   If your baby cries, find a happy baby.

   If you have on pants, find pictures of everyone wearing pants.

   If you have blond hair, find someone else with blond hair.

   If you have a purse, find a woman with a purse.

   Find a person who cannot walk yet.

   When I snap my fingers, find three men.

   When I hold up four fingers, find four babies.

   If you are a girl, find a picture of a girl who does not look like you.

3. Object movement directives
   These ball and beanbag games require recognition of family members, actions, position and quantity concepts, and attributes. Use the same pictures used in the conditional directives.

   Throw the beanbag on a person who shaves his face.

   Roll the ball to a little family member.

   Bounce the ball on a picture of a child not a girl.

   Throw the ball across all the pictures.

   Put the beanbag under a picture of a man standing.

   Throw the beanbag on a sad baby.

   Kick the ball to a picture of a woman sitting.

   Bounce the ball to an unhappy man.

   Roll the ball to a child having fun.

   Get two beanbags and throw them on two parents.

   Put the beanbag between a boy and a girl.

   Throw the ball on the picture of a sleeping baby.

   Bounce the ball beside the pictures of two men.

   Roll the ball around the pictures of three women.

4. Hide and seek
   Have one child hide the pictures according to positional directions, then relate the directions (changing "put" to "find") to another child to find the item.

> Put a picture of a man under the book on the desk.
>
> Hide a picture of a baby behind the doll chair.
>
> Hide a picture of a woman in the cabinet on the top shelf.
>
> Hide a boy picture at the bottom of the locker.
>
> Put a Daddy picture in the bookcase behind a book.
>
> Put a baby picture at the end of the shelf under a puzzle.
>
> Hide a girl picture next to the box on the floor.
>
> Put the pictures of children under the cover of the baby bed.
>
> Put the pictures of parents in the middle of the crayon box.
>
> Hide a pair of baby pictures inside the closet.
>
> Hide a picture of a man behind something brown.
>
> Put a picture of a girl under something soft.
>
> Hide a picture of little people near something purple or orange.
>
> Put a picture of big people beside something hard.

Questions

1. Reasoning questions—Function (3-5 years)
   Pictures needed
   a. Level 1 (3-4 years)

> What do parents do with children?
>
> What does Daddy do with a car?
>
> What does Mama do with pots and pans?
>
> What does a family do with clothes?
>
> What does Daddy do with a razor?
>
> What does Daddy do with a necktie?
>
> What does Mama do with a purse?
>
> What does a baby do with diapers?
>
> What does a baby have a bottle for?
>
> What does Mama do with her mouth?
>
> What does Daddy do with his hands?

b. Level 2 (4-5 years)

Why does Mama carry diapers for baby?

Why does Mama need a stove?

Why does Daddy need a hairbrush?

Why does Mama use detergent?

Why does Daddy need keys?

Why do parents like newspapers?

Why do babies cry?

Why do babies crawl?

Why do parents need telephones?

Why do parents hug children?

Why do parents go to work?

Why do babies sleep in beds with rails on the sides?

2. Reasoning questions—Situational/Adaptive (3-6 years)

a. Level 1 (3-4½ years)

What does Mama do when:	we're hungry?
	we're dirty?
	it gets dark?
	we need to cross the street?
	she's tired?
	the baby cries?
	she's proud of you?
What does Daddy do when:	his whiskers grow?
	he's on vacation?
	you do something he asked you to?
	you can't button your shirt?
What does a baby do when:	she's wet?
	he loses his toy?
	she can't walk?

b. Level 2 (4½-6 years)

What would Mama do if:	you had a fever?
	you ran out in the street?
	you didn't say "please"?
	she had no more milk?
	she lost her purse?
	you brought her flowers?
	you wouldn't share with your friends?
	she didn't want to cook?
	Grandma came to visit?
What would Daddy do if:	it were your birthday?
	your ball rolled in the street?
	you drew him a pretty picture?

3. Reasoning questions—How (3-6 years)

a. Level 1—Manner (3-4 years)

How does Mama: hug?
How does Daddy: sound?
                cook?
                read stories to us?
                drive?
                sing?
                work?
                look?

How does Baby: smell when dirty?
                play with toys?
                feed herself?
                drink his bottle?

b. Level 2—Method/Ordered sequence (4-5 years)

How does Mama: relax?
How does Daddy: go shopping?
                clean house?
                get ready for work?
                cook hamburgers outside?
                take care of the yard?
                play ball with you?
                make the car go?

How does Baby let you know what she wants?

c. Level 3—Degree-quantity (4-6 years)

How many parents do you have?

How many sisters do you have?

How many brothers do you have?

d. Level 4—Cause (4½-5 years)

How does Mama make herself look pretty?

How does Daddy catch a fish?

How does Daddy make popcorn?

How does Mama get music to listen to?

4. Time-based questions (5-6 years)

When does Mama: give us cereal?
When does Daddy: wash dishes?
                make us go to bed?
                come home from work?
                work in the garden?
                turn on the TV?
                wear a raincoat?
                answer the phone?

When does Baby: throw food?
                sleep a long time?

Narratives

The Messy Baby

The baby is learning to feed himself. He dips his spoon in the applesauce and takes it to his mouth. Some of the food spills on his shirt and the chair!

He picks up a piece of meat with his fingers and chews it up. He gets ketchup on his face!

He takes a drink of milk and spills it all over his pants.

Mama is so proud of her big baby. "Now I don't have to feed you. I just have to clean you up!" she laughs.

> What is the baby learning to do?
> How many things does he eat?
> Which does he eat with a spoon?
> How does Mama feel?
> Why does she laugh?

My Parents

My Mama and Daddy both work. Daddy is a dentist. He helps take care of children's teeth. Mama is a teacher. She teaches big boys and girls how to use computers at school.

My parents work hard all day, and *then* they come home and take care of our family! Sometimes Mama cooks, and sometimes Daddy cooks. They are both good cooks! I like Mama's apple pie and Daddy's spaghetti.

My brother and I think we have a good Mama and Daddy! We love them!

> What kind of job does Daddy have?
> Where does Mama work?
> How do they cook?
> How do the children feel about their parents?

A Family Party

The Thomas family is having a big party. All the uncles and aunts and cousins are here. So are the grandparents.

It is Grandma Thomas's birthday. She is the oldest person in the family and has a big birthday cake! What a *lot* of candles there are!

Now Grandma is opening her presents. Uncle Mark gave her a pretty necklace. Cousin Frances gave her a plant to put in her room. What is in that big package? Oh, it is a big patchwork quilt that Aunt Willene made for her!

That's enough presents! Now Grandma cuts her cake. Everybody eats cake and homemade ice cream. Grandma looks so happy! We all have a good time.

Who is the party for?
Is Grandma young?
Why are there a lot of candles?
How many presents did she get?
When did Grandma cut the cake?

Animals

Gather realistic toys and pictures of domestic animals, and have illustrated animal storybooks available.

Use the ENABLE I puppet figures of the cow and chicken, and the ENABLE II puppet figures of a pig, turkey, and sheep. These ENABLE II flannel board pictures illustrate two of the narratives:
52. The Dairy Farm
53. The Sheep Farm

Directives

Compound and complex directives of two to five steps (3½-5 years)

1. Body parts game
    Children seated in a circle respond to teacher directives that focus on the body parts and actions of animals depicted in pictures.

    Find the animal the farmer raises for wool.

    Touch the animal we'd buy if it were Thanksgiving.

    If you see five animals, put them in a row.

    Touch all the animals with hair except the pig.

    Hop on the animal that gobbles and the animal that clucks.

    Put your nose on the animal with a snout.

    Touch your thumbs to the animal that has horns.

    Touch your elbows to the animals with wings.

    Tiptoe around a picture of an animal that says "oink."

    Sit beside an animal that sits on a nest.

    Turn upside-down a picture of an animal that farmers shear.

    Put together all the four-legged animals.

    Put together both the animals that don't have hooves.

    Make a row of animals with hair.

    Put the animal that says "baa-baa" behind the cow.

    Put the animal that has an udder in front of the turkey.

    Touch the animals that play in mud.

    Put the animals that eat grass close together.

    Join hands across the animal that says "moo-moo."

    Find five animals that live on a farm.

2. Conditional directives—Attributes and functions
   Children seated in a circle respond to conditional directives involving attributes and functions of pictured or toy animals in order to earn animal stickers.

   If you see two birds, put your little finger on each.

   If the animal gives us milk, pat it.

   Find the animal you'd need if you wanted eggs.

   Find the animal the farmer raises for wool.

   Touch the animal we'd buy if it were Thanksgiving.

   If you see five animals, put them in a row.

   If you see the smallest animal, put it first in the row.

   If you see the biggest animal, put it last in the row.

   If a pig eats lots of food, put it next to last.

   If you see an animal with wool, put it in the middle.

   Touch the animal you'd need if you wanted ham or bacon.

   Get the animal you'd see if you were at a dairy farm.

   Touch the mama animal you'd need:

   > if you wanted a baby lamb.

   > if you wanted a baby calf.

   > if you wanted baby chicks.

   > if you wanted piglets.

   Find the animal you'd need if you wanted beef.

   Show me the animal we'd have if we had fried chicken.

   Get the animal who gives us what we need to make cheese and butter.

3. Object movement directives
   Tape pictures of animals to the sides of cans. Lay cans on sides for kicking and rolling, and upright for throwing, bouncing, and placing the balls or beanbags.

   Throw the ball to the right of a brown bird.

   Put the ball to the left of a white bird.

   Roll the ball between the cow and the sheep.

   Kick the ball into the can with a turkey on it.

   Bounce the ball over all the animals.

   Throw the beanbag behind the chicken can.

   Put the beanbag next to the fattest animal.

   Put the beanbag above the thinnest animal.

   Put the beanbag between the animals whose ears you cannot see.

   Bounce the ball near the animal with the longest tail.

   Throw the beanbag behind the animal with the shortest legs.

   Kick the ball into the can of an animal with toes.

   Lay the beanbag in front of an animal with a curly tail.

   Throw the beanbag outside the can of a feathery animal.

4. Barn positions
   Use a toy barn and plastic toy animals, or a paper cutout of a barn and animal stickers or cutouts.

   Put the chicken over the barn, and the turkey under the barn.

   Put the cow to the right of the barn, and the sheep to the left.

   Put the pig at the bottom of the barn, and the chicken at the top.

   Put the animals with feathers in the middle of the barn.

   Put the animals with wings in the corner of the barn.

   Put all the animals other than the pig and sheep behind the barn.

   Put each of the animals with toes in front of the barn.

   Put the big animals inside the barn, and the little animals outside.

   Put the animal that chews a cud far away from the barn.

   Put the animal that feeds piglets near the roof of the barn.

   Put the turkey by the barn door, and the chicken in the window.

   Put the pig on the highest part of the barn, and the sheep beside the lower part.

Questions

1. Reasoning questions—Function (3-5 years)
   a. Level 1 (3-4 years)

What does a pig do with:	its hooves?
	corn?
	its snout?
	mud?

   | What does a turkey do with: | its wings? |
   | | its beak? |

What does a chicken do with:	a nest?
	eggs?
	corn?
	its feet?

What does a cow do with:	grass?
	water?
	hay?
	its tail?

What does a sheep do with:	its ears?
	its eyes?
	its mouth?
	its legs?

   b. Level 2 (4-5 years)

Why do farmers raise:	cows?
	sheep?
	turkeys?
	pigs?
	chickens?

Why do cows need barns?
Why do these animals need farmers?
Why do chickens need nests?
Why do farmers need fences?
Why does a farmer want pigs to get fat?

2. Reasoning questions—Situational/Adaptive (3-6 years)

a. Level 1 (3-4½ years)

What does a farmer do when he needs a sheep's wool?
What does a farmer do when a chicken lays eggs?
What does a farmer do to get a cow's milk?
What does a farmer use to keep animals warm?

b. Level 2 (4½-6 years)

What does a chicken do if it is scared?
What does a pig do if it is hot?
What does a cow do if it is hungry?
What does a farmer use if he needs to herd sheep?
What does a turkey farmer do if it is Thanksgiving?

3. Reasoning questions—How (3-6 years)

a. Level 1—Manner (3-4 years)

How do: cows move?
          pigs look?
          turkeys sound?
          chickens feel?
          sheep run?

b. Level 2—Method/Ordered sequence (4-5 years)

How do farmers care for animals?
How do dairy farmers milk cows?
How does a farmer get wool?

c. Level 3—Degree/Quantity (4-6 years)

How many legs does a sheep have?
How many horns does a cow have?
How many hooves does a pig have?
How many wings does a chicken have?
How many tails does a turkey have?

d. Level 4—Cause (4½-5 years)

How do we get bacon and ham?
How do we get eggs?
How do we get beef?
How do we get ice cream and cheese?

4. Time-based questions (5-6 years)

When do: farmers milk cows?
            animals sleep?
            farmers gather eggs?
            we usually eat turkey?

Narratives

The Dairy Farm

A dairy farm is a place where cows are cared for to produce milk to sell.

Dairy farmers have an important job. Early in the morning and again in the evening, the dairy farmer and all the helpers hook the cows to milking machines to gather the milk.

They store the milk in clean milkhouses until it is ready to be shipped to factories. There it will be made clean and safe from germs. Then the milk is poured into milk cartons or prepared to be made into butter, cheese, ice cream, or other dairy products.

Dairy farmers work hard to keep their barns, equipment, and cows clean and nice. That way we always have good, healthy milk products.

    Why do dairy farmers work hard?
    When are the cows milked?
    Where is the milk sterilized and packaged?
    How many things are made out of milk?

The Sheep Farm

Mrs. Jamal took her class for a visit on a sheep farm. They saw many woolly sheep eating grass in a big green field. A sheep dog guarded them and kept them all together and safe.

The little girls in the class liked seeing the baby lambs best. One little lamb was drinking milk from its mother.

The little boys in the class liked it when the farmer showed them how he sheared the wool off one sheep. He bundled the wool into a pile. It was ready to ship to market. There it would be made into wool sweaters and blankets.

The farmer gave each child in Mrs. Jamal's class a little strand of wool to wrap around a finger. It felt soft and fuzzy.

    Where did Mrs. Jamal's class go?
    What animal guarded the sheep?
    What did the girls like best on the sheep farm?
    When did the boys like the visit best?
    What happened to the sheep's wool?

Porko the Prize Pig

Billy Brown had a little pet named Porko. Billy took care of him from the time the pig was a baby.

Billy fed Porko lots of corn and mash. He wanted him to grow big and fat. Then Billy was going to show him at the county fair. The biggest pig would win a prize.

Soon the day of the fair arrived. Billy washed his pig. He took him to the fair in his daddy's truck.

Many boys walked their pigs in front of the judges. But Billy's pig won first prize!

"What a fine hog!" said the judges. (Big pigs are called hogs.)

Then a man named Mr. Lucas offered to buy Porko. Billy was sad because he had come to love Porko, but he was proud because he knew he had done a good job.

"You are going to be a good pig farmer!" said Billy's daddy.

When did Billy begin to care for Porko?
Why did he feed him lots of food?
What do we call a big, fat pig?
How did Billy feel about selling Porko?
What do you think Billy will be when he grows up?

Home

Gather pictures and storybooks of homes, rooms, garages, porches, and yards. Use the *ENABLE* posters of the inside and outside of a house. You also may want to use a larger playhouse with a kitchen, bathroom, bedroom, and living room.

These ENABLE II flannel board pictures illustrate two of the narratives for this unit:
    54. A Weekend at Home
    55. Backyard Fun

Directives

Compound and complex directives of two to five steps (3½-5 years)

1. Rooms of the house
   This activity can be implemented at home by parents using the actual rooms in their house, or used at school in a directive-response game. In a game format, use a playhouse or the *Enable* poster of the inside of a house. If pictures are used, substitute the word "find" for "go to" in the directions.

   Go to the kitchen and touch the cooking place.

   Find the room for cleaning and toileting and touch the sides of the room. (*wall*)

   Walk to rooms that have chairs and find the room with a couch.

   Touch the top and bottom of each room and tell me what they are called. (*ceiling, floor*)

   Go to a room for sleeping and touch the places that hold clothes. (*closets, chest of drawers*)

   Find the places in the kitchen where you could get something to drink. (*sink, refrigerator*)

   Find a room that has shelves for holding dishes and cans of food, and count the shelves.

   Find a room where you can brush your teeth, and touch the racks for holding towels.

   Open and shut the door to the room with the most windows.

   Go to the smallest room and jump, and then walk to the biggest room and sit down.

   Stand in front of a place where you could keep your car.

Walk to the middle of a room that has something that gets hot and something that gets cold. (*stove, refrigerator*)

Go to the hall of the house and run back and forth.

Raise and lower a window at the front of the house.

Find the part of the house where smoke rises and sit beside it.

Find the rooms where you would not sleep and turn the lights on and off.

Go to a room used for talking and playing and count the corners of the room.

Go to a place that has a rail to hold onto and walk up and sit in the middle. (*stairs*)

2. Conditional directives

These directions can be given at home, or in a game with children pointing to the appropriate place.

If you are hot, open the window.

If you are hungry, go to the kitchen and open the refrigerator.

If you are thirsty, get a glass and turn on the water faucet in the kitchen.

If you are sleepy, go to a room with a bed.

If you are barefooted and want to go outside, get your shoes out of the closet.

If it is dark, find the light switch and turn the light on.

If it is too bright, pull the shade down (or close the curtains).

When you're happy, jump around the outside of the house.

When you're dirty, go to the room that has soap and towels.

If you are cold, stand in front of the fireplace.

If you want to watch cartoons, find a room with a TV or radio.

If you want to be quiet, go in the bedroom and shut the door.

If you can't find clean clothes, go to the utility room.

If you are finished playing, go to the room for bathing.

Bring a friend to your house if you are lonesome.

3. Object movement directives

On the floor, tape the outline of a roofed house with four rooms (living room, bedroom, kitchen, bathroom) and a garage. In each room, place toy furniture, or materials typically found in these rooms, or pictures of a furnished room of that type. Children move balls and beanbags according to directives.

Throw a beanbag in the middle of each room.

Kick a ball over the roof of the house.

After you throw a beanbag in the bedroom, bounce a ball in the living room.

Throw a ball toward the door of the house, then kick it away from the house.

Throw beanbags in the rooms on the right side of the house.

Bounce balls across the left side of the house.

Line beanbags in a row along the bottom front of the house.

Throw the orange beanbags into the kitchen, and the brown beanbags in the bathroom.

Throw beanbags in every room except the one where we eat.

Kick a couple of balls beside the house.

Put three beanbags in rooms that don't have bathtubs.

Roll a ball into any room other than one with a bed.

Get a pair of beanbags and throw them together in a room where people wake up in the morning.

Bounce a ball into a room with the longest floor.

4. Listen and hide

This game can be played at home. Parent gives the child or children directions as to where to hide. If the right hiding place is achieved, the child wins a snack for being the best listener.

Hide in the garage beside the garbage can.

Hide in the backyard behind a tree.

Hide on the front porch in front of a window.

Hide under the roof beside a door.

Hide under a table, in a room for washing dishes.

Hide inside a closet in a hallway.

Hide in the room where Mama keeps bandages.

Hide in the corner of the bedroom.

Hide between the wall and a chair in the living room.

Stand still close to a place for looking outside.

Hide next to the door to the bathroom.

Hide near a lamp in a room with a chair.

Hide under a mantel in a room where families relax.

Questions

1. Reasoning questions—Function (3-5 years)
   Use pictures.
   a. Level 1 (3-4 years)

      What do you do in a:

bedroom?	bathroom?
living room?	utility room?
kitchen?	garage?

      What do you do with a:
      window?
      door?

   b. Level 2 (4-5 years)

      Why do we have:

homes?	light switches?	stairs?
floors?	rugs?	doorbells?
chimneys?	walls?	fences?
roofs?	door knobs?	backyards?
halls?	gates?	porches/patios?
mantles?	curtains?	shower curtains?

2. Reasoning questions—Situational/Adaptive (3-6 years)
   a. Level 1 (3-4½ years)

      What place do you go at home when/Where do you go when:
      you're hungry?
      you're tired of playing inside?
      you're sleepy?
      you want to potty?
      you feel bad?
      you're cold?
      you're thirsty?
      you're dirty?
      you want to play ball?
      you need to ride in a car?
      your teeth are dirty?
      you want to roast marshmallows?

   b. Level 2 (4½-6 years)

      What would you do if you wanted to go inside the house?

      What would you do with your dirty clothes after you take them off?

      What would you look for to tell the time?

      What would you get to hang up clean clothes?

      What would you do with wet boots in the house?

      What can you do with walls?

      What can you do with a fireplace?

      What can we do to keep the dog in the yard?

3. Reasoning questions—How (3-6 years)
   Use materials, pictures, or experiences.
   a. Level 1—Manner (3-4 years)

   How do:
   rugs feel?
   lights look?
   doorbells sound?
   chimneys feel?
   kitchens smell?

   b. Level 2—Method/Ordered sequence (4-5 years)

How do you:	take a bath?
How does Mama:	set the table?
How does Daddy:	wash dishes?
	get dressed?
	cook supper?

   c. Level 3—Degree/Quantity (4-6 years)

   How many rooms are in your house?
   How many doors are in your house?
   How many windows are in your house?
   How many trees are in the yard?

   d. Level 4—Cause (4½-5 years)

   How do you make a door open?
   How do you get rested at home?
   How do we get water cold at home?

4. Time-based questions (5-6 years)

When do we:	play outside?
When does Mama:	cook lunch?
When does Daddy:	go to work?
	eat breakfast?
	wash clothes?
	come home?
	go inside?
	get undressed?

Narratives

A Weekend at Home

It was Saturday, and it was cold outside. It was too cold to go out and play. Daddy built a fire in the fireplace.

Mama said, "Let's cook hot dogs, popcorn, and hot chocolate. We can have a winter picnic! We can eat on the living room rug in front of the fire!"

Daddy brought a quilt and put it on the floor. The children helped Mama cook the food. Then Mama, Daddy, Bitsy, and Larry sat on the floor and ate the good food.

> How was the weather outside?
> What did Daddy do to make it warm inside?
> How did they get ready for the winter picnic?
> Did the family have a good time together?

Backyard Fun

Brady and his friend Jamie were playing in the backyard. They were playing ball.

Brady would throw the ball as far as he could. His dog Muttsy would run and bring the ball back.

Jamie would kick the ball a long, long way. Muttsy would grab the ball in her mouth and bring it back.

It was a good game! The boys had fun, and Muttsy had fun.

Mama opened the door and came onto the back porch. "Would you like a snack?" she asked. "I have ice-cream bars for you boys and dogbones for Muttsy!"

"Yea-aa!" said the boys.

"Ruff, ruff!" said Muttsy.

What a nice ending for a game!

> Where were the boys playing?
> Who brought the ball back?
> How did she bring it back?
> How many snacks did Mama have?
> Do you think they'll play the game again?

Helping Mama Clean

One day Mama was working hard. She was cleaning house.

She vacuumed the floors. She dusted the furniture.

Marcus and Nessa felt sad because Mama was working so hard. "We will help you, Mama. What can we do?" asked the children.

"Thank you, you sweet children! You *can* help me. Marcus, take this bag and empty all the trashcans into it. Nessa, bring all the dirty clothes and towels to me in the utility room."

Marcus got all the trash. He and Mama tied up the bag and Marcus put it outside in the big garbage can.

Nessa brought all the dirty clothes. She and Mama sorted the clothes and put the light-colored ones in the washing machine.

Then both children helped Mama fold all the clothes from the dryer and put them away.

Mama gave the children a big hug. "I'm proud of my little helpers!" she said.

Why were the children sad?
How did Marcus help Mama?
What did Nessa do to help?
How did Mama feel?

Furniture

At home, actual furniture can be used for these games and activities. At school, use playhouse furniture and furniture pictures.

These ENABLE II flannel board pictures illustrate two of the narratives:
56. Living Room Fun
57. Making the Beds

Directives

Compound and complex directives of two to five steps (3½-5 years)

1. Furniture-room association
   This game can be played at home, using actual furniture; or at school, using the taped floor outline of a house with four rooms described in the previous unit. The outlined rooms may contain either toy furniture or pictures of furniture.

   Go to the kitchen and pull the chairs out from the table.

   Walk to the bathroom and turn on the water faucet.

   Jump to the living room, sit on the couch, and touch the couch back.

   Take long steps to the bedroom and turn down the covers on the bed.

   Walk to the kitchen, turn on the light, and put your hands on the sink.

   Hop to the bathroom, wash your hands in the sink, rinse them, and turn off the water.

   Go to the living room, talk on the telephone, and hang it up.

   Walk around the outside of the house, walk through the inside of the house, and stop beside the stove in the kitchen.

   Count the chairs by the kitchen table, and crawl fast around the table.

   Sit beside the couch and watch a cartoon on TV from beginning to end.

   Pull out all the drawers of the bedroom chest, and find the ones that are the most full and the most empty.

   Touch all the furniture in the living room that has four legs.

   Find all the things in the bathroom that hold water and touch all except the one that can be flushed.

   Walk to the kitchen, stand in the middle, and count everything that can be turned on and off.

179

Find the part of the stove that can hold things inside and the part that heats up things at the top.

Open and close the door to the tall furniture in the kitchen for keeping food cold and fresh.

Go to the bathroom and count the sides of the bathtub and the faucets of the bathtub.

Run to the living room, put a magazine in the middle of the coffee table, and touch a rocking chair.

Find the antenna, channel switch, and on/off switch on the television.

Walk to every room that has a lamp and touch the bottom and top of the lamp.

2. Conditional directives

At home, these directives can be given routinely. At school, the teacher gives the condition, and the child is allowed to reason through the response.

If you are tired, go to the bedroom and lie on the bed.

If you want a cold drink, get one out of the refrigerator.

If your teeth are dirty, go to the bathroom and brush your teeth at the sink.

If it is raining outside, play with your toys in the living room.

If you want a couple of cookies, find the cookie jar beside the refrigerator.

If you are missing a sock, find another one in your chest of drawers.

If the television is too loud, turn the volume switch down.

If the telephone rings, pick up the receiver and say "hello."

If you are afraid of the dark, turn on the lamp.

If the food is ready on the stove, put it on the table.

If it is cold outside, get your sweater and gloves out of the drawer.

When you're tired of playing, sit on the couch and watch TV.

When you're finished eating, go to the bathroom and brush your teeth and wash your hands.

When you have a few books, sit in the chair and read.

When you're taking a bath, wash all over with soap.

If Mama cooked you a good dinner, say "thank you" before you leave the table.

3. Object movement directives

Children move balls and beanbags in relation to furniture or furniture pictures.

Roll a ball across the top of the chest of drawers.

Throw a beanbag in the middle of the bed.

Throw a beanbag at the handles on a chest of drawers.

Roll a ball in front of a television.

Roll a ball through the legs of a table.

Hide a beanbag under the cushion of the couch.

Put beanbags on the back, under the legs and under the seat of the chair.

Put down the lid of the potty, and throw a ball over the potty seat.

Put the telephone receiver on the red beanbag and put a blue beanbag on the telephone dial.

Roll a ball to the left of the refrigerator and then roll it to the right.

Put a beanbag on the tallest kitchen furniture.

Put a beanbag on the longest living room furniture.

Drop a ball in the deepest bathroom furniture.

4. Listen and hide
Parent or teacher gives "hiding" directions in relation to furniture. If the child hides correctly, a sticker is awarded for good listening.

Hide away from the bed in the bedroom.

Hide on the left side of the couch.

Hide under the middle of the table.

Hide behind the chest of drawers.

Hide by something brown in the bedroom.

Hide in front of something green in the kitchen.

Hide in front of the kitchen furniture other than something cold.

Hide inside where you take a bath in the bathroom.

Hide on the right side of the coffee table in the living room.

Hide under a desk in the bedroom (or living room).

Hide in the bedroom but not under the bed.

Hide in any room other than the bathroom.

Hide near something in the living room.

Hide below a rocking chair in the living room.

Questions

1. Reasoning questions—Function (3-5 years) Use pictures.
   a. Level 1 (3-4 years)
      What do you do with a:

bed?	table?	chair?
television?	potty?	bathtub?
telephone?	stove?	couch?

   b. Level 2 (4-5 years)
      Why do we have:

refrigerators?	volume	water faucets?
ovens?	changers?	coffee tables?
drawer	oven doors?	bathtub drains?
handles?	lamp cords?	refrigerator shelves?
table legs?	telephone dials?	

2. Reasoning questions—Situational/Adaptive (3-6 years)
   a. Level 1 (3-4½ years)

   What piece of furniture do you use when:
   you're hungry?
   you're dirty?
   you're tired?
   you want to heat soup?
   you need to potty?
   you need more clothes?
   you need something cold to drink?
   you want to talk long distance?

   b. Level 2 (4½-6 years)

   What would you do if you were in bed and got cold?

   What would you do if the refrigerator was too crowded?

   What could you do if there were no more seats on the couch?

   What could you do if the bathtub water was too cold?

3. Reasoning questions—How (3-6 years)
   Use materials, pictures, or experiences.
   a. Level 1—Manner (3-4 years)

   How do:
   bed mattresses feel?
   dirty tables feel?
   telephones ring?
   refrigerators feel?

   b. Level 2—Method/Ordered sequence (4-5 years)

   How do you:
   make a bed?
   get ready for a bath?
   clean off a table?
   clean the living room?

   c. Level 3—Degree/Quantity (4-6 years)

   How many chairs are in the kitchen?

   How many drawers are in the chest of drawers?

   How many people can sit on the couch?

   Which is the biggest piece of furniture?

   Which is the tallest piece of furniture?

   Which is the shortest piece of furniture?

   Which is the roundest piece of furniture?

   How many shelves are in the refrigerator?

   d. Level 4—Cause (4½-5 years)

   How do you keep food fresh?

   How does Mama cook food?

   How do you talk on the telephone?

   How do you make a television work?

4. Time-based questions (5-6 years)
>   When does:
>>   Mama cook in the kitchen?
>>   the family watch television?
>   When do we:
>>   talk on the telephone?
>>   make the bed?

Narratives

Living Room Fun

It was the weekend. The whole family was relaxing in the living room. Daddy was reading the paper on the couch. Mama was talking to the baby in her playpen. Felina and Juan were playing a game of checkers at the coffee table.

Daddy said, "I like Saturdays because I don't have to work."

Juan said, "We like Saturdays because we can play at home."

Mama smiled. "I like Saturdays, too, even though that's when I have to do more cooking!"

>   When did this story happen?
>   Why did Daddy and Juan like Saturdays?
>   How did Mama feel?

Making the Bed

Ben and John were brothers. They slept in twin beds in their room.

One day Mama said, "You are big boys now. It is time for you to learn to make up your own beds. I will show you how to do it."

Mama showed them how to pull up and smooth the sheet and blankets. They learned how to tuck them into the sides of the bed. Then they learned how to pull up the quilt and fluff the pillow.

Ben and John were surprised! Their beds looked so nice!

"I can't wait to tell my teacher what I can do!" said Ben.

"Me, too!" said John. "Big boys are good helpers!"

>   Who were Ben and John?
>   What did Mama teach them?
>   How did they make up their beds?
>   How did they feel about what they learned to do?

Ready for Bed

Mama looked outside. It was getting dark.

"Children, children!" she called. "Time to come in and take a bath!"

The girls came running into the kitchen.

"Oh no!" said Mama. "You are *so-o* dirty! Go in the utility room and take off your dirty clothes. Put them in the hamper. Then run into the bathroom."

Mama went into the bathroom and turned on the warm water. Then she poured bubble bath in the water.

"Oh boy! Bubbles!" said the girls!

They sat in the warm water and had a nice bath. They played with their bath toys and scrubbed dirt off each other.

Mama helped them rinse and dry. Then they put on their warm pajamas.

Mama tucked the girls into bed and read them a story.

"Goodnight, sleepyheads!" Mama said as she turned off the light. But the girls were already asleep!

> When did this story take place?
> How did the children get clean?
> Why did Mama put bubbles in the water?
> Do you think the girls slept well?

Utensils

The actual and toy utensils introduced in ENABLE I can be used again in this unit. Additional utensils are a skillet, spatula, cookie sheet, and pitcher. It will be helpful to provide a sorting tray for the silverware, a toy storage cabinet for the dishes, and a toy table and stove.

These ENABLE II flannel board pictures illustrate two of the narratives for this unit:
58. Using the Silverware
59. Breakfast Time

Directives

Compound and complex directives of two to five steps (3½-5 years)

1. Utensil arrangement
   These directives can be given at home in one-to-one interaction between parent and child, or at school in a game format.

   Take four knives and arrange them together to make a square.

   Put the skillet on the stove and the cookie sheet in the oven.

   Turn the cup upside down, and put the spoon in the bowl.

   Pour the juice out of the pitcher into the glass until the glass is full.

   Set a place at the table, using a plate, glass, knife, fork, and spoon.

   Get the utensil for frying and the one for turning eggs and put them on the stove.

   Empty all the dishes, rinse them off, and put them in the dishwasher.

   Arrange three spoons to make a triangle.

   Line up the bowls in a row, and put the plates beside them.

   Sort the silverware into the tray. Put the knives on the left, the forks in the middle, and the spoons on the right.

   Put lemons, sugar, and water into a pitcher and stir it to make lemonade.

   Put bread on the cookie sheet. Spread butter on the bread, and put it in the oven to make toast.

   Wash the dishes, dry them, and stack them on the shelves.

   Pour cereal and milk into a bowl, then sprinkle sugar on top.

   Use the spatula to get the cookies off the cookie sheet.

   Put a pot and skillet on top of the stove, and put a pan inside the oven.

Give me three forks and four spoons.

Put all the dishes except glasses on the table.

Set the pitcher in the middle of the table.

Starting with the plates and ending with the silverware, set the table.

2. Conditional directives

This activity can be played in the Housekeeping Corner as part of "pretending."

If you want to eat soup, get a bowl and a spoon.

If you want to cook eggs, get a skillet and a spatula.

If you want to eat meat, get a fork and knife.

When you want to cook supper, get a pot, a pan, and a spatula.

If you want to make chocolate milk, stir milk and chocolate syrup into a pitcher.

If you want to set the table, get four plates, four glasses, and four spoons, knives, and forks.

If you want something to put your dinner on, get a plate.

If you want to store your silverware, get a tray.

If you want to make cookies, get a cookie sheet and mixing bowl.

If you want to spread peanut butter on your crackers, use a knife.

If you want a utensil for picking up meat, get a fork.

If you want a utensil for eating soup, get a spoon.

If your dishes are clean, put them on the cabinet shelf.

If you need something to make orange juice in, get a pitcher.

3. Object movement directives

Children move balls and beanbags positionally in relation to plastic utensils.

Line up three cups and roll the ball to knock them over.

Put a red beanbag under a red plate and a blue beanbag beside a blue cup.

Throw the green beanbag between a pair of green bowls.

Bounce the ball over the silverware tray.

Throw one ball over the skillet and another ball into a pan.

Throw all the beanbags except the orange one into the pitcher.

Kick the ball across the cookie sheet.

Hit the beanbag with the spatula.

Run across the room with a beanbag on a spoon.

Roll the ball in front of the dishes.

Throw the ball behind the knives.

Fill the empty pot with beanbags.

Bounce the ball around the dish cabinet.

Throw the ball in the middle of the cookie sheet.

Roll the ball to the right of the pots and pans.

4. Listen and find

Parent or teacher hides utensil, then gives child specific direction for finding the object. Child who correctly finds two hidden utensils is rewarded with a snack.

Find what we use to hold juice on the top shelf of the cabinet.

Find a pair of forks below the silverware tray.

Find what we use to make toast inside the bottom oven.

Find the spoons in the cups on the left side of the cabinet.

Find the utensil for spreading and cutting in the middle of the drawer.

Find what we use for stirring on the corner of the table.

Find what we use to hold soup on the lower cabinet shelf.

Find all the red utensils except the cups beside the stove.

Find all the round utensils inside the bottom cabinet.

Look in the left side of the drawer and find all the long utensils.

Find the tallest container on the shelf.

Find the shortest container on the shelf.

Find what we use for cutting inside the dishwasher.

Questions

1. Reasoning questions—Function (3-5 years)
   Use objects or pictures.

   a. Level 1 (3-4 years)

      What do you do with:
      plates?
      knives?
      spoons?
      forks?
      pots and pans?
      bowls?

   b. Level 2 (4-5 years)

      Why do we have:
      spatulas?
      cabinets?
      pitchers?
      silverware
      trays?
      skillets?
      detergent?
      cookie sheets?
      dish towels?
      dishwashers?
      napkins?

2. Reasoning questions—Situational/Adaptive (3-6 years)
  a. Level 1 (3-4½ years)
    What utensils do you use when:
      you eat soup?
      you cook bacon?
      you pour juice?
      you spread butter?
      you eat lunch?
      you get food out of a skillet?
      you bake cookies?
      you drink hot cocoa?
      you make pudding?

  b. Level 2 (4½-6 years)
    What utensils would you need if you were making a salad?
    What would you do if you wanted to cook and the skillet was dirty?
    What could you do if another person came to eat with you?
    What would you do when everyone finished eating?

3. Reasoning questions—How (3-6 years)
  Use materials, pictures, or experiences
  a. Level 1—Manner (3-4 years)
    How do: fork tines feel?
             spatulas look?
             clean dishes feel?
    How does a hot skillet smell?

  b. Level 2—Method/Ordered sequence (4-5 years)
    How do you: set a table?
                 sort silverware?
                 wash dishes?
                 make lemonade?

  c. Level 3—Degree/Quantity (4-6 years)
    How many utensils do you use to set a table place?
    Which is the tallest utensil?
    Which is the largest utensil?
    Which utensil holds the most?
    How many kinds of silverware are there?

  d. Level 4—Cause (4½-5 years)
    How do you get dishes clean?
    How do you eat meat?
    How do you cut meat?

4. Time-based questions (5-6 years)
  When do we:
    set the table?   clear off the table?
    use a skillet and a spatula?   use a pitcher?

Narratives

Using the Silverware

One day Phillip's mother said to him, "It is time for you to learn to use a fork and a knife."

Phillip liked that. He was tired of only using a spoon like a baby.

"I will show you how," said his mother.

She showed him how to stick the fork tines into pieces of food and pick them up. She showed him how to hold the meat with his fork and cut it with his knife.

Phillip had to practice, but soon he could use a fork and knife pretty well.

"I can learn anything I want, if I just try," he said.

> What did Phillip's mother want him to learn?
> How did Phillip feel about that?
> Why did Phillip practice?
> How did he feel after he learned to use them?

Breakfast Time

Breakfast is a busy time at our house. Mama and Daddy both work, and my brother and I go to school. So we *all* help to cook breakfast!

I cook the toast, and my brother makes the orange juice.

Daddy makes the coffee and sets the table.

Mama cooks the eggs and bacon.

Then we all eat together.

After we eat, Brother and I carry all the dishes to the sink and wipe off the table. Mama and Daddy take turns putting the dishes in the dishwasher, and Brother and I take turns taking out the trash.

We all have fun while we work together!

> When is it busy at our house?
> How does the family prepare breakfast?
> How do they clean up after they eat?
> Do you think the family does a good job?

A Big Dinner!

Mama was having company to eat dinner with the family. She was cooking a big, big meal!

Mama had to use *so many* utensils to cook that dinner! She cooked pots of vegetables. She baked a chicken in a pan in the oven. She cooked a skillet of rice and a cookie sheet full of rolls. Her oven and stove were full, and in the refrigerator, she had fruit salad and a lemon pie!

Mama cooked so much that there was no room on the table for all the food. People had to bring their plates to the counter and serve themselves.

Mama said you could call that a buffet. I call it having a good dinner!

Why was Mama cooking so much?
How did she cook the chicken and rolls?
Where did she keep the pie?
Why did Mama put the food on the counter?
What is a buffet?

Simple Tools and Machines

Along with the actual and toy tools and machines used in ENABLE I, the following are added: dishwasher, microwave oven, typewriter, computer, and lawn mower. Use ENABLE II flannel board pictures 60-64 of those items. ENABLE I flannel board scenes 21, 22, and 23 also can be used for activities in this unit. These ENABLE II flannel board pictures illustrate two of the narratives:

65. Quick Work
66. Granddad's Yard

Directives

Compound and complex directives of two to five steps (3½-6 years)

1. Tool and machine association

   These directions may be given at home at appropriate times; or at school as listening practice or in a game format, using real, toy, or pictured objects.

   Put the glasses and cups in the top part of the dishwasher, and the bowls, plates, and silverware in the bottom.

   Put all the light-colored clothes in the clothes washer, pour in detergent, close the top, and push (turn) the starter button.

   Take the clothes out of the dryer and sort them by size before folding them.

   Put the shirt on the ironing board, and pretend to iron it.

   Bring the dish to put in the microwave, cover it with a napkin, set the timer, and push the starter button.

   Turn on the radio and turn the station button until you find a station playing fast music.

   Plug in the record player, put a record on it, and then put the arm on the record.

   Turn the computer on, put the correct disk in the disk drive, and push the "enter" button.

   Put a page in the typewriter and roll it in; then type all the numerical keys.

   Lean the ladder against the house, climb up three steps, and then climb down.

   Hold the nail on top of the board carefully, and hammer it deep into the board.

Take the broom and sweep all the dirt into a pile before sweeping it into the dustpan.

Dig one deep hole and two shallow holes in the ground.

Rake the leaves into a pile, rake them into a bag, and tie up the bag.

Put on your boots before helping Daddy to push the lawn mower.

2. Conditional directives

Display pictures of the items indicated, and have students point to and name the one that completes the sentence. (These are indicated by the italicized words.)

When you want to cook something fast, put it in the *microwave*.

If you want to get dishes very clean, wash them in the *dishwasher*.

If you want the *clothes washer* to do a good job, sort the clothes first into light and dark piles.

If you want your clothes to look nice, take them out of the *dryer* as soon as it stops running.

If you don't want to burn yourself, never touch a hot *iron*.

If you want to avoid an accident, always unplug the *iron* before taking it off the *ironing board*.

If you want to listen to the news, turn on the *radio*.

If you want to listen to your favorite record, put it on the *record player*.

If you want to print your name, type it with a *typewriter*.

If you want to play a game, use the *computer*.

If you want to go up high, climb a *ladder*.

If you want to build something, use *hammer*, *nails*, and boards.

If you want a clean floor, sweep with a *broom*.

If you want to plant a bush, dig a hole with a *shovel*.

If you want to jump in a pile of leaves, use a *rake* to make the pile.

If you want a pretty lawn, mow it with a *lawn mower*.

3. Object movement directives

Children are required to move objects relevant to the tool or machine, or to move balls and beanbags positionally in relation to the object.

Take the clean dishes out of the dishwasher and put the dirty ones in.

Take the little clothes out of the washer and put them in the dryer, but hang up the bigger clothes to dry.

Open the door to the microwave, put the dish in the middle, and shut the door.

Wind the cord around the handle on the iron, and fold up the ironing board.

Put a purple beanbag on the right side of the radio, and a green beanbag in front of the radio.

Move the joystick to the computer back and forth.

Type all the letters in the middle of the typewriter and two letters on the left side.

Lay the ladder on the floor and throw two beanbags between the first and second rung.

Count out four nails, and hammer them in the four corners of the board.

Sweep the beanbags with the broom and push them into the can.

Shovel dirt into a pail until it is full.

Throw a ball over the rake after you lean it against the wall.

Push the lawn mower around the tree and into the shed.

4. Listen and do

Children respond to a sequenced direction in relation to a tool or machine.

Take all the things we drink from out of the dishwasher, but leave the other dishes in.

Put four big pieces of clothing and five little pieces of clothing in the clothes washer.

Take all the towels out of the dryer, fold them, and put them in a basket.

Put the dish in the microwave, put the timer on "3 minutes" and push the button to start.

Pull up the radio antenna, and turn the volume up loud.

Get three records, put them beside the record player, and take one record out of its container.

Plug in the electric typewriter, push the "on" button, and hit the space bar.

Count the parts of the computer, and find a computer game disk.

Step on the first and third ladder rung, but don't step on the second rung.

Hit two little nails and one big nail with the hammer.

Sweep the floor, empty the dustpan, and put the broom in the closet.

Dig a long row and a short row in the garden with the shovel.

Clean off the lawn mower, and pull it backward.

Questions

1. Reasoning questions—Function (3-5 years)
   Use objects or pictures

   a. Level 1 (3-4 years)
      What do you do with:
      clothes washers?
      record players?
      clothes dryers?
      ladders?
      brooms?
      radios?
      shovels?
      rakes?
      irons and ironing boards?
      hammers and nails?

   b. Level 2 (4-5 years)
      Why do we have:

dishwashers?	keyboards?
detergent?	lawn mowers?
microwaves?	monitors?
timer buttons?	space bars?
typewriters?	ladder rungs?
volume controls?	machine doors?
computers?	electric cords?

2. Reasoning questions—Situational/Adaptive (3-6 years)

   a. Level 1 (3-4½ years)

      What do we use to:
      get dishes clean?
      listen to music and news?
      wash dirty clothes?
      dry clothes fast?
      write letters?
      play games?
      get on top of the house?
      nail things together?
      get the floor clean?
      make the yard neat?
      get wrinkles out of clothes?

   b. Level 2 (4½-6 years)

      What tools and machines do you use in a kitchen?

      What tools and machines do you use at school?

      What tools and machines do you use in a utility room?

      What tools and machines do you use in a yard?

3. Reasoning questions—How (3-6 years)
   Use materials, pictures, or experiences.
   a. Level 1—Manner (3-4 years)

       How does:
           a dishwasher sound?
           an iron feel?
           a typewriter sound?
           a computer sound?
           cut grass from a mower smell?
       How do clothes out of the dryer feel?

   b. Level 2—Method/Ordered sequence (4-5 years)

       How do you:
           load a dishwasher?
           start a microwave?
           play a game on the computer?
           turn on a record player?

   c. Level 3—Degree/Quantity (4-6 years)

       How many dishes will the microwave hold?
       Which machine is the loudest?
       Which machine is the biggest?
       How many songs are on one record?
       How many dishes are in the dishwasher?
       How many clothes are in the washer (dryer)?

   d. Level 4—Cause (4½-6 years)

       How do you get wrinkles out of clothes?
       How do you print words on paper?

4. Time-based questions (5-6 years)

       When do we:
           use dishwashers?
           sweep the floor?
           use dryers?
           listen to the radio?
           use microwaves?

Narratives

Quick Work

When Mama picked up the children from school one day, she said, "We have to cook supper quickly and eat fast! Tonight is Open House at your school."

When they got home, Mama popped a casserole into the microwave oven and set the table. While supper was cooking, she took the clothes out of the dryer, folded them, and put a load of dirty clothes in the washer.

After the family ate, Mama loaded the dirty dishes into the dishwasher. The children got dressed to go to Open House. Soon the family was in the car driving back to school.

"Thank goodness for all those machines in my kitchen!" said Mama. "We can cook and clean up fast!"

    Why did Mama want to cook and eat supper fast?
    How did Mama cook the casserole?
    When did she wash and dry clothes?
    What was Mama glad to have?

Granddad's Yard

Justin was visiting his grandparents. On Saturday, his granddaddy said, "This is the day I work in my yard. Want to help me, Justin?"

"You bet!" said Justin, and he followed Granddaddy out into the backyard.

"First we have to mow the front and backyard," said Granddaddy. "You can ride with me on the riding lawn mower."

All morning, Justin and his granddaddy mowed the lawn. They waved at the neighbors. They waved at two squirrels. They watched Grandma put fresh water in the birdbath.

Then Granddaddy worked in his garden, while Grandma and Justin raked up some pine needles on the hill.

Granddaddy pulled up the weeds in his garden and dug up some potatoes with his shovel. Justin and Grandma put them in a basket and carried them in the house. And guess what? They had those potatoes for lunch—baked, with cheese and bacon on top! Um-m-m, good!

    When does Granddaddy work in the yard?
    How did he mow the yard?
    Why did Granddaddy use a shovel?
    When did they eat the potatoes?

Playing a Computer Game

One day at school, Joy and Jackie's teacher said, "I have something new to show you today. It is called a computer."

The children were so excited! Mrs. Brannon showed them all the parts of the computer. She showed them how to type their names on the keyboard and see the letters come up on the monitor screen.

Mrs. Brannon said, "I have three computer games for us to learn to play. Today we will play a game with Sticky Bear. He is learning to recognize shapes."

Mrs. Brannon showed the children how to put the disk in the drive and start the game. She let each child have a turn at the keyboard. They liked the Sticky Bear game very much.

"Can we play this all day today?" asked Joy.

Mrs. Brannon laughed. "No," she said, "but every day we will play computer games one time."

"Yea-a-ay!" said the children.

> What did Mrs. Brannon show the children first?
> How did they see their names?
> Which game did they play?
> Why do you think the children liked the computer?

Clothing

Extra-large actual clothing and doll clothing items are helpful for this unit. Use the large boy and girl figures and magnetic vinyl clothing items from ENABLE I, plus these magnetic vinyl clothing items: swimming suit, belt, pajamas, boots, jewelry (necklace and bracelet), purse, and umbrella. These ENABLE II flannel board pictures illustrate two of the narratives:

67. A Rainy Night
68. A Shopping Trip

Directives

Compound and complex directives of two to five steps (3½-5 years)

1. Clothing association

   These directives may be given at home or school at appropriate times, or in a "listen and do" group game, using either real clothing and children, dolls and doll clothing, or the puppet figures and magnetic vinyl clothing.

   Put all the clothing in a pile; and when you're finished, pull out the clothing we wear on the top part of our body.

   Find clothing we wear at night, and put it on a boy.

   Gather all the clothing that has buttons, and button two buttons on one thing.

   Pull out all the clothing we wear on our feet, and show me the pair of footwear with long tops.

   Find one thing we wear in hot weather and four things we wear in cold weather.

   Put on the socks and shoes, and fold the socks down.

   Dress (the little girl) for rainy weather, and don't forget what you (she) need(s) to hold over your (her) head.

   Pull out clothing that has zippers or snaps or laces.

   Sort out clothing with sleeves, and point to the sleeves that are long.

   Sort out clothing that covers all or part of children's legs.

   Count all the clothing a child would wear to play outside.

   Point to all the left shoes, and then point to all the right shoes.

   Put on what you wear on your feet in the winter.

   Get the gloves and find the middle finger of each glove.

Find something you can wear around your waist.

Find something girls wear or carry to "dress up."

Point to the legs of something children wear at night.

Open and close what girls carry to keep things in.

2. Conditional directives

   Put all the items of clothing in a pile in the middle of a circle of children. Give conditional directives, but do not name the clothing item needed to fill the condition. Children listen, then name the clothing item and find it in the pile.

   If you want to go outside and not be barefooted, put on your _____ . (shoes)

   When you want to pull on something to wear with your shoes, get your _____ . (socks)

   If you want something to cover your legs, get a pair of _____ . (pants)

   If you want something to cover the top part of your body, put on a _____ . (shirt)

   If you are a girl and you want to look nice, put on a _____ and _____ . (dress, jewelry)

   If it is very cold, always wear a _____ outside. (coat)

   If the weather is cool but not cold, get a _____ to wear. (sweater)

   If it is raining outside, put on a _____ and carry an _____ . (raincoat, umbrella)

   If it is cold or wet, wear _____ outside on your feet. (boots)

   When your hands get cold, put on a pair of _____ . (gloves)

   If you need something to wear on your head, wear a hat or a _____ . (cap)

   When the weather is hot and you want to swim, put on a _____ . (swimming suit)

   If you want to hold up your pants, put on a _____ and buckle it. (belt)

   If you're ready to go to bed, get into your _____ . (pajamas)

   If you're going to a party, you might want to wear some _____ . (jewelry)

   If you want jewelry for your neck, put on a _____ . (necklace)

   When you want jewelry for your arm, wear a _____ . (bracelet)

   If you need to carry money, carry it in a _____ . (purse)

3. Dressing race
   At one end of the room, make two piles of duplicate clothing items (or have duplicate items in one pile). Children form two lines at the other end of the room. Give a directive that involves putting on, taking off, fastening, or unfastening clothing. Two children race to choose clothing from the pile and comply with the request. (Older children may run back to tag the next player for a relay race.) The game should not focus on competition but rather the fun of trying to manipulate clothing speedily.

   Run to the clothing and put on a pair of socks and shoes.

   Jump to the clothing and pull on a pair of long pants.

   Zip and snap the pants, then unzip and unsnap them.

   Walk to the clothing, pull on a dress, and button the top button.

   Button and fold a shirt, and put your hands on the pocket.

   Hop to the clothing, find a sweater and a coat, and put on the coat.

   Skip to the clothing, put on a raincoat, and pull up the hood.

   Find a pair of gloves, and put on the left glove.

   Put on and take off a swimming suit.

   Thread a belt through pants loops and buckle it.

   Put on pajamas and do a somersault.

   Take off your shoes and put a boot on your right foot.

   Open and close an umbrella.

   Get all the jewelry except the bracelets and put them in a purse.

   Take the laces out of a pair of shoes.

4. Clothing parts
   Use the *ENABLE* figures and magnetic vinyl clothing items.

   Touch the top of the cap visor.

   Point to all the sleeves except the one on the dress.

   Touch all the pant loops that the belt goes through.

   Touch four different clothing fasteners.

   Find all the pockets on the left.

   Touch the sleeves that are long.

   Find the buttons and buttonholes on the raincoat.

   Find the thumb place in the mittens.

   Point to the buckle of the belt and the belt holes.

   Point to the top of the pajamas.

   Point to the heel and toe of the boots.

   Show me where the purse opens and closes.

   Touch the handle of the umbrella.

Questions

1. Reasoning questions—Function (3-5 years)
   a. Level 1 (3-4 years)

   What do you do with:
   - shoes?
   - gloves?
   - socks?
   - pants?

   What do you do with a:
   - dress?
   - cap?
   - coat?
   - shirt?
   - raincoat?
   - sweater?

   b. Level 2 (4-5 years)

   Why do we have:
   - swimming suits?
   - jewelry?
   - belts?
   - purses?
   - pajamas?
   - umbrellas?
   - boots?
   - pockets?
   - snaps?
   - buttons?
   - laces?
   - zippers?

2. Reasoning questions—Situational/Adaptive (3-6 years)
   a. Level 1 (3-4½ years)

   What do you wear (or carry) to:
   - protect your feet?
   - keep you dry?
   - keep you warm?
   - play in the water?
   - keep money in?
   - keep hands warm?
   - hold pants up?
   - keep your head dry?

   b. Level 2 (4½-6 years)

   What clothes do you need:
   - when it's cold?
   - so you won't be barefooted?
   - when it's wet?
   - when it's hot?
   - to wear to school?
   - when it's nighttime?
   - to go to a party?
   - when it's daytime?
   - when the weather is rainy?

3. Reasoning questions—How (3-6 years)
   Use real clothing and experiences.
   a. Level 1—Manner (3-4 years)
      How do:
         coats feel?
         shoes feel?
      How does:
         an open umbrella look?
         a closed umbrella look?
         a belt look?
         a raincoat feel?

   b. Level 2—Method/Ordered sequence (4-5 years)
      How do you:
         get ready to play in the snow?
         get ready to go outside when it's raining?
         get ready to go to bed?
         get ready to go shopping?

   c. Level 3—Degree/Quantity (4-6 years)
      How many shoes is a pair?
      How many fingers are on one glove?
      How many sleeves does a jacket have?
      How many buttons are on your shirt?
      How many pockets are on your pants?
      Which clothes are the longest?
      Which clothes are the shortest?

   d. Level 4—Cause (4½-5 years)
      How do you fasten and unfasten clothing?
      How does an umbrella keep you dry?

4. Time-based questions (5-6 years)
   When do we:
      wear boots?
      wear pajamas?
      wear jewelry?
      carry a purse?
      use a belt?
      open an umbrella?

Narratives

A Rainy Night

Aunt Allison took Jo-Jo and his baby sister Lana for a walk one night. She pushed Lana in the stroller, and Jo-Jo ran alongside.

It was very cloudy, so Aunt Allison put raincoats and boots on the children, and she stuck an umbrella in her purse.

They walked and walked. Soon after they turned around to walk back home—sure enough, it started to rain! Jo-Jo squealed, and Baby Lana laughed to feel and smell the rain.

Aunt Allison pulled out her umbrella and put it up. She put Jo-Jo's hood over his head.

"Now we can just walk in the rain but not get wet!" she said.

And they walked happily home!

> What did Aunt Allison do with the children?
> How did the baby go?
> Why did they wear raincoats?
> When did it rain?
> What happened when it started to rain?

A Shopping Trip

Mama looked out the window. "This is a pretty day for a shopping trip!" she said. "There are a few clouds, but it is sunny and warm."

Mama and LaKeena put on their prettiest dresses to go out. Mama wore blue high-heeled shoes and a blue dress. LaKeena wore a yellow and green dress with a sash, a green necklace and bracelet, and yellow socks. Both Mama and LaKeena carried purses. LaKeena had some money to buy a bow for her hair.

They went to a nice clothing store. Mama bought LaKeena and her sister some new jeans, shirts, sweaters, and underwear to start school.

LaKeena bought herself a yellow bow.

Then they had a pizza before they went home.

"I love my school clothes, and so will my sister, Natalie!" said LaKeena.

> How was the weather the day of the shopping trip?
> What did LaKeena wear shopping?
> Why did LaKeena carry her purse?
> When did they eat pizza?

The Lost Boots

Chip had been waiting a long time for the first snow.

One morning he woke up and there was snow all *over* the ground!

Chip jumped up and began to dress to go outside and play.

"Don't forget your gloves and boots!" said Mom.

But Chip couldn't find his boots anywhere! He looked all through his closet. He looked under his bed. He looked in the basement. He even looked in his brother's closet!

"You can't go outside without boots!" said Mom.

Chip sat down and started to cry.

"Don't cry, Chip!" said his big sister, Martha. "I'll help you look."

So they looked all over the house.

Suddenly Martha said, "Look what I found, Chip!" And there were his boots!

"Where *were* they?" said surprised Chip.

"At the bottom of the your toy box!" laughed Martha.

What do you think Chip did next?
Why did Chip look for his boots?
Where did he look?
Who helped Chip?
Where were the boots found?

School

This unit focuses on materials frequently used in an early childhood school setting. These include crayons, scissors, paper, paint and paintbrushes, easels, chalk, blackboards, books, glue (or paste), blocks, and puzzles. Use of the exact school materials will be especially helpful. The items are shown in these ENABLE II flannel board scenes:

69. Tabletop with crayons, paper, scissors, and glue
70. Blackboard with chalk; and an easel, paint, and paintbrushes
71. Blocks, open and closed books, and puzzles

These situational pictures illustrate two of the narratives:

72. A Picture of Mama
73. Cleaning the Classroom

Directives

Compound and complex directives of two to five steps (3½-5 years)

1. School materials association

   Set up the easel, paint, and paintbrushes. Place chalk on the blackboard ledge. Put other school materials in a pile. Begin the activity by naming "all the things we use at school." Then give individual directives to each child.

   Get the box of crayons and pull out the brown and black ones.

   Get the scissors and cut off a corner of the paper.

   Go to the easel, dip the paintbrush into the paint, and mark around the paper.

   Walk to the blackboard and draw a few long lines with the chalk.

   Open a book and turn to the second page.

   Lift the top of the glue, and put a small dot of glue in the middle of the page.

   Count out five blocks, and build a house.

   Draw circles on the paper with the orange and purple crayons.

   Cut up from the bottom of the page, and then cut to the right.

   Get the paintbrush, and paint both of the top corners of the paper.

   Draw a "happy face" on the blackboard with the chalk.

   Clip a clean sheet of paper onto the easel.

   Get three books, and look for a picture of a boy.

Cut out a circle, and glue it on the green paper.

Arrange the blocks to build a long road.

Take all the pieces out of the puzzle, and turn them over.

Put the puzzle back together.

Make two piles of blocks, and show me the pile that has *more* blocks.

Draw a line down the paper with the yellow crayon.

Cut on the long line with the scissors.

Look at the end of the book, and show me the last picture.

Go to the blackboard, and underline all the circles with your chalk.

2. Conditional directives
   Use the same materials as above.

   If you want to make a square, cut out four long strips of paper. When you've finished cutting, arrange the strips together to make the square.

   If you want to draw a happy face, use a blue crayon for the eyes and a red crayon for the mouth.

   If you want to paint an "X", mark sideways from right to left first, then sideways from left to right.

   If you want to draw your mother, pick up the chalk and begin with her head.

   If you want to glue a balloon picture, put glue in the middle of a circle. After you've finished gluing the balloon, trace with the glue the line for the string.

   Put the little block in front of the big block, but put the biggest block behind both blocks.

   After you've worked the puzzle, put it on the shelf.

   If you want to draw a rainbow, use all the crayons except brown and black. When you draw the rainbow, make curved, not straight, lines.

   If you want to paint a tree, use brown and green paint.

   If you build a train with the blocks, put the red block last.

3. Conceptual directives
   Use the same materials as above. Some prepared worksheets may be needed.

   Crayons

   Trace on the dotted lines with the green crayon, and color inside the line with the red crayon.

   Get all the crayons out of the box, except the black ones.

   Draw a circle around all the foods that are the same.

   Mark an "X" on the food that is different.

   Copy a square and a triangle.

Scissors and paper

Cut fast around the circle, but stay on the line.

Don't cut off the corners of the triangle.

Cut through the middle of the page of paper.

Cut below the picture, but cut the whole picture out.

Cut on the straight lines, then cut on the curved lines.

Easel, paint, and paintbrushes

Put on your paint smock before you paint.

Use the big paintbrush with the red paint, and the little paintbrush with the yellow paint.

Paint away from the sides and toward the center of the page.

Dip the brush into the jar, and wipe some of the paint on the jar top.

Put the ship template over the paper on the easel.

Paint back and forth to paint the whole ship.

After you finish painting, put the top on the paint jars and wash the brushes.

Hang your painting on the art line, and wash all the paint off your hands.

Blackboard and chalk

Draw a long line from the left side of the board to the right.

Make two more lines just like the first one.

Draw circles between the top and bottom lines.

Erase the line in the middle after you're finished.

Use the colored chalk to draw a picture of a sunny day.

Draw a picture of a rainy day beside the first weather picture.

Paper and glue

Open the glue, and squeeze a little bit into a jar top.

Don't squeeze the glue bottle too hard.

Dip the back of the paper into the glue, but don't get too much glue.

Stick the glue side of your picture to the paper.

Cut off little pieces of paper and glue them onto the circle to make a red ball.

Books

Open your book and point to the picture.

Point to the picture of the child who is walking. (*other actions*)

Listen to this story and answer my questions.

Find the child under the table. (*other positions*)

Turn to the middle of the book and point to the child not playing. (*other actions*)

Puzzles and blocks

Put the pieces of the puzzle together to make a rooster.

Start with the piece that looks like a tail.

Turn the piece around so it will fit there.

Wiggle the piece so you can fit it in.

Stack up the blocks to make a tower.

Make a bridge that looks like this one.

Line up the blocks to make a wall.

Build something and tell me about it.

Questions

1. Reasoning questions—Function (3-5 years)
   a. Level 1 (3-4 years)

   What do you do with:

crayons?	blocks?
books?	paintbrushes?
scissors?	chalk?
glue (or paste)?	puzzles?

   b. Level 2 (4-6 years)

   Why do we have:

   paper?
   paint?
   easels?
   blackboards?

2. Reasoning questions—Situational/Adaptive (3-6 years)
   a. Level 1 (3-4½ years)

   What do you use to:

   color a picture?
   listen to a story?
   cut paper?
   stick things together?
   paint a picture?
   build a tall building?
   write on the board?
   put a picture together?

   b. Level 2 (4½-6 years)

   What school materials would you need if you wanted to:

   draw a rainbow?
   trace and cut out a circle?
   use your paintbrush?
   use your chalk?
   build a house and train?
   hold paper to paint?
   look at many pictures?
   glue a flower picture?

3. Reasoning questions—How (3-6 years)
Use actual school items.

  a. Level 1 (Manner) 3-4 years

    How do:
      crayons feel?
      paintbrushes look?

    How does:
      paint feel?
      glue smell?
      glue feel?
      drawing with chalk sound?

  b. Level 2—Method/Ordered sequence (4-5 years)

    How do you:
      make a collage?
      get ready to paint?
      draw a happy face?
      use a book?
      cut out a square?
      clean blackboards?

  c. Level 3—Degree/Quantity (4-6 years)

    How many crayons are in a box?

    How many finger holes do scissors have?

    Which is the longest thing we mark with?

    How many pieces are in your puzzle?

    How many blocks does it take to stack a tall tower?

    How many legs are on an easel?

  d. Level 4—Cause (4½-5 years)

    How do you make green paint?

    How do you make a paper airplane?

4. Time-based questions (5-6 years)

    When do we:
      need crayons?
      fold our paper and put it in our bag?
      clean a blackboard?
      play with blocks?

Narratives

A Picture of Mama

Juanita wanted to draw a picture for her daddy.

"Why don't you draw him a picture of your mama?" said her teacher, Mrs. Luevano.

"OK!" she said, and took out her crayons and her paper.

She used her brown crayon and drew Mama's head, body, legs, and arms.

Then she drew black hair, black eyes, and a red mouth.

Last, she colored a purple and yellow dress and purple shoes.

"Daddy will love that pretty picture!" said Mrs. Luevano.

Juanita felt proud of her hard work. She folded the picture and put it into her bag to take home.

> Why did Juanita draw a picture?
> How many crayons did she use?
> How did she draw the picture?
> How did Juanita feel about her picture?

Cleaning the Classroom

It was the end of the school day, and all of Mrs. Quon's kindergarten students had gone home.

Mrs. Quon looked at her room. "Oh, no! *What* a mess!" she said.

She sighed and began to clean it up.

She put all the tops on the paint jars and washed the jars and paintbrushes. She put fresh paper on the easels. Then she erased and washed all the blackboards.

"This looks better!" she said.

Then she began to put all the books in the racks, the crayons in the boxes, and the glue and scissor cans on the shelves.

Last of all, she wiped off all the work tables and swept the floor.

Mrs. Quon looked around her room. She felt good now.

"On Monday, we'll all come back to a neat and tidy room!" she said.

And she gathered her things to go home for the weekend.

> What time of day was it?
> How did Mrs. Quon's room look?
> What did she do first to clean it?
> What did she do last?
> How will the room look Monday?

The First Day of School

Michael was three years old, and today he was starting nursery school!

"Hello, Michael!" said his new teacher, Mrs. Morgan. "Come in this school room and meet your new friends!"

All day long, Michael had a good time. He and his friends built things with the blocks. They worked puzzles. Mrs. Morgan read them a story, and she gave the children a good snack.

When Michael's grandmother came to pick him up, he started to cry.

"What's wrong, Michael?" said Mrs. Morgan. "I thought you liked school."

"I do," cried Michael. "I don't want to go home!"

Mrs. Morgan and Grandma laughed. "But you will be coming to school every morning!" they said.

Michael stopped crying and started to smile.

"Get me up early in the morning, Grandma!" he told her, taking her by the hand to leave.

> How old was Michael?
> Where did he go and what did he do?
> Why did Michael cry?
> How did he feel when he found out he would be coming back to school?

Health and Safety

Health and Safety, a typical late preschool, kindergarten, or first grade unit, attempts to build on children's accomplishment of basic self-help skills (independent toileting, cleaning, feeding, and dressing). The unit aims to help young children develop awareness of what it takes to keep their bodies and minds healthy and growing. Directives, questions, and narratives emphasize eating well, keeping clean, playing and exercising, resting, learning and working, and keeping safe. These goals are illustrated in the following ENABLE II flannel board scenes:

74. Eating well
75. Keeping clean
76. Playing and exercising
77. Resting
78. Learning and working
79. Keeping safe

These situational pictures illustrate two of the narratives:

80. The Exercise Class
81. Safety First!

Directives

Compound and complex directives of two to five steps (3½-5 years)

1. Health and safety categories
   Use the *ENABLE* flannel board pictures and others gathered from magazines.

   Show me the child eating and drinking well to grow strong.

   Point to children getting fresh air and playing outside.

   Show me three ways to move and get exercise.

   Point to two important ways to keep clean.

   Show me a child getting enough rest.

   Find children looking and listening at school.

   Touch children working with their hands at school.

   Point to children learning when to cross a street.

   Show me a child eating meat, vegetables, and fruit.

   Touch children jumping, hopping, and riding.

   Point to the child throwing a ball and the child who catches it.

   Show me children learning to do school work.

   Point to a child drinking something that will help him grow strong.

215

2. Conditional directives

Play an "if-then" game with conditions for staying healthy and growing strong. The game can be played by having the children complete the sentence verbally or point to the correct picture.

Eating well

If you don't want to choke on your food, *chew it slowly.*

If you want to grow strong, eat *a few bites* of everything on your plate.

If you want to eat food that is good for you, every day eat some *meat, vegetables, fruit, bread, and eggs.*

If you want to have strong bones and teeth, drink your *milk.*

Keeping clean

If we want to keep from getting sick, we try to stay *clean.*

If we want to keep our bodies clean, every day we *take a bath.*

Before and after we eat our food, we should *wash and dry our hands* and *brush our teeth.*

If we want to keep our nose clean, we should *use a tissue.*

After we use a tissue, we should *throw it in the trash.*

When we cough or sneeze, we should *cover our mouth and nose.*

If we want to keep our hair clean, we should *shampoo* it often.

Playing and exercising

If we want to get plenty of fresh air, we need to *play outside.*

If we want to get exercise every day, we can *run, jump, hop, skip, climb, ride tricycles.* (Any one or two of these answers will do.)

If we want to exercise our arms, we can *play ball.*

If we play ball with friends, we can learn to *throw and catch.*

If we want to exercise our legs, we can *run, jump, hop, skip, ride tricycles.*

Resting

If we want to stay healthy, at night we should *sleep well.*

If we want to get enough rest, we can also *take a nap every day.*

Learning and working

If we want to learn to do good work at school, we should *look and listen* to teachers.

If we pay attention at school, we can learn to *think.*

If we learn to cut, color, and glue, we learn to *do our own work.*

If we want to do our own work, we have to learn to *cut, color, and glue* (or) *do what teacher tells us to do.*

Safety

> If we don't want to get hit by cars, we should *stay out of the street.*
>
> Before we cross a street, we have to *look both ways* for cars.
>
> If we see broken glass, we should *stay away from it* (or) *have a grown-up pick it up.*
>
> If we see a hot stove (or iron), we should *not touch it.*
>
> If we are climbing, we should *hold on tight.*

3. Associative and sequenced action directives
   This game can be used to extend auditory and visual memory for following directives.

   a. Visual memory
      Show pictures of three to five of the following objects or actions, then ask children to name three things they saw.

      > Bed, quilt, pajamas, pillow, rest mat
      >
      > Running, jumping, hopping, climbing, riding tricycle
      >
      > Throwing, catching, bouncing, kicking, rolling (ball)
      >
      > Meat, vegetable, fruit, milk, bread (*Child may name by object, not category*)
      >
      > Drying hands, bathing, blowing nose, brushing teeth, shampooing hair
      >
      > Listening, looking, cutting, coloring, gluing
      >
      > Busy street, hot stove, broken glass, ladder

   b. Auditory memory
      Give three action directives, and ask the child to demonstrate the action or point to appropriate pictures.

      > Jump, run, and hop.
      >
      > Show me eating, drinking, and wiping face.
      >
      > Find bathing, covering mouth and nose, and brushing teeth.
      >
      > Show me resting, looking, and listening.
      >
      > Bounce, catch, and throw a ball.

Questions

1. Reasoning questions—Function (3-5 years)
   a. Level 1 (3-4 years)

   What do you do with:
   food?
   beds?
   books?
   towels?
   soap and water?

   b. Level 2 (4-5 years)

   Why do we have:
   meat, vegetables, and fruits?
   toothbrushes and toothpaste?
   jump ropes?
   tissues?
   school?
   stoplights?
   bandages?
   balls?
   milk?
   tricycles?

2. Reasoning questions—Situational/Adaptive (3-6 years)
   a. Level 1 (3-4½ years)

   What do you do (or use) to:
   get rest?
   keep clean?
   get exercise?
   learn?
   eat good food?
   keep from getting hurt?

   b. Level 2 (4½-6 years)

   What do you do if you're tired after lunch?
   What can you do to make your legs strong?
   What can you do to make your arms strong?
   What can you do to grow strong and healthy?
   What can you do to keep from "getting germs"?
   What can you do to learn to be a "good thinker"?
   What can you do to stay "squeaky clean"?
   What can you do to keep from being run over by a car?
   What can you do to keep from falling?

3. Reasoning questions—How (3-6 years)
   Pictures may be needed.
   a. Level 1—Manner (3-4 years)
   How do:
   vegetables taste?
   vegetables smell?
   we chew food?

   How does:
   a bed feel?
   milk taste?
   toothpaste taste?
   meat taste?
   soap smell?
   soap feel?
   fruit smell?
   `shampoo smell?
   a busy street sound?

   b. Level 2—Method/Ordered sequence (4-5 years)
   How do (can) we:
   get our bodies clean?
   learn to work?
   get exercise?
   stay safe?

   c. Level 3—Degree/Quantity (4-6 years)
   Explain while counting on fingers.
   How many times a day do we eat?
   How many ways can you clean yourself?
   How many times do you eat in a day?

   d. Level 4—Cause (4½-5 years)
   How can you burn yourself?
   How can you cut yourself?
   How can you keep from falling?

4. Time-based questions (5-6 years)
   When do you:
   rest?
   learn?
   play outside?
   eat breakfast?
   eat lunch?
   eat supper?
   stay out of the street?
   pay attention (or) look and listen?

Narratives

The Exercise Class

Mrs. Sumner was a teacher who *really* believed that exercise was good for children. She believed that little children should get exercise *every day*!

So every day that it didn't rain or snow, Mrs. Sumner took her class outside. There the children would swing and slide. They would run races, jump ropes, and play hopscotch. Several times a week, they would play ball.

When the weather was too cold or too rainy, Mrs. Sumner's class would exercise inside their classroom. They would jump on the trampoline, ride tricycles, and throw beanbags in baskets.

Mrs. Sumner's boys and girls had a good time getting their exercise.

> What did Mrs. Sumner believe?
> How did the children get exercise outside?
> Why would they exercise inside sometimes?
> How did the children feel about the exercise?
> Do you think it made them strong?

Safety First!

Jamal was a little boy who was *always* getting hurt.

He burned himself on a stove. He cut his hand on some broken glass. He fell off his bike and skinned his knee!

"*What* would I do without bandages?" said Jamal's mama.

"It is time for you to learn safety, Jamal!" she said.

So Jamal's mama started reading stories to him about safety. She took him for walks and showed him things that were dangerous—like broken glass and the busy street.

Mama took him around the house and showed him things not to touch—like the hot iron, an electric plug, and bottles of medicine and cleaning materials.

One day, Jamal ran up to Mama and gave her a hug.

"What was that for?" asked Mama.

"Look!" said Jamal. "I don't have on any bandages. I know how to be safe now!"

"Thank goodness!" said Mama.

How did Jamal hurt himself?
What did Mama teach Jamal?
Why did Jamal hug Mama?
How did Mama's safety lessons help?

Learning to Think

"You are growing up, Penn!" said his mama. "It is time for you to learn to think."

"How do you learn to think?" asked Penn. "Is it hard?"

"No," said his mama. "You just have to look and listen a lot. You will do that in school."

The next day Penn started kindergarten.

At kindergarten, Penn's teacher talked a lot. She told them stories and showed them how to do new things. She talked a lot!

"I want to talk!" Penn told his mama. "Teacher talks too much."

"First you have to learn to think!" said Mama. "Remember that, and look and listen for a while."

"But when do I know if I can think?" asked Penn.

"You'll know, because your teacher will start to ask you questions," answered Mama, and she smiled.

A week went by. Penn learned to cut out a circle. He learned to recognize some numbers and sets. He learned to write his name.

One day, the teacher asked Penn a question. And Penn answered it. When he got through, Teacher said "Good thinking, Penn!"

Penn sat up straight. He smiled. "I can think now!" he thought. "Teacher will let me talk more!"

And sure enough, that's what happened.

What did Mama say Penn should learn?
What happened at kindergarten?
How did Penn have to learn to think?
When did he know he could think?

Community People and Places

Orientation to their community is the first "widening of the world" to youngsters' environments beyond their immediate home and family. ENABLE I featured basic information about the more common community elements typically noted by younger children, in the categories of transportation, community helpers, and shopping. Building on that base, ENABLE II offers activities and narratives about six additional community places and eight community helpers. Flannel board pictures include:

82. Hospital scene, with nurse and doctor
83. Dentist's office and dentist
84. Gas station-auto shop and mechanic
85. Transportation center, with bus driver and taxi driver *
86. Movie theater
87. Television station, with newscasters and weatherperson

These situational pictures illustrate two of the narratives:

88. A Visit to the TV Station
89. Getting a Check-Up

*Residents of large cities may wish to substitute subway and subway driver.

Directives

Compound and complex directives of two to five steps (3½-5 years)

1. People and place association and function
   These directives can be given as part of role-playing games. In activities prior to these games, children can prepare costumes and materials typical of the helpers and scenes.

   Hospital—Nurse, doctor, and patient

   Nurse, help the patient lie on the table and take his temperature.

   Doctor, examine the patient's eyes, nose, ears, and throat.

   Nurse and Doctor, put a cast on the middle of the patient's left leg.

   Patient, ask the nurse to help you walk on crutches.

   Nurse, put the patient in a wheelchair and take her to her hospital room.

   Nurse, help the ambulance attendants to get the patient out of the ambulance.

Dentist's office—Dentist, assistant, and patient

Dental Assistant, help the patient lean back in the chair.

Assistant, put a drape around the patient's neck.

Dentist and Assistant, wash and dry your hands and cover your mouths.

Dentist, examine the top and bottom teeth in the patient's mouth.

Assistant, clean the patient's teeth and rinse his mouth.

Dentist, teach the patient the best way to brush his teeth.

Dentist, tell the patient she has no cavities and help her make another appointment in six months.

Gas station-Auto shop—Mechanic, clerk, and customer

Customer, drive into the gas station, put gas in your car, and pay the clerk.

Mechanic, check the car to see if it needs oil and water.

Mechanic, put air in the four car tires and clean the windshield.

Customer, pay the clerk for the mechanic's work and also buy a newspaper.

Transportation center—Ticket salesperson, bus driver, taxi driver, and passenger

Passenger, buy a ticket from the ticket salesman and get in line for the bus.

Bus driver, pull over to pick up the passenger, and open the bus doors.

Passenger, get on the bus, give the driver the ticket, and sit on a right middle seat.

Bus driver, drive slowly, stop for the red lights, and stop to pick up two more passengers.

Passenger, pick up the telephone and call for a taxi cab. Don't forget to give your address.

Taxi driver, drive to the passenger's house and honk.

Taxi driver, help the passenger carry her bags to the taxicab. Put them in the trunk.

Movie theater—Ticket salesperson, ticket collector, concession salesperson, and customer

Customer, buy a ticket and give it to the ticket collector.

Customer, buy popcorn and soda pop at the concession stand.

Customer, go sit in a back seat and watch the movie.

Concession salesperson, pop popcorn and put it in boxes.

Ticket salesperson, count the money and sort it into piles.

Ticket collector, say "Ticket, please" first, and then say "Thank you."

Television station—Newscaster and weatherperson

    Newscaster, get your papers and sit in your chair.

    Newscaster, say "Good evening," and tell some news.

    Weatherperson, show the weather pictures and tell whether it is rainy or sunny today.

    Weatherperson, tell what the weather will be like tomorrow.

2. Conditional directives

Use situational pictures of the various settings. Children point to the correct picture identified in a conditional directive, or complete the sentence verbally by naming the person or place.

    If you had a sore throat, a _____ might give you a shot. (*nurse*)

    If you had the flu, Mama might give you medicine prescribed by a _____ . (*doctor*)

    If you fell out of a tree, an ambulance would take you to a _____ . (*hospital*)

    If you were sick enough to stay in a hospital, you would be called a _____ . (*patient*).

    If you break a tooth, your mother should take you quickly to see a _____ . (*dentist*)

    If your teeth need cleaning, it is usually done by the _____ . (*dentist's assistant*)

    When your car has a flat tire, get it fixed at the _____ . (*auto shop*)

    If your car needs a new battery, an _____ can put it in for you. (*auto mechanic*)

    If your car is almost out of gas, go to a _____ . (*gas station*)

    If you don't have a car, you can go places on a _____ or in a _____ . (*bus, taxi*)

    If you ride in a vehicle driven by someone else, you are called a _____ . (*passenger*)

    If you want to ride on a bus or subway, you must buy a _____ from the _____ . (*ticket, ticket salesperson*)

    If there are many people riding with you, you are probably riding a _____ . (*bus*)

    If you go someplace in a _____ , you need to pay the driver money. (*taxi or bus*)

    If you want to see a story on a big screen, go to a _____ . (*movie theater*)

    If you want to see a movie, buy a ticket from the _____ and give it to the _____ . (*ticket salesperson, ticket collector*)

    When you want to know what kind of clothes to wear to school, watch the _____ on television. (*weatherperson*)

    If you are a newscaster, you work at a _____ . (*television station*)

    If Daddy and Mama wanted to know what happened today, they would watch the television _____ . (*newscaster*)

3. Descriptive phrase game
   Place situational pictures of community people and places on the floor, and give children body and object movement directives related to the pictures.

   Walk a circle around the picture of a place where you go when you are sick.

   Throw a beanbag on the picture of the person who takes care of your teeth.

   Put your elbows on a place and a person for car repairs.

   Jump in front of the place you go to see a story and eat popcorn.

   Pedal a tricycle back and forth from the place you go to get a ride.

   Hop across the place where a newscaster works.

   Run between the place to fix broken arms and the place to fix broken teeth.

   Lie down on a place that has the longest vehicles.

   Throw a beanbag behind a pump for getting gas.

   Stand on the person you might call to come to get you and drive you somewhere.

   Hop on top of the person who talks about rain and sunshine.

Questions

1. Reasoning questions—Function (3-5 years)
   a. Level 1 (3-4 years)
      What do you do with:
         gas tanks?
         taxis?
         buses?
         televisions?

   b. Level 2 (4-5 years)
      Why do we have:
         hospitals?
         gas stations?
         movie theaters?
         nurses?
         auto mechanics?
         newscasters?
         dentists?
         taxi drivers?
         weatherpersons?
         doctors?
         transportation centers?
         television stations?

2. Reasoning questions—Situational/Adaptive (3-6 years)
   a. Level 1 (3-4½ years)

   What do you do if:
   you have a high fever?
   your teeth need checking?
   your car is out of gas?
   you need a ride to town?
   you want to see a movie?
   you need to know the weather?

   b. Level 2 (4½-6 years)

   What do you do when:
   a doctor says you need a shot?
   it's time for the news?
   you buy a ticket to the movie?
   you need to ride a taxi?
   your dad's car won't start?
   you fall and knock a tooth out?

3. Reasoning questions—How (3-6 years)
   Pictures may be needed.
   a. Level 1—Manner (3-4 years)

   How do:
   nurses dress?
   movie theaters look?
   hospitals smell?
   gas stations look?
   newscasters sound?
   transportation centers sound?

   How does popcorn taste?

   b. Level 2—Method/Ordered sequence (4-5 years)

   How can we:
   help a doctor check us?
   get in to see a movie?
   get to ride a bus?
   pretend to be a newscaster?

   How do we behave in a dentist's chair?

   c. Level 3—Degree/Quantity (4-6 years)

   How many helpers wear white clothes?

   How many places do you buy tickets?

   d. Level 4—Cause (4½-5 years)

   How can you keep from getting cavities?

   How do doctors and nurses help us get well?

   How do we get tickets?

4. Time-based questions (5-6 years)

When do you:
see a doctor?
watch the news?
get a filling?
call a taxi?

Narratives

A Visit to the TV Station

Kimmee's daddy was a weatherperson. He worked at a television station. One day, he invited Kimmee's preschool class to visit the station.

The children were so excited! They rode the bus to the television station.

There were so many things to see! The man who worked the television camera showed them the big camera and let the children look through it.

The station director showed them the big operating panel with all its buttons and switches. She let them turn on and off the big lights that shine on the people who are being filmed.

Then came the most fun of all! Kimmee's daddy introduced the class on television during his weather show. And Kimmee got to point to a weather chart!

Wouldn't *you* like to visit a television station?

Where was Kimmee's class invited?
How did they get there?
How many things did they see?
What was the most fun thing the class did?

Getting a Check-Up

"It's time to get you a good check-up," said Mama. "I want to do it before school starts."

Louis knew that meant going to see a doctor.

"But I'm not sick, Mama!" said Louis.

"And we want to *keep* you well!" Mama replied.

So on Tuesday, Louis and Mama rode a taxi to see Dr. Aarons.

"Hello, Sport!" said Dr. Aarons, as he swung Louis up on his examining table. "Let's see how you're doing!"

Dr. Aarons looked in Louis's mouth and ears. Then he looked in Louis's nose and listened to his heart. He tapped Louis's knees and elbows with a little hammer.

"That tickles!" said Louis.

Next, Dr. Aarons's nurse weighed Louis and took his temperature.

"You have a very healthy boy!" Dr. Aarons told Mama. "Louis is growing up strong!"

"What good news, Louis!" said Mama. "Let's go to the movies to celebrate!"

> Why did Mama take Louis to the doctor?
> How did Dr. Aarons "check" Louis?
> How did the nurse help?
> Why did Mama want to take Louis to the movies?

The Sore Tooth

Poor Merinda! She had a very sore tooth!

Mama took her to see the dentist. Merinda was afraid. She was scared the dentist would hurt her.

When Merinda got up in the dentist's chair, Dr. Weyman smiled at her. "Don't worry, we'll make it *stop* hurting! I promise!" he said.

Dr. Weyman looked in Merinda's mouth. He looked carefully at every tooth. Then he said, "We can fix this quickly!"

Dr. Weyman told Merinda and her mama that one of her big teeth was ready to come in. It was pushing against her baby tooth and making it hurt.

Before Merinda could blink, Dr. Weyman had pulled out the baby tooth. It didn't even hurt! Then he rubbed some medicine on Merinda's gum.

"By tomorrow, that big tooth will be poking through, and your mouth won't hurt anymore!" Dr. Weyman said.

Then he gave Merinda a sticker that said "I lost my first baby tooth!"

When Merinda left Dr. Weyman's office, she hugged her mama. "I like coming to see the dentist!" she said.

> What was wrong with Merinda?
> Why was Merinda afraid?
> How did the dentist help her?
> Why do you think Merinda liked Dr. Weyman?

Foods

Actual foods, play foods, or food pictures can be used with this unit. While ENABLE I focused on food categories (fruits, vegetables, and meats), ENABLE II places emphasis on specific mealtimes—breakfast, lunch, and supper (or dinner, according to the word most commonly used in your area). Flannel board pictures show typical foods eaten at these meals:

90. Breakfast
91. Lunch
92. Supper (dinner)

These situational pictures illustrate two of the narratives:

93. A Lazy Breakfast
94. Making Soup

Directives

Compound and complex directives of two to five steps (3½-5 years)

1. Mealtime association
   These directives may be given at home, using actual foods, or at school, using toy or pictured foods.

   Show me a food that people eat during the first meal of the day.

   Show me a couple of foods used to make a sandwich.

   Find all the things we could drink at breakfast except coffee.

   Tell me two green foods we might eat at supper.

   Point to several foods Mama could use to make soup.

   Show me foods other than lettuce we could use to make a salad.

   Find some foods that might be served as dessert.

   Show me two foods we could eat with a spoon.

   Tell me some meats we eat during the last meal of the day.

   Starting with oatmeal, point to and name several breakfast foods made from grains.

   Point to a hot lunch food and a cold lunch food.

   Point to a food that tastes sweet and is served last at dinner.

   Find some foods served in the middle of the day.

   Point to all the foods we cut with knives.

2. Food attributes
   These directives may also be given at home or at school during mealtime.

   Find a food that can be scrambled or fried.

   Find a fruit that makes juice for us to drink at breakfast.

   Point to two things we might spread on our toast.

   Point to a pair of spices we might shake on our eggs.

   Touch two things we might pour on our cereal.

   Find a long, skinny meat we eat at breakfast.

   Point to something hot that Daddy drinks and something cold that you drink.

   Point to all the round fruits.

   Find fruits that are canned and fruits that are fresh.

   Show me a couple of yellow vegetables and one orange vegetable.

   Touch a meat we use to make spaghetti.

   Find a round red vegetable we usually eat in salads.

   Point to two foods we spread on most sandwiches.

   Point to a pie meringue and a pie crust.

   Point to a big dessert and a little dessert.

   Show me a food you can bake, fry, or boil.

3. Conditional directives
   These directives may be given for children to respond to by pointing or "cloze."

   If you were just waking up in the morning, you'd want to eat _____ . (*breakfast*)

   If you wanted a hot breakfast, you could ask for _____ . (*bacon and eggs, oatmeal, hot chocolate*)

   When you eat cereal, you need to cover it with _____ . (*milk*)

   When you make a sandwich, you start with two pieces of _____ . (*bread*)

   If you eat soup, be sure it's not too _____ . (*hot*)

   If you're eating chicken noodle, you're not eating a sandwich, you're eating _____ . (*soup*)

   If you want a good dessert, you need to make (or buy) _____ . (*cake, pie*)

   If you want to have steak, you have a good _____ . (*meat*)

   If you eat crackers or chips with lunch, they will taste _____ . (*salty*)

   If you bite into apples, carrots or celery, you will eat food that is_____ . (*crunchy*)

   If you want to eat a good dinner, always eat a _____ . (*meat, vegetable, fruit*)

   If you want something to put on rice or potatoes, you could use _____ . (*butter, gravy*)

Questions

1. Reasoning questions—Function (3-5 years)
   a. Level 1 (3-4 years)

      What do you do with:
      - salt?
      - gravy?
      - mayonnaise?
      - pickles?
      - jelly?
      - sugar?

   b. Level 2 (4-5 years)

      Why do we have:
      - orange juice?
      - eggs?
      - ice cream?
      - breakfast?
      - bread?
      - supper?

2. Reasoning questions—Situational/Adaptive (3-6 years)
   a. Level 1 (3-4½ years)

      What do you need to:
      - make a sandwich?
      - put on top of cake?
      - fix a bowl of cereal?
      - make salad?
      - make food salty?
      - peel fruit?

   b. Level 2 (4½-6 years)

      What foods do you need for:
      - breakfast?
      - making soup?
      - lunch?
      - a cold day?
      - supper?
      - cooking spaghetti?

3. Reasoning questions—How (3-6 years)
   Use real food and meal experiences.
   a. Level 1—Manner (3-4 years)

      How does:
      - gravy taste?
      - a tomato look?
      - ice cream feel?
      - macaroni feel?
      - meat smell?
      - spaghetti smell?
      - a banana look?
      - celery taste?

    b. Level 2—Method/Ordered sequence (4-5 years)

        How do you:
            make a sandwich?
            fix a fruit salad?
            ice a cake?
            make hot chocolate?

    c. Level 3—Degree/Quantity (4-6 years)

        How many things can you put on toast?
        How many vegetables do you see (can you name)?
        How many fruits have stems?
        How many breakfast foods do you see (can you name)?

    d. Level 4—Cause (4½-5 years)

        How do you make a vegetable salty?
        How do you make food sweet?

4. Time-based questions (5-6 years)

        When do we:
            usually eat eggs and toast?
            have the first meal of the day?
            eat supper?
            usually eat a sandwich?
            eat lunch?

Narratives

A Lazy Breakfast

One Saturday Lani and her family woke up late.

"I'm too sleepy to cook breakfast this morning," said Mama.

"That's OK," said Daddy. "I'm not very hungry!"

"I'll fix breakfast!" said Lani.

"You're too little!" said Daddy.

"Let her try!" laughed Mama.

So Lani went in the kitchen. She got bowls and spoons out of the cabinet and put them on the table. Then she put cereal and milk on the table.

"Oops, I forgot something!" she said, and she whispered something in Daddy's ear.

"I can do that!" laughed Daddy, and he came in the kitchen and helped Lani make orange juice.

She put the orange juice on the table and got out the glasses.

"Breakfast is ready!" called Lani.

Lani's mama and daddy were so proud of her for making the breakfast. "Now we can be lazy on Saturdays but not be hungry!" laughed Mama.

> What did Mama say when she got up?
> How did Lani fix breakfast?
> How did Daddy help her?
> When can the family be lazy now?

Making Soup

Leo was visiting his Aunt Maria. She was such a good cook! Every day Leo thought about what she would cook next!

One day, Aunt Maria said, "Leo, help me make the soup today!"

"All right!" said Leo. "What do I do?"

"You can wash the vegetables and hand them to me," she said.

Aunt Maria put some cubes of meat, salt, and a can of tomatoes into a big pan of water on the stove. She turned the stove on.

While that was cooking, Aunt Maria cut up each vegetable that Leo washed and gave her. She cut up potatoes, onions, celery, and carrots. Then she and Leo put the vegetables into the soup pot on the stove. They put the top on the pot.

"Now we wait!" said Aunt Maria.

The soup cooked for a long time. It cooked all afternoon.

At supper, the family ate the good soup.

"I helped cook this!" Leo told Uncle Horatio.

"Well, you did a fine job!" said Uncle Horatio, smacking his lips. "Um-m, this tastes *good*!"

> How did Leo help Aunt Maria?
> How did they make the soup?
> How many vegetables did Aunt Maria cut up?
> When did they eat the soup?

The Fastest Sandwich

One Sunday Daddy said, "Let's do something different for lunch!"

"What?" asked Mama, Bo, and Suzy.

"Let's have a sandwich making contest!" he said. "We'll put out lots of different foods to make sandwiches. The person who makes a sandwich the quickest wins a prize. And—the person who makes the *best* sandwich wins a prize!"

"What are the prizes?" asked Mama.

"The last two pieces of cake in the refrigerator!" laughed Daddy.

So Daddy put out bread, mayonnaise, mustard, cheese, meats, lettuce, tomatoes, and pickles.

"Get ready . . . go!" shouted Mama, and everybody started making sandwiches fast.

When all the sandwiches were made, Mama decided the winners.

Bo made the best-tasting sandwich, but Daddy made the fastest sandwich!

"I knew you'd win one of those pieces of cake!" laughed Suzy and Mama.

What did Daddy want to do?
How could you win the contest?
Why did Daddy want to win?
How did he win?

Playtime

While the Playtime unit in ENABLE I focused on a park, the circus, and the zoo, this ENABLE II unit features McDonald's (with emphasis on soda pop, hamburger, and French fries), a birthday party (with emphasis on cake, ice cream, balloons, and presents), children's "outside" toys (tricycle, wagon, and kites), and again the zoo (this time emphasizing monkeys, bears, and tigers). Visits to the actual places or experiences with the items should be utilized. If this is not possible, the teacher should collect and use pictures and storybooks about them. (Appropriate situational pictures may be found in *TOTAL Tales, On Vacation* and *TOTAL Tales, At the Zoo*.) Use these flannel board pictures to illustrate two of the narratives:

95. All the Animals
96. Outside Fun

Directives

Compound and complex directives of two to five steps (3½-5 years)

1. Playtime association
   Set up "pretend" centers representing McDonald's (chairs, toys, play or cutout food items, napkins, straws, trays, "counter"), a birthday party (real or toy cake with candles, ice-cream cutouts, a balloon, and gift on top of the table), "outside" (actual tricycle, wagon, and small kite), and zoo (toys or pictures of a gorilla, chimpanzee, polar bear, and tiger). Children respond to directives relevant to these items and places.

   Go up to the counter at McDonald's and order a soda.

   Get a napkin and a straw and put them on your tray.

   Salt all of your French fries and put some ketchup on a few.

   Put your napkin on your lap and your straw in your drink.

   Go to the birthday party and give your present to the birthday boy (girl).

   Blow up a balloon and tie a string around its neck.

   Get your plate of cake and ice cream and sit down.

   Count the candles on the birthday cake and sing "Happy Birthday."

   Go outside, get on your tricycle, and pedal it.

   Put a friend in the wagon and pull her (him) around the room.

   Take your kite outside, hold it up in the air, and run.

   Find the cages with the big monkey and the big cat.

   Find the zoo and go to the cage with the big white bear.

Go to the restaurant and put two things to eat on your tray.

Go to the party and play a game with the balloons.

Go to the zoo and look at the animals that roar.

Put the kite in the wagon, and then ride the tricycle across the yard.

Go to the zoo and look at the animals but don't touch the cages.

2. Conditional directives
   Use the play centers or pictures. When giving the directives, hesitate to allow the child a chance to guess what place or item fills the condition.

   If you want something to eat, go to the *restaurant*.

   When you want to have a good time, go to a *birthday party*.

   If it is your birthday, open the *present*.

   If you like to ride by yourself, get on the *tricycle*.

   If you want to see wild animals, go to the *zoo*.

   When you want to buy food already cooked, go to *McDonald's*.

   If you want to play a balloon game, go to the *birthday party*.

   If you like to play outside when it's windy, play with your *kite*.

   If you want to hear a tiger roar, go to the place with *wild animals*.

   When you want to eat and play on a playground, go to *McDonald's*.

   When you go to a birthday party, hug the *birthday person*.

   If you like to sit and be pulled around, find a *wagon*.

   When you want to see animals that come from all over the world, go to a *zoo*.

   If you like to pedal, get on a *tricycle*.

3. Object movement directives
   Children move balls and beanbags in relation to pictures of individual playtime items and places that are placed on the floor.

   Put a beanbag in the middle of a utensil for carrying hamburgers and french fries.

   Roll a ball under the wagon and between the wheels.

   Throw a beanbag and hit the things that float in the air.

   Put a beanbag on top of the picture of an animal that climbs trees.

   Kick a ball near the place where we can buy soda.

   Bounce a ball across the food with candles on it.

   Throw a beanbag near the vehicle with three wheels.

   Throw beanbags on all the animals except the polar bear.

   Roll a ball along the top of a counter.

   Bounce a ball beside the toy that the wind blows up high.

   Put a beanbag in front of the animals that can stand up on two feet.

   Put a pair of beanbags under a picture of the food made from potatoes.

   Put a beanbag on the corner of the package with a surprise inside.

Throw the ball over the toy that has handlebars.

Kick a ball in front of a zoo picture and throw it behind the zoo picture.

4. Attribute and detail directives
   Children find pictures of specific items relevant to playtime.

   Touch the place with booths and counters.

   Show me the toy with more wheels.

   Find the place with many animals.

   Touch the food you can scoop up and put in a cone.

   Point to a food that you find between two parts of a bun.

   Point to a time for blowing out candles.

   Find a toy that looks like a rectangle on wheels.

   Show me the toy that looks like a diamond on a string.

   Point to the animal that runs the fastest.

   Point to the animal that jumps the farthest.

   Find something for wiping ketchup off your mouth.

   Show me something made of paper, sticks, and string.

   Find the biggest monkey and the animal with white fur.

Questions

1. Reasoning questions—Function (3-5 years)
   Use pictures.
   a. Level 1 (3-4 years)
      What do you do with:
         hamburgers?
         candles?
         kites?
         soda?
         tricycles?

   b. Level 2 (4-5 years)
      Why do we have:
         trays?
         parties?
         napkins?
         wagons?
         straws?
         zoos?

2. Reasoning questions—Situational/Adaptive (3-6 years)
   a. Level 1 (3-4½ years)
      What do you do if you want to suck your drink?

      What do you do with your present at the birthday party?

      What do you do when you want a turn on the tricycle?

What do you do when the waiter gives you your drink at McDonald's?

What do you do when you spill ice cream on your dress?

What do you do with kites on a windy day?

    b. Level 2 (4½-6 years)

What would you do if your balloon popped?

What would you do if your kite got tangled in a tree?

What would you do if you dropped your tray of food?

What would you do if the tiger roared?

3. Reasoning questions—How (3-6 years)
Use materials, pictures, and experiences.

    a. Level 1—Manner (3-4 years)

How do:
hamburgers smell?
French fries taste?
straws feel?

How does:
a gorilla look?
a kite fly?
ice cream taste?
icing feel?
a tricycle wheel feel?

    b. Level 2—Method/Ordered sequence (4-5 years)

How do you:
wrap a present to take to the birthday party?
fly a kite?
ride a tricycle?

    c. Level 3—Degree/Quantity (4-6 years)

How many French fries are in a bag?

How many wheels does a tricycle have?

How many candles would your birthday cake have?

How many of the zoo animals have tails?

Which is the longest food?

Which is the coldest food?

How many sides does a wagon have?

    d. Level 4—Cause (4½-5 years)

How does a kite fly?

How do you put candles out?

How do you use a straw?

4. Time-based questions (5-6 years)

When do you:
have your birthday party?
fly a kite?
go to McDonald's?
play outside?

Narratives

All the Animals

Uncle Van was having a good time this Saturday. He was showing his little nieces, Lee Song and Lark, around the big zoo.

They watched the tiger eat its lunch.

"Oh-h-h! I don't like those big ol' teeth!" said Lark.

"They help the tiger eat its food," smiled Uncle Van.

They looked at the big polar bear swimming in the cold water.

"He has so-o much fur!" said Lee Song.

"That's to keep him warm when it's very cold!" Uncle Van told her.

The little girls liked the chimpanzees the best. They thought they were *so* funny, when they ate bananas and made funny faces!

"Why do they have such long arms?" asked Lark.

"So they can climb and swing in the trees!" said Uncle Van.

The little girls hugged their uncle tightly.

"What's that for?" he asked, surprised.

"You know *everything*!" they said, happily.

> When did Uncle Van take the girls to the zoo?
> How (did he tell them) do tigers use their big teeth?
> Why (did he say) do polar bears have thick fur?
> What did the girls like about their uncle?

Outside Fun

"Let's play outside, LeRoy!" said his big brother, Jovan.

"Stay inside the fence!" said Mama, as the two little boys ran out the back door.

LeRoy got on his tricycle. "Bud'nnn, bud'nnnn!" he said, making motorcycle sounds. "I'm a policeman chasing a car going too fast!"

Jovan was running around the backyard, holding his kite up. Finally the wind blew the kite up in the air.

"I wish I could fly like that kite!" Jovan said to himself.

Boom! The kite suddenly fell down and hit the ground.

"Pull me, pull me!" shouted LeRoy, running up with the little wagon.

"OK, if you'll play like you're hurt, and I'm taking you to the hospital!"

LeRoy promptly flopped into the wagon and closed his eyes.

"Ah-h-h-h!" sang Jovan, as he pulled LeRoy in the "pretend ambulance."

"What's wrong?" called Mama, running out of the house.

"We're 'tending he's hurt, Mama! Will you play you're a doctor and fix him up?" asked Jovan.

Mama grinned and said, "Wait a minute!" Then she ran in the house.

When she came out, she washed LeRoy's face with a damp cloth and put two bandages on his forehead.

"Good doctorin', Mom!" said Jovan. The two boys ran off to play again.

"Good opportunity to wash a little face!" laughed Mama to herself.

> Where were the boys going to play?
> What are three things they played with?
> How did they use the wagon?
> Why was Mama glad to be a "pretend doctor"?

The First Trip to McDonald's

Mama, Daddy, and Alvis were taking Baby Blaine to McDonald's for the *first* time.

Blaine couldn't talk yet—but she could feed herself with her fingers! So Mama got her some French fries. Boy, did Blaine love those fries! She ate and ate. But she spilled half of them on the floor!

Suddenly, Blaine started to scream!

"Why is she crying?" asked Alvis.

Before Mama could answer, Blaine reached over and grabbed a fistful of Alvis's fries. She stopped screaming and stuffed them in her mouth!

"She was trying to tell us to get her more French fries!" laughed Mama.

> Where did the family take the baby?
> What happened to half of Blaine's fries?
> Why did she scream?
> What made her happy again?

Nature

While the nature unit in ENABLE I focused on the "backdrop" of nature (sky, earth, and water), this ENABLE II nature unit focuses more on nature's creatures. These are featured in the ENABLE II puppet figures of a bird, butterfly, bee, spider, frog, snake, and squirrel.

Because there is a variety of types of each one of these creatures, gathering a number of different pictures and storybooks is recommended. Creating a "creature center" of actual nature items and pictures of items associated with these creatures (such as nuts, nests, cocoons, hives, webs, tadpoles, and snakeskins) is helpful and fun!

These flannel board pictures illustrate two of the narratives:
97. Catherine the Squirrel
98. A Walk in the Woods

Directives

Compound and complex directives of two to five steps (3½-5 years)

1. Nature's creatures association
   Children are seated in a circle. Pictures of the creatures, their natural environments, and items associated with them are placed in the middle of the circle. Children find the picture described in the directive given to them.

   Make the creature with feathers, a beak, and wings fly.

   Match the caterpillar and the cocoon to the creature each will grow into.

   Show the class the bug that buzzes and makes honey.

   Find the bug that crawls, and put it on its web.

   Show me the creature that lives on both land and water.

   Point to the long creature that has no legs and crawls on its stomach.

   Put the funny little animal with sharp claws beside something it likes to eat.

   Pick up the creature that hops on two legs, and put it on its nest.

   Put the butterfly on the pretty plant where it gets food.

   Put together all the creatures that fly, and touch one that climbs.

   Touch the creature without legs and the creature with the most legs.

First find the creature that can sting you, and then find the creature that hops very fast.

Gather all the creatures except the one with fur.

Put the creatures that make no sounds in one pile, and the ones that do make sounds in another pile.

Find the biggest and the smallest creatures that fly.

Get the creature that can swim and the one that can spin a web.

Point to where a bee gathers the pollen for its honey and to where it makes the honey.

Put the nuts and the seeds with the creatures that eat them.

2. Conditional directives
   Children are seated in a circle, with the pictures placed in the middle.

   If a bird is ready to lay eggs, show me what it builds first.

   Find the place a butterfly lands if it wants food.

   Touch the place a bee goes when it wants to go "home."

   Show me what a spider builds to help catch its food.

   Show me some things a squirrel might eat if it were hungry.

   Show me some creatures you might see if you were looking up in a tree.

   Show me what a bird spreads out when it wants to fly.

   Point to what a tadpole loses when it turns into a frog.

   If you heard the sound, "rib-it!" show me what creature you might see.

   Show me three creatures you should not play with if you do not want to get stung or bitten.

   Show me what a squirrel uses when it wants to eat nuts.

   Show me the creature that hunts worms when it wants to feed its babies.

3. Object movement directions
   Line up pictures of nature's creatures. Children move balls and beanbags in relation to the pictures as directed.

   Put the green beanbag on the back of the bird and the yellow beanbag in front of the bird's feet.

   Kick the ball across the butterfly and roll it near the bee.

   Bounce the ball around the spider.

   Kick the ball between the frog and the snake.

   Put the beanbag on the animal that chatters.

   Hide a beanbag under the creature that sits on a log or a lily-pad.

   Roll a ball on the back of the long creature.

   Drop beanbags on the creatures that do not fly.

   Bounce a ball on each creature that can walk on legs.

4. Parts and details

Children show the described parts and details.

Touch the antennas and wings of two creatures.

Find the creature with two legs and two animals with four legs.

Point to the creature that sometimes has poison in its bite.

Find the flying creatures that have six legs.

Find the tiny creature that has the most legs.

Show the animal with sharp claws and teeth.

Show the creature with big eyes and a long tongue.

Point to the creature with thin, colorful wings.

Point to the creature that sleeps coiled up like a circle.

Find the creatures without wings and the one that has scaly skin.

Questions

1. Reasoning questions—Function (3-5 years)
   Use pictures.

   a. Level 1 (3-4 years)

   What do:

   birds do with nests?
   squirrels do with nuts?
   bees do with hives?
   frogs do with bugs?

   b. Level 2 (4-5 years)

   Why do:

   birds build nests?
   squirrels have sharp teeth?
   butterflies like flowers?
   frogs have long tongues?
   snakes crawl fast?

2. Reasoning questions—Situational/Adaptive (3-6 years)

   a. Level 1 (3-4½ years)

   What do you do if you see a snake?

   What do you do if you hear a bee?

   What can you do to feed a squirrel?

   b. Level 2 (4½-6 years)

   What should you do if a bee stings you?

   What should you do if you find a hurt bird?

   What should you do if you find a bee hive?

3. Reasoning questions—How (3-4 years)
   Use materials, pictures, and experiences.
   a. Level 1—Manner (3-4 years)
      How do:
      birds sing?
      butterflies look?
      frogs sound?
      snakes look?

   b. Level 2—Method/Ordered sequence (4-5 years)
      How do:
      birds build nests?
      squirrels save their food?

   c. Level 3—Degree/Quantity (4-6 years)
      How many legs do bees have?
      How many legs do spiders have?
      How many antenna do butterflies have?
      How many wings do birds have?

   d. Level 4—Cause (4½-5 years)
      How do bees get honey?
      How do spiders make webs?

4. Time-based questions (5-6 years)
   When do:
   birds build nests?
   squirrels dig up nuts they've saved?

Narratives

The Disappearing Tadpoles

One spring, Brad and his big brother Larry were playing near a little stream close to their house.

"Look at these little swimming things!" Brad shouted to Larry. "What *are* they?"

"Those are little tadpoles. They just hatched from eggs that frogs laid. Someday they'll grow into frogs." Larry said.

"These little things look like little black fishes, not frogs!" said Brad. "Frogs have legs and fat stomachs!"

"Just watch them for a few weeks!" Larry said.

So every week Brad went down to the stream. After a couple of weeks, the tadpoles had gotten much fatter and their tails had gotten shorter.

Then the next week, Brad found that the tadpoles had started to grow legs! He was so surprised!

A week later, Larry and Brad went down to the stream again.

"Where are my tadpoles?" asked Brad.

Larry pointed to some little frogs hopping at the edge of the stream.

"*That's* the tadpoles! They've all turned into frogs!" Larry said.

Brad was amazed. "I'm sorry I didn't believe you, Larry!"

> Where did Brad and Larry find the tadpoles?
> Why didn't Brad believe Larry about the tadpoles?
> What happened to the tadpoles?
> When did Brad say he was sorry?

Catherine the Squirrel

Catherine was a friendly little squirrel. She lived in the Witt's backyard. She loved the Witt family, and they loved her.

When Catherine was hungry, she climbed up on the Witt's kitchen window and scratched on the screen. Someone in the family would see her and go outside and bring Catherine some food.

Catherine liked to eat lots of things. She liked to eat peanuts, graham crackers, grapes, and apple slices with peanut butter. But most of all, Catherine liked to eat pecans!

Eating pecans made Catherine so happy! She would stand on her two hind feet, swish her furry tail, and go CRUNCH, CRUNCH, CRUNCH! with her teeth.

The Witt family laughed to see Catherine eat those pecans!

Catherine loved the Witt family because they fed her so many pecans. When she had baby squirrels, she brought them to their backyard. She knew the Witts would love and feed her babies, just like they loved and fed her.

Now the Witts feed *three* little squirrels—Catherine, Catlin, and John.

That takes a *lot* of pecans!

> When did Catherine scratch on the Witt's screen?
> How many things did Catherine like to eat?
> How did Catherine look when she ate pecans?
> Why did Catherine bring her babies to the Witt backyard?

A Walk in the Woods

Granddaddy and Maury were taking a walk in the woods. It was a pretty Fall day.

Granddaddy showed Maury a fat snake coiled up on a rock in the sunshine.

"Soon it will be so cold that he will sleep all Winter in a hole in the ground!" whispered Granddaddy, and they tiptoed by Mr. Snake without waking him.

A beautiful yellow butterfly flew past Maury's nose and settled on a large yellow flower.

"What's *it* doing?" Maury whispered to Granddaddy.

"It's sucking the last nectar out of the flowers. Soon the flowers will die from the Winter cold," Granddaddy said.

"Buz-z-z . . . bz-zz." The buzzing sound got louder, and Granddaddy pointed to a beehive hanging in a tree.

"I'll bet that's full of honey that the little bees have worked all Summer to make. Now they won't be hungry this Winter!"

"Granddaddy, do we need to buy a lot of food so *we* won't be hungry this Winter?" asked Maury, worried.

Granddaddy laughed. "No, people have grocery stores where they can buy food *all* year."

"Poor little bees and butterflies! I wish *they* had grocery stores in the Winter," said Maury.

> What three animals did Granddaddy and Maury see?
> Why was the butterfly on the flower?
> How did Granddaddy say the bees got ready for Winter?
> What worried Maury about Winter?

Seasons

This unit features the particular attributes of the four seasons of the year. Teachers and parents are encouraged to collect diverse pictures representing each season. A flannel board poster is provided for each season:

    99. Fall
   100. Winter
   101. Spring
   102. Summer

Situational pictures are provided for two of the narratives:

   103. The Spring Garden
   104. The First Snow

Directives

Compound and complex directives of two to five steps (3½-5 years)

1. Seasonal association

   Glue the four large posters on colored construction paper in seasonal colors (Fall, orange; Winter, white; Spring, green; Summer, yellow). Make sure each child understands which poster board stands for which season. (You may wish to print the season name in large letters on the board.) Children line up at one end of the play area. Put the posters on the floor at the opposite end of the play area, and place a large pile of seasonal pictures or objects between the posters and the line of children. Directives involve finding the described object or picture and placing it on the correct poster.

   Find a crisp red leaf and place it on the orange board.

   Get a blossoming yellow flower and put it in the middle of the green board.

   Look for a man made of snow and put it at the top of the white board.

   Find a vegetable garden and put it at the bottom of the yellow board.

   Look for a squirrel burying nuts and put it in the center of the Fall board.

   Get the child dressed in coat and boots and put it on the left side of the Winter board.

   Find the child flying a kite and put it in the right bottom corner of the Spring board.

   Look for a man mowing the yard, and put it beside the garden on the Summer board.

Find children waiting for a school bus and put them under the squirrel on the Fall board.

Get a frosty window and put it at the bottom of the Winter board.

Find a nest of baby birds and put it on the top left corner of the Spring board.

Look for a family at the beach and put it over the garden on the Summer board.

Get the football and sweater and put them beside the squirrel on the Fall board.

Find the gloves and muffler and put them on the right side of the white board.

Look for the package of flower seeds and put it next to the flower on the yellow board.

Find the shovel and pail and put it near the bottom of the Summer board.

2. Conditional directives

Use the seasonal posters again. Children perform body movements according to conditional directives.

If you want to slide down a snowy hill, stand on the Winter board.

If you want to jump into a pile of leaves, jump on the Fall board.

When you want to plant a flower garden, crawl over to the Spring board.

If you want to watch butterflies, sit on the Summer board.

If you like cool, but not cold, weather, carry a sweater to the orange board.

When it rains a lot, carry your umbrella to the green board.

If you like to wear shorts and go barefooted, jump on the yellow board.

If you like to sit in front of a warm fire, sit on the white board.

When you want to pick pumpkins, stand on the Fall board.

If you like to ice skate, tiptoe onto the Winter board.

When you want to pick strawberries, carry a bucket to the Spring board.

If you like tomatoes and corn, go to the Summer board.

3. Object movement directives

Collect a football or soccer ball, a "snowflake" (prepared by cutting out two snowflake shapes, gluing the edges, and stuffing them with cotton or paper), a "seed bag" (green beanbag), and a tennis ball or softball. Children move these as directed in relation to seasonal pictures.

Kick the football (or soccer ball) into a pile of leaves.

Put the snowflake near a picture of a snowy day.

Throw the seed bag near the empty garden.

Roll the tennis ball (or softball) over the hot, sunny day.

Bounce the soccer ball on the apple tree.

Drop the snowflake on a picture of a sled.

Throw the seed bag on top of the tree with new leaves.

Bat the softball under the picnic table.

Kick the football near the school bus door.

Place the snowflakes near the picture of icicles.

Drop the seed bag on a picture of a windy day.

Throw the softball over the swimming pool.

4. Sensory seasonal attributes

Display the *ENABLE* seasonal posters. Children listen to the description of a sensory attribute, touch the appropriate seasonal picture, and name the season in which the attribute may be enjoyed.

Feel the crisp, crunchy leaves and see their bright red and yellow colors.

Smell the hot chocolate and hear the scraping sound of the snow shovel.

Hear the song of the birds and the buzz of the bees and see the yellow and red flowers.

Feel the warmth of the sun and touch the smooth, green grass.

Smell the spicy apple pie and feel the cool, brisk breeze.

Feel the freezing cold on your nose and the crunching snow under your boots.

Feel the softness of the baby bunny's fur and smell the fresh-cut flowers.

Smell the hamburger on the grill and hear the sounds of children playing in the yard.

Feel the smoothness of the ripe pumpkin and the roughness of cornhusks.

Taste the cold sweetness of snow ice cream and feel the tingling cold on your tongue.

Smell and feel the wet, black dirt of the garden.

Touch the gritty sand and the shiny seashell.

Questions

1. Reasoning questions—Function (3-5 years)
   Use pictures.
   a. Level 1 (3-4 years)
      What do you do with:
        umbrellas?
        flowers?
        mittens?
        rakes?

   b. Level 2 (4-5 years)
      Why do we have:

apple trees?	snow shovels?
kites?	sandpiles?
seeds?	sleds?
fireplaces?	barbecue grills?
sweaters?	pumpkin vines?

2. Reasoning questions—Situational/Adaptive (3-6 years)
   a. Level 1 (3-4½ years)
      What do you do with fallen leaves in the Fall?

      What do you do to get ready to play in the snow?

      What do you do to grow flowers in the Spring?

      What do you do with summer vegetables?

   b. Level 2 (4½-6 years)
      What would you do to play outside on a cool Fall day?

      What would you do to get warm after playing in the snow?

      What would you do if it rains in the Spring?

      What would you do to help you float in a swimming pool?

3. Reasoning questions—How (3-6 years)
   Use materials, pictures, and experiences.
   a. Level 1—Manner (3-4 years)
      How do:
        Fall leaves feel?
        new green leaves feel?
        ocean waves feel?
        ocean waves sound?

      How does:
        a pumpkin look?
        Spring wind sound?
        Spring wind feel?
        snow feel?
        hot chocolate taste?
        Summer sun feel?

    b. Level 2—Method/Ordered sequence (4-5 years)

        How do you:
            dress for a Fall day?
            build a snowman?
            plant a garden?
            cook hot dogs on a grill?

    c. Level 3—Degree/Quantity (4-6 years)

        How many warm clothes do you wear in the Winter?

        How many foods do squirrels eat?

        Which is the coldest season?

        Which is the hottest season?

        Which is the greenest season?

        How many colors are there of Fall leaves?

    d. Level 4—Cause (4½-5 years)

        How do you care for a garden?

        How does a squirrel save food?

        How do you keep warm in the Winter?

        How do you keep cool in the Summer?

4. Time-based questions (5-6 years)

        When do:
            leaves change colors and fall?
            you see lots of ice and snow?
            leaves and plants start to grow?
            you go swimming?
            squirrels save nuts?
            you see football games?
            children play outside?
        When does the weather stay hot for a long time?

Narratives

The Spring Garden

"Let's plant a garden, Beth!" said Grandma. "What would you like to grow?"

"Pansies and petunias!" Beth answered happily.

"Oh, that will be pretty!" said Grandma.

So Grandma and Beth drove to the nursery and bought some tiny pansy and petunia plants. Then they drove home and went out to the empty flower garden.

Grandma hoed and loosened up the dirt while Beth shook fertilizer out of a pail and over the dirt.

Next, Grandma dug small holes, which Beth filled with the little flower plants.

Last, Grandma and Beth sprinkled water around each plant.

When they finished, they looked at their pretty pink and purple garden and hugged each other with pride.

"There is nothing prettier than your own garden!" said Grandma. And Beth smiled and nodded.

> Why did Grandma and Beth go to the nursery?
> How did they plant the garden?
> What did they do last?
> How did they feel when they were through?

The First Snow

"Oh, my goodness!" said Rand's mama as she opened the curtains of his room.

"What's the matter, Mama?" asked Rand, sitting up in the bed.

"Look at *all* that snow! It is all the way up to our window ledges!"

Rand jumped up and looked out the window. All he could see was snow and *more* snow!

Rand's daddy stopped at his door. "I'm going to try to dig a path to the street," he said. "The snow plows should be along soon."

Rand quickly got dressed and went to the kitchen. He and Mama sat at the table, drinking hot chocolate and watching Daddy and other men in the neighborhood as they cleared a path from their houses to the street.

"Whir-r-r-r . . . whish-whish!" Along came the snow plow. Soon the street in front of their house was clear, and piles of snow lay along the sides of the street.

"*Now* we can play outside!" Rand said happily, and he ran to put on his snowsuit and boots.

"I'd better keep the chocolate warm," Mama said to herself. "Everybody will be coming back in soon, and they'll be cold."

> What did Mama see out the window?
> How did the neighborhood "dig out" of the snow?
> How did the snow plow sound?
> Why did Mama want to keep the chocolate warm?

The Seasons of Color

"Fall is my favorite time of year!" said Mama.

"Why?" asked Sarah.

"Because of all the beautiful color everywhere in the Fall!" said Mama.

"Summer has a lot of color, too!" said Sarah. "The grass and trees are green, the sky is blue, and you see so much color in the growing flowers and vegetables."

"That's true!" said Mama. "But I love the red, gold, and orange of the Fall leaves, the orange pumpkins, the bright blue Fall sky, and the crisp red apples and green pears."

"Summer and Fall *both* are beautiful times of color. I'm glad we have *different* seasons," said Sarah.

"I *agree!*" said Mama.

> Why did Mama love Fall?
> Why did Sarah love Summer?
> How many colors of Fall did they name?
> What did Mama and Sarah say they were glad about?

Holidays

Like the Seasons unit, Holidays calls attention to the dimension of time. Holidays are exciting time periods that highlight the environment of young children. This unit emphasizes the basic points and pleasing attributes of the more popular holidays—Halloween, Thanksgiving, Christmas, Valentine's Day, Easter, and the Fourth of July. (The religious aspects of these holidays are not emphasized.)

It will be helpful to provide a variety of holiday pictures and storybooks. It also is helpful and fun to use relevant holiday items—a pumpkin, masks, trick-or-treat bags, cornucopia, Indian and Pilgrim hats, turkey feathers, gifts, Christmas ornaments, stockings, star, valentine card, envelope, eggs, basket, toy bunny, flag, drum.

A flannel board poster is provided for each holiday:
    105. Halloween
    106. Thanksgiving
    107. Christmas
    108. Valentine's Day
    109. Easter
    110. Fourth of July

Situational pictures are provided for two of the narratives:
    111. Dyeing Easter Eggs
    112. The Special Christmas Present

Directives

Compound and complex directives of two to five steps (3½-5 years)

1. Holiday association
   Place a variety of holiday items on the floor. Children interact with items as described in the directive.

   Pick up the round thing you use to make a jack-o'-lantern face on Halloween.

   Find what people call a horn of plenty, and put it in the middle of the table.

   Get what you find under a tree on Christmas.

   Cut out the shape that makes a valentine.

   Find what you dye pretty colors for Easter.

Hold up the symbol of our country.

Get what you put treats in on Halloween.

Find what our Indian friends wore on their head on the first Thanksgiving.

Get what you put on top of a Christmas tree.

Put the valentine inside what you would use to mail it.

Find what eggs and candy are carried in at Easter.

Pick up what is always played in a parade.

Get what trick or treaters wear on their face on Halloween.

Find what covers the big bird that later will be our Thanksgiving dinner.

Look for the long things that hang on our mantle at Christmas.

Find a heart-shaped candy we eat on Valentine's Day.

Get the toy children sometimes are given on Easter.

Find something that has stars and stripes on it.

2. Conditional cloze game

Children listen to the condition and cloze with the holiday it describes.

If you are working with a knife, spoon, and pumpkin, then it is _____ . (*Halloween*)

When Mama is cooking turkey and making pumpkin pie, it may be _____ . (*Thanksgiving*)

If you have red paper and green ribbon, you may be wrapping presents for _____ . (*Christmas*)

When Mama makes cookies that look like red hearts, it is probably _____ . (*Valentine's Day*)

If Daddy helps you dye eggs yellow and blue and pink, it may be near _____ . (*Easter*)

If you are eating ice cream and watching a parade, it may be _____ . (*the Fourth of July*)

If Mama helps you dress up like a black cat, you could be getting ready for _____ . (*Halloween*)

If your teacher reads a story about Pilgrims and Indians, it may be close to _____ . (*Thanksgiving*)

When Daddy puts up a fir tree in the living room, you are getting ready for _____ . (*Christmas*)

If a friend gives you a card that says "I love you," it may be _____ . (*Valentine's Day*)

If you go to a party to hunt eggs, it may be a party for _____ . (*Easter*)

When people watch fireworks at a picnic, it may be a party for _____ . (*the Fourth of July*)

3. Object movement directives
   Gather a trick-or-treat bag, feather, Christmas present, valentine cookie cutter, toy egg, and drum. Children move the holiday-related items in relation to the holiday pictures.

   Put all the Halloween pictures in the trick-or-treat bag.

   Put the feather on the picture of the turkey.

   Put the present beside the picture of the Christmas tree.

   Put the Easter egg on the picture of the Easter bunny.

   Hit the drums with the drumsticks three times.

   Put the cookie cutter on the picture of valentines.

   Take out of the bag all the Halloween pictures except the one of a pumpkin.

   Put the feather on the top of the picture of an Indian.

   Place the present under the picture of Christmas stockings.

   Put the cookie cutter under the picture of a mailman.

   Roll the egg over to the basket picture.

   Put the drum on top of all the Fourth of July pictures except the one of the flag.

4. Sensory holiday attributes
   Display the *ENABLE* holiday posters. Children listen to the description of a sensory attribute, touch the appropriate holiday picture, and name the holiday at which the attribute may be enjoyed.

   Touch the holiday when you could smell tart apples and taste sweet candy.

   Find the holiday when you could hear vegetables being chopped up and smell spicy pie.

   Look for the holiday where you could smell and touch the sharp pine needles.

   Show me the holiday where you could cut and color cards for people you love.

   Find the holiday when you could smell and taste cookies shaped like pink bunnies and yellow chicks.

   Touch the holiday when you could see brightly colored firecrackers exploding in the night sky.

   Find the holiday when you feel the brisk, dark air and see lighted pumpkin faces.

   Get the holiday when you can smell turkey and dressing.

   Find the holiday when you see snow on the ground and hear carols being sung.

   Touch the holiday when a heart gift means love.

   Get the holiday where baskets hold candy and colored eggs.

   Find the holiday when you can smell hot dogs cooking and hear "The Star Spangled Banner."

Questions

1. Reasoning questions—Function (3-5 years)
   Use relevant objects or pictures.

   a. Level 1 (3-4 years)

   What do you do with:
       a pumpkin at Halloween?
       a turkey at Thanksgiving?
       a present at Christmas?
       a heart on Valentine's Day?
       a basket at Easter?
       a drum at Fourth of July?

   b. Level 2 (4-5 years)

   Why do we have:
       trick-or-treat bags?
       Thanksgiving dinner?
       Christmas trees?
       envelopes?
       dye?
       our flag?

2. Reasoning questions—Situational/Adaptive (3-6 years)

   a. Level 1 (3-4½ years)

   What do you say to people on Halloween?

   What do we eat on Thanksgiving?

   What do we give people at Christmas?

   What do we give people on Valentine's Day?

   What do we dye on Easter?

   What do we hold up high on the Fourth of July?

   b. Level 2 (4½-6 years)

   What do you do to hide your face on Halloween?

   What do we give thanks for at Thanksgiving?

   What do you do to decorate your house at Christmas?

   What do you do to send valentines to people?

   What do we hunt on Easter?

   What do we celebrate on the Fourth of July?

3. Reasoning questions—How (3-4 years)
   Use materials, pictures, and experiences.

   a. Level 1—Manner (3-4 years)

   How does:
       bobbing for apples feel?
       pumpkin pie taste?
       a lighted Christmas tree look?
       a valentine look?
       Easter candy smell?

   How do fireworks sound?

b. Level 2—Method/Ordered sequence (4-5 years)

How do you:
    cut out a jack-o'-lantern?
    set the table at Thanksgiving?
    decorate a Christmas tree?
    make a valentine?
    make up an Easter basket?
    get ready for a Fourth of July picnic?

c. Level 3—Degree/Quantity (4-6 years)

How many ways can you dress up for Halloween?
How many pies should you have at Thanksgiving?
How big is the Christmas tree?
How many valentines can you make?
How many colors can you dye your eggs?
How many stripes are on the flag?

d. Level 4—Cause (4½-5 years)

How do you make scary sounds on Halloween?
How do you make a cornucopia?
How do you make Christmas bright?
How do you make someone happy on Valentine's Day?
How do you decorate Easter eggs?
How do you cut a Fourth of July watermelon?

4. Time-based questions (5-6 years)

When (in what month) is Halloween?
When (in what month) is Thanksgiving?
When (in what month) is Christmas?
When (in what month) is Valentine's Day?
When (in what month) is Easter?
When (in what month) is the Fourth of July?

Narratives

Halloween Fun

It was Halloween.

"I have a *good* idea!" said Mama to Amy. "Let's dress Baby Bobby like a black cat. You'll be dressed as a witch, and he can go trick-or-treating with you!"

"OK!" said Amy. "That will be fun. Do you have a trick-or-treat bag for him to carry?"

"Here it is!" said Mama. "Help me dress Bobby and paint his face."

Bobby giggled and laughed as Mama and Amy dressed him in a black suit and painted whiskers under his nose.

"Say 'trick-or-treat,' Bobby!" said Amy.

"T'i-or-t'ee!" the little boy said.

Amy took Baby Bobby out on his first Halloween night. They went to all the houses on the block. At every one, Bobby held out his bag and said, "T'i-or-t'ee!"

And at every house, people smiled and said, "What a cute little cat! Here's a treat for you!"

Amy was so proud of her baby brother! And Bobby's mama had a very sticky smile to wash that night!

> What was Mama's good idea?
> Where did Mama and Amy paint Bobby's whiskers?
> Why did everybody smile at Baby Bobby?
> How did the children feel about their Halloween?

Dyeing Easter Eggs

Mrs. Hanna's class was dyeing Easter eggs. Each child had three eggs to dye.

First, the children prepared the bowls of dye. They mixed vinegar, hot water, and the dye tablets. Then they stirred the mixture.

Some children drew pictures on the eggs with a wax crayon. Then they dipped the boiled eggs in the bowls of colored water.

Soon, piles of pink, yellow, blue, purple, green, and orange eggs lay drying on a newspaper.

Some of the children punched out paper hats, faces, hands, and feet and glued them on the eggs.

The children had a good time. "We're all ready for the Easter egg hunt now!" they said, as they started to clean up the messy table.

How many eggs did each child have?
How did some children draw pictures on the eggs?
How did other children decorate the eggs?
What did the children have to do before the Easter Egg hunt?

The Special Christmas Present

Nathan had a special friend who lived across the street from him. Her name was Mrs. Lewis, and she was an old lady with no family of her own.

Nathan liked to visit Mrs. Lewis. In the Summer, they would swing on her porch and drink lemonade. In the Winter, they would rock in front of her fireplace and play with her parakeet together.

One Christmas, Nathan wanted to give his friend a special present. He wanted to buy it himself.

"Can I do some jobs to earn some money, Mama?" asked Nathan.

Nathan's mom smiled and hugged him. She let Nathan carry out the trash, sweep the kitchen floor, and unload the dishwasher. Nathan saved his money every day for two weeks.

Finally, Nathan's daddy took him shopping. They walked all over the mall, but Nathan couldn't find exactly the right present to give to Mrs. Lewis.

Finally, Nathan's eyes lit up. "This is it! This is my present!" Nathan said, and he picked up a beautiful, soft, red wool shawl.

"Mrs. Lewis will look so-o pretty in this!" Nathan sighed happily.

The next day was Christmas Eve. Nathan walked across the street, carrying the big present. He knocked on Mrs. Lewis's door.

When Mrs. Lewis opened the present, she was so surprised. "Why, Nathan, how *lovely*!"

"I bought it 'specially for you!" smiled Nathan. " 'Cause I love you!"

Tears came to Mrs. Lewis's eyes. "This is the most wonderful Christmas I've ever had!" she said, and she hugged Nathan as hard as she could.

Why did Nathan want to save his money?
How did he earn money?
How did Mrs. Lewis and Nathan feel about each other?
When did Nathan give Mrs. Lewis her present?

Weather

This unit provides activities to develop understanding of the six most common weather terms: sunny, rainy, cloudy, windy, hot, and cold. Experiences with the actual weather condition will facilitate comprehension of each weather concept. It will be helpful to collect a variety of pictures that illustrate the weather.

A flannel board poster is provided for each weather concept:
- 113. Sunny
- 114. Rainy
- 115. Cloudy
- 116. Windy
- 117. Hot
- 118. Cold

Situational pictures illustrate two of the narratives:
- 119. Winter and the Birds
- 120. A Hot Summer Day

Directives

Compound and complex directives of two to five steps (3½-5 years)

1. Weather association

    Display the *ENABLE* weather posters. Children sit in a circle, with a pile of objects and clothing relevant to each concept (such as a swimming suit, fan, glass of ice, muffler, raincoat, gloves, umbrella, blanket, sweater, kite, balloon, weather thermometer, coat, rainboots, snowboots, snow shovel, sand shovel and pail, empty package of hot chocolate). Directives require children to make an association between the weather concept and an object.

    > Put the swimming suit between the pictures of hot and sunny weather.

    > Find something you wear for rainy weather, and put it beside the picture of cloudy weather.

    > Gather two things that are fun to play with during windy weather, and put the picture of wind on top of them.

    > Hold the umbrella near the picture of rainy weather, and open and close it.

    > Get the picture of cold weather, and put on everything you would need to play outside.

Stand by the picture of hot weather, take off the winter clothing fast, and turn on the fan.

Put the snow shovel by the picture of cold weather, and put the sand shovel and pail by the picture of hot weather.

Jump around a picture of the kind of weather you need to play outside.

Put the rainboots near the picture of weather you see before you have thunder and lightning.

Put the glass of ice in the middle of the picture of hot weather.

Lay the long thing that tells how hot or cold it is near the pictures of hot and cold weather.

Point to the type of weather where fluffy white and gray things hide the sun.

Point to a machine that makes the air feel like windy weather.

Wrap a blanket around you and hold the picture of cold weather.

2. Conditional directives
   Use the weather posters again. Children perform body movements according to conditional directives.

   Pick up what we should carry if it's cloudy and we are walking to the store.

   Hold up what will go up high in the sky if the weather is windy.

   Get what we can drink to warm up when the weather is cold.

   Show me what Daddy could use if there were snow all over our sidewalk.

   If it was raining, point to everything we'd need to go outside.

   If the red mark is down at the bottom of the thermometer, point to what we would wear.

   If the red mark is near the top of the thermometer, point to what we would wear.

   If you heard thunder, point to a picture of what you would see in the sky.

   If cloudy goes with rainy and snow goes with cold weather, put the weather picture that goes with hot beside it.

3. Typical weather directives
   These directives are regularly given by parents and teachers during specific weather conditions.

   Hot, Sunny

   Play in the shade so you won't get too hot.

   Come inside when the sun is overhead.

   Don't walk barefoot on the hot concrete.

   Don't stay in the sunshine too long.

   Wear a hat (or sunglasses) when you play in the sun.

   After you've played outside a while, come in and get a drink.

Cloudy, Rainy

Take your umbrella in case it rains.

Come inside if you hear thunder.

Look at the clouds covering the sun.

Put on your raincoat and rainboots and put your hood over your head.

Look out the window at the rain and lightning.

Don't play outside if you hear thunder and see lightning.

Windy

Look at the branches swaying and hear the sound the wind makes.

Put on a sweater if the wind is cold.

Feel the cool wind on your face.

Watch your balloon blow in the wind.

Cold

Dress warmly before you go out.

Don't play in the cold too long.

Come inside if your gloves get wet with the snow.

Rub your hands when they get cold.

Put on two pairs of socks before you put on your boots.

Questions

1. Reasoning questions—Function (3-5 years)
   a. Level 1 (3-4 years)

   What do you do with:
   kites?
   ice?
   sunglasses?
   umbrellas?
   gloves?
   raincoats?

   b. Level 2 (4-5 years)

   Why do we have:
   sweaters?
   fans?
   sun lotion?
   rainboots?
   mufflers?
   thermometers?

2. Reasoning questions—Situational/Adaptive (3-6 years)
   a. Level 1 (3-4½ years)
      What do you use to:
         keep dry?
         cool off?
         play in the wind?
         keep warm?
         keep sun out of your eyes?

   b. Level 2 (4½-6 years)
      What would you do if:
         it was cloudy and you heard thunder?
         it was warm and very windy?
         snow got inside your boots?
         you didn't want to get a sunburn?
         you got too hot playing outside?
         the wind started to blow and dark clouds covered the sun?

3. Reasoning questions—How (3-6 years)
   Use real weather situations.
   a. Level 1—Manner (3-4 years)
      How does:
         rain feel?
         wind sound?
         snow feel?
         sun look?
      How do clouds look?

   b. Level 2—Method/Ordered sequence (4-5 years)
      How do you:
         get ready to play in the sun?
         get ready to go outside in the rain?
         fly a kite when it is windy?

   c. Level 3—Degree/Quantity (4-6 years)
      How many things do you wear when it's cold?
      How many things do you wear when it rains?

   d. Level 4—Cause (4½-5 years)
      How does it rain?
      How can we get warm after playing in the cold?

4. Time-based questions (5-6 years)
      When:
         does it rain?
         is it the coldest time of year?
         is it the hottest time of year?

Narratives

Winter and the Birds

All night long it had snowed. Now the sun was shining, but it was *very* cold outside.

"The birds will be hungry!" Aunt Iva told Sherman and Stacey. "We have to help them find food or they will die!"

"Oh, no! What can we do?" the children asked their aunt.

Aunt Iva took out a board. She spread peanut butter on it and sprinkled bird seed and crumpled graham crackers on top. Then she said to the children, "Now let's break some leftover breakfast toast into a bowl."

They put the food out in the middle of the back yard.

All day, Aunt Iva, Sherman, and Stacey were happy. They watched the hungry birds eat the food they had put out in the cold for them.

"We did a good deed today!" said Aunt Iva. "Does that make you feel happy?"

"YES!" answered the children.

How was the weather?
Why did Aunt Iva want to feed the birds?
How did they make food for the birds?
How did they feel about helping the birds?

A Hot Summer Day

It was the middle of the summer. Outside, the sun was shining brightly, and it was a very hot morning.

"What a good day to go swimming!" said Mikey.

He and his mom packed a bag and drove to the swimming pool.

When they got there, Mikey was ready to run jump in the water.

"Wait!" said Mom. "I have to put sun lotion on you so you won't get a sunburn. *Then* you have to put on your water wings so you will be safe in the water."

Mikey sighed, but he put on the water wings and let Mom put on the lotion. Then he jumped in the water and began to splash happily about. Mom swam for a while, too.

Soon the sun was high in the sky and *very* hot. "Now we have to go home and rest, Mikey!" called Mom.

Mikey did not want to go. He grumbled all the way home. But he was so tired from the heat and the water exercise that he almost fell asleep at the lunch table. He barely had time to stretch out on his bed before he was fast asleep.

Mom smiled as she softly kissed Mikey. "I think *I'll* take a nap, too," she said, yawning.

    When did Mikey and his mom go swimming?
    Why did she want him to wear sun lotion?
    Why did she want him to wear water wings?
    How did Mikey feel about going home to rest?
    Why do you think Mikey and Mom were so tired?

A Sudden Storm

Sharon and Ann were playing outside. They were having fun riding their tricycles up and down the sidewalk. All of a sudden, some leaves blew up in Ann's face.

"It is getting windy!" she said to Sharon.

"Yes," said Sharon, "and look at all those big black clouds!"

"Where did the sun go?" asked Ann, with surprise.

"The clouds covered it up," answered Sharon. "I think it might rain!"

Ka-BOOM! The girls jumped, scared by the sudden sound of thunder.

"Let's go inside now!" Both girls rode their tricycles into the garage and ran inside the house.

"Oh, good, girls!" said Mom. "I'm glad you came in. I think we're going to have a storm!"

About that time, the girls heard the rain beginning to pelt the roof. They stood at the living room window and watched the storm, and they heard thunder. A couple of times, they saw streaks of lightning.

"I like to watch rainstorms when we're inside, but I don't like to be outside in them!" said Sharon.

"Me, too!" said Ann.

    How did Sharon know it was getting ready to rain?
    Why did the girls go inside?
    Where did they stand to watch the storm?
    How did they like the storm?

Friends

Learning to be a social being—one of a group—is an important responsibility of the preschooler. This unit focuses on aspects of learning to behave so that peers and adults want to be a friend. A variety of pictures can help children in generalizing these concepts. Flannel board posters are provided for these concepts:

121. Sharing
122. Cooperating
123. Helping
124. Being considerate

Use these situational pictures to illustrate two of the narratives:

125. Learning to Work Together
126. Learning to Be a Friend

Directives

Compound and complex directives of two to five steps (3½-5 years)

1. Social considerations

   Display the four *ENABLE* Friends posters along with a variety of pictures that illustrate sharing, cooperating, helping, and being considerate. Children respond to directives.

   Point to the boy sharing his food with a friend.

   Show us the girls cooperating to make a wall picture.

   Touch the picture of the boy helping his teacher get ready for snack time.

   Find the boy being considerate to the little hurt child.

   Find a picture of helping, and put it next to a picture of being considerate.

   Get the picture of the child helping the grown-up, and give it to the teacher.

   Find three pictures of children sharing either food or toys, and put them in a row.

   Get two pictures of children cooperating, and put one at either end of the "sharing" picture row.

   Point to children trying to be friends in the first three pictures on the bottom row.

   Point to considerate children, and put the pictures in the last place on the top row.

271

Show me a picture of a child being considerate to a grown-up.

Get a picture of a grown-up being considerate to a child, and put it with the last picture.

2. Conditional directives

Children listen to the condition and cloze with an appropriate action.

Being Considerate

If you are chewing gum and a friend walks by, *give him a piece of gum.*

If the library lady is carrying lots of books, *help her carry some of the books.*

When your sister runs out of toothpaste, *share yours with her.*

If a friend drops his cookie, *give him a piece of yours.*

Cooperating

If your friend wants to build a town with blocks, *share your blocks and help him.*

If you and your friend want to paint a picture, *let her choose the paint.*

If Mama wants to set the table, *offer to help her.*

When a friend wants to play hide and seek, *let him hide first.*

Sharing

If your friends are hungry and you have cookies, *give them some.*

If your friend wants to look at your book, *give her a turn.*

When friends are visiting, *let them play with your toys.*

If a friend has no toys, *share yours with him.*

Helping

If Daddy wants to wash his car, *help him wash it.*

When Mama is trying to cook and Baby Sister is crying, *play with Baby.*

If Teacher needs a book on her desk, *go get it for her.*

3. Ways To Be Friends

During the routine of the day, give typical directives that call children's attention to concepts of "friendliness."

Help your neighbor put away the toys.

Share the crayons with your friends.

Be considerate and let your friend have a turn on the tricycle.

Cooperate with your friend to play the piano.

Help Mama put the clean clothes in the bedroom.

Share your chips with your sister.

Be considerate and turn the TV volume down.

Help teacher collect the lunch money.

Share your story with the class.

Be considerate and let someone else be first.

Cooperate and follow the rules of the game.

Questions

1. Reasoning questions—Function (3-5 years)
   a. Level 1 (3-4 years)

   What do you do with:
   - games?
   - snacks?
   - bandages?
   - toys?

   b. Level 2 (4-5 years)

   Why do we:
   - help people?
   - share toys?
   - cooperate in a game?
   - take turns?

2. Reasoning questions—Situational/Adaptive (3-6 years)
   a. Level 1 (3-4½ years)

   What do you do to:
   - help Mama clean up?
   - cooperate with a friend?
   - be considerate at school?
   - share snacks?

   b. Level 2 (4½-6 years)

   What would you do if:
   - a friend lost his gloves?
   - Mama was tired?
   - Teacher needed some help?
   - your friend won a game?

3. Reasoning questions—How (3-6 years)
   a. Level 1—Manner (3-4 years)

   How does:
   - a smile look?
   - it feel to have a friend who shares?
   - it feel to have someone help you finish a job?

   b. Level 2—Method/Ordered sequence (4-5 years)

   How can you:
   - be considerate of a friend with a skinned knee?
   - help Teacher get ready for a snack?
   - cooperate with teacher in doing your work?

   c. Level 3—Degree/Quantity (4-6 years)
   Explain while counting on fingers.

   How many ways can you help Mama?

   How many ways can you cooperate with Teacher?

   How many ways can you be considerate of friends?

d. Level 4—Cause (4½-5 years)

How can you make a friend happy?

How can you make grown-ups proud of you?

Narratives

A Sick Friend

Reesa was a little girl in Mrs. Jenkins's kindergarten class. One day she was not at school.

"Reesa had to have her tonsils taken out," Mrs. Jenkins told the class. "It will take a few days for her to get well."

"Let's make her a present," said Lyndon.

"What a considerate thing to do!" said Mrs. Jenkins.

The children decided to draw Reesa a big card and to have an ice cream cake sent to her. Mrs. Jenkins said, "Ice cream is good for a child with a sore throat."

When Reesa came back to school, she was so happy. She hugged all her friends and her teacher.

"Your present made me feel so happy!" she told them. "You are sweet friends."

What happened to Reesa?
How did the children try to be considerate?
What did they send Reesa?
How would you feel if your friends did this for you?

Learning to Work Together

It was almost Christmas. Mrs. Ryals and her class decided to have a Christmas program for their parents.

"We'll have to cooperate," said Mrs. Ryals.

"What does that mean?" asked the children.

"That means we'll all have to work together and each do our own part."

So that's what the children did. Several of the children painted boxes and boards to decorate the stage. Some children sang, and others dressed up to play a part. Some played angels, and others played shepherds.

The program was held the day before Christmas holidays began. All the parents and friends of the children came to see it.

It was a wonderful program. Every child did his or her part!

The parents were proud. The teacher was proud. But most of all, the children were proud of themselves.

Friends help each other and cooperate!

> When did the children decide to have a program?
> What does cooperating mean?
> How did the children cooperate?
> What happened because they cooperated?

Learning to Be a Friend

Tal was an unhappy little boy. He had no friends. It was no fun to play alone.

Tal went to his teacher. "I'm sad," he said. "Nobody likes me. I want some friends."

Teacher said, "To have a friend, you have to *be* a friend. Children don't like to play with children who won't share their toys or who always have to be first. Try playing with whatever the others are playing with."

Tal went over to the play corner. Two boys were playing with the blocks.

"Can I play?" he asked.

"Sure!" one boy answered. "We're building a town and a road. Can you build a house here?"

"I can!" Tal said, and he started to work.

The children worked quietly for a while. Soon they were finished.

"What a beautiful town and road!" said Teacher.

"Thanks for helping, Tal!" said one of the boys. "Want to swing now?"

Tal nodded happily. It was so much fun to cooperate and play together! He was learning how to be a friend.

> Why was Tal unhappy?
> How did Teacher help him?
> How did Tal try to get some friends?
> What happened at the end?

Ball Games

Ball games are one of the earliest forms of competition experienced in childhood. Most preschoolers are provided with activities to develop their object movement skills through rolling, throwing, catching, kicking, and bouncing balls. Teachers realize these activities strengthen the children's gross and fine motor proficiency. Competition is seldom a part of these early activities. But as children develop more social and motor competence, competition is introduced and children learn to apply these object movement skills in games that have rules.

This unit's activities are organized around four of the more popular ball games: football, basketball, soccer, and bowling. It is helpful and fun to gather and have available some of the game paraphernalia, such as a football, football helmet, pads, cleats, a numbered jersey, and pictures of the football field and goal posts; a basketball, commercial or teacher-made hoop, sneakers, picture of a basketball court; a soccer ball, knee pads, and pictures of a goalie and soccer net; a bowling ball and bowling pins, bowling shoes, a score pad, and pictures of a bowling alley.

A flannel board poster is provided to illustrate each game:
    127. Football
    128. Basketball
    129. Soccer
    130. Bowling

These situational pictures illustrate two of the narratives:
    131. Doren and the Soccer Game
    132. Playing Basketball and Learning to Count

Directives

Compound and complex directives of two to five steps (3½-5 years)

1. Game association
   Prepare a "set-up" situation for each game: miniature version of goalposts, basketball hoop, soccer net, and ten bowling pins. Place a sack with balls and related materials in front of a line of children. Children respond to directives.

   Find the brown pointed ball, put it in front of the goal posts, and try to kick it over them.

   Bounce the basketball as you turn all the way around, and then throw it in the basket.

Get the ball that you cannot use your hands to move, and kick it toward the net.

Pick up the bowling ball, walk forward, and roll it hard to knock over the pins.

Get the football cleats and the football jersey, and put them on the bottom and top of your body.

Bounce the basketball to your neighbor and catch it when she bounces it back.

Have your friend bounce the soccer ball to you, and try to bat it back with your knee or elbow.

Swing the bowling ball back and forth a couple of times, then roll it across the floor.

Turn around and throw the football over everyone's head to the person at the end of the line.

Throw the basketball three times at the basket, and then give it to the next child in line.

Kick the soccer ball sideways down the line from child to child.

Roll the bowling ball one time to try to knock down the pins on the left side, then roll it toward the pins on the right side.

2. Conditional directives
   Use the same set-up as above.

   If you want to play football, put on the jersey, helmet, and cleats.

   When you play football, kick the ball over the goal post.

   Show me a picture of where you play if you are playing basketball.

   Put on what you wear when you play basketball.

   Point to where you would stand if you were the soccer goalie.

   Show me where you would keep score if you were bowling.

   Show me which ball you would need if you were playing a game that only lets you roll the ball.

   Find the ball you need if you are playing the ball game that does not let you use your hands to move the ball.

   Get the ball you move if you are trying to make a touchdown.

   If you have the heaviest ball, then roll it toward the pins.

   If you have the lightest ball, kick it with your toes toward the net.

   If you have the ball that is not round, throw it as far as you can.

3. Ball game rules
   Use the *ENABLE* ball game posters, balls, and other relevant materials.

   Find the picture of a grassy field with lines across it and goal posts at each end.

   Point to the place on a football field where you carry the ball to make a touchdown.

   Find the place on a football field where you kick the ball to get "extra" points.

   Find a picture of the place where basketball players "slam-dunk" the ball.

Point to the place where basketball players get "out of bounds."

Find a picture of the person who can use hands to stop a soccer ball.

Put the soccer ball where it has to stop to get a point.

Point to the "X" mark you get when you knock over all the bowling pins to get a strike.

Put the basketball under the hoop and the football between the goal posts.

Roll the bowling ball toward the middle of the pins.

Get what you wear to keep from hurting your knees in a soccer game.

Bounce the basketball as many times as you can.

Questions

1. Reasoning questions—Function (3-5 years)
   a. Level 1 (3-4 years)

   What do you do with:
   - a football?
   - a soccer ball?
   - a basketball?
   - a bowling ball?

   b. Level 2 (4-5 years)

   Why do we have:
   - goal posts in football?
   - bowling pins?
   - an end zone in football?
   - points?
   - football helmets?
   - score pads?
   - a basketball hoop?
   - a soccer net?
   - game boundaries?
   - a soccer goalie?

2. Reasoning questions—Situational/Adaptive (3-6 years)
   a. Level 1 (3-4½ years)

   What do you do to:
   - make a touchdown?
   - get points in basketball?
   - win a soccer game?
   - get a strike when bowling?

   b. Level 2 (4½-6 years)

   What would you do if:
   - you didn't want to get hurt playing football?
   - you wanted to give the basketball to another player?
   - the soccer ball was coming toward you?
   - your bowling ball was too heavy?

3. Reasoning questions—How (3-6 years)
   These are best asked while watching an actual or televised game.
   a. Level 1—Manner (3-4 years)
      How does:
         a bowling ball feel?
         a bouncing basketball sound?
         a football move?
         winning a ball game feel?

   b. Level 2—Method/Ordered sequence (4-5 years)
      How do you:
         dress for a football game?
         get points in a football game?
      How can you:
         keep the other team from winning in basketball?
         get to roll the ball again when bowling?

   c. Level 3—Degree/Quantity (4-6 years)
      How many points do you get for a touchdown?
      How many points do you get for a basket throw?
      How many points do you get for a bowling strike?
      How many points do you get for a soccer goal?

   d. Level 4—Cause (4½-5 years)
      How do you move:
         a football?
         a soccer ball?
         a basketball?
         a bowling ball?

4. Time-based questions (5-6 years)
      When (at what time of year) do people:
         play football?
         play basketball?
         play soccer?

Narratives

Going Bowling

"Do you know what I'd like to do tonight?" asked Daddy.

"What?" said Mama.

"Let's go bowling!" And so they did. Monica and Aaron had never gone bowling before. It was their very first time!

When they reached the bowling alley, Daddy rented shoes for everyone. Then they went to a bowling lane, and they each picked a bowling ball.

"These are heavy!" said Monica.

"They have to be heavy to knock down those pins. I'll buy French fries for the first person to knock down all the pins!"

The family bowled and bowled, but everybody kept knocking down only three or four pins.

Finally, in the last frame of the game, Aaron knocked down all the pins!

"Where are my French fries?" he asked.

"I tell you what! Let's *all* get hamburgers and French fries, and then we'll play another game. Aaron, you get the biggest bunch of fries!"

"*That* sounds like a winner!" said Mama and the children.

> Where did the family go?
> What did Daddy promise for knocking over all the pins?
> Do you think the family were good bowlers? Why?
> What did Mama think about Daddy's last idea?

Doren and the Soccer Game

Doren was a little boy who loved to play ball. One Christmas, he got a soccer ball.

His big brother taught him how to move the ball without using his hands. Doren practiced and practiced, and he became very good at kicking the ball with his feet and striking it with his knees, shoulders, and head.

Soon Doren joined a soccer team. He was so proud of his soccer uniform!

After the first practice, Doren's coach told his daddy, "This little boy does his best when he plays soccer."

That Saturday was the first soccer game. The whole family came to watch.

Doren played so hard! He ran hard and kicked hard, but the other team was ahead.

Then, near the end of the game, the soccer ball moved in front of Doren. As hard as he could, he kicked that ball right into the net!

Yea! The team got a point!

Soon they scored again, and they won the game!

Who do you think was the proudest family that day?

> When did Doren start to play soccer?
> How did he get to be good at the game?
> How did Doren play during his first team game?
> What happened at the end of the game?

Playing Basketball and Learning to Count

Mrs. Stephens's kindergarten class was learning about numerals and sets. Every day the class counted things and found the numeral for how many they counted.

One Friday, Mrs. Stephens said, "Who likes to play basketball?"

Everyone in the class answered, "I do!"

"Today," she said, "we will do our number lesson and play basketball at the same time!"

Mrs. Stephens took her class into the gym and onto the basketball court. The coach lowered the basket hoop for the children, and he pulled over a big drum full of basketballs.

"This is how we will play the game," said Mrs. Stephens. "Two children at a time will dribble the ball (that means bounce the ball with one hand) as many times as they can. We will count how many times they dribble. Then we will mark on paper each one's score," she said.

"Next, each child will try to throw the basketball into the hoop five times. We will write down how many times each person gets the ball in the basket."

The children had so much fun playing this game. "This is a *lot* more fun than doing numbers in class!" they said.

And when the game was over, Mrs. Stephens had *another* surprise—popcorn and grape juice for the whole class!

"This is the *best* Friday we've ever had!" said the children.

> How was the class learning about numerals?
> What happened on Friday?
> Why were they counting dribbles?
> How did they feel about the game and the surprise?

Music

Activities in this unit are organized around musical instruments commonly used as part of rhythm bands in early childhood settings. Teachers are encouraged to use the actual instruments in these activities. Flannel board posters are provided that illustrate:

133. Things You Strike (drums, triangles, cymbals, rhythm sticks)
134. Things You Shake (bells, castanets, rattles)
135. Things You Blow (horns, flutes, kazoos)

Situational pictures illustrate two of the narratives:

136. The Homemade Band
137. Baby's First Parade

Directives

Compound and complex directives of two to five steps (3½-5 years)

1. Instrument function

    Children are seated in a circle, with instruments lying on a blanket in the center. Teacher gives each child a directive concerning an instrument or instruments.

    Get two instruments that you strike with sticks, and hit them together once.

    Find the horn with three buttons, and blow it loudly.

    Get the metal thing you shake, shake it softly, then put it back on the blanket.

    Find the round metal things you strike together, and play them three times.

    Get the rhythm sticks, and hit them together very fast at first and then more slowly.

    Find all three shaking instruments, and shake two of them at the same time.

    Hit the drum, then blow the horn, then shake the castanet; and last, blow the kazoo.

    Count the instruments you play by striking, and play the one that is a kind of shape that is not round.

    Get the instrument babies like, and shake it slowly.

    Blow the horn with the softest sound, and then blow the loudest horn.

Ring the bells, strike the cymbals together, and shake the rattle.

Get all the horns, give each one to a child; and everyone, blow them all at the same time.

2. Conditional directives

Use the same set-up as above.

If you want to play drums, get both drumsticks.

When you blow a horn, hold it tightly against your mouth.

If you want to sing "Jingle Bells," get the bells.

If you want to dance a Mexican dance, use the castanets.

If you want to have a parade, get the horns, drums, and cymbals.

When you want to play soft music, get the triangles and flutes.

When you want to play loud music, get the rhythm sticks, drums, cymbals, and rattles.

If you want to have a band, give every child one instrument.

Play your instrument when the teacher points at you.

If you want to sound funny, play the kazoo, rattle, and rhythm sticks.

3. Matching rhythms and sound levels

Give each child an instrument. Play an instrument according to a certain rhythm or sound level, and give each child a chance to imitate. (You may prefer to use a drum or cymbal.) Suggested rhythms and sound levels include:

Slow, slow, fast, fast

Fast, slow, slow, fast, fast

Soft, soft, loud

Loud, soft, loud, soft

Loud, loud, soft, soft, soft

Fast, fast, fast, slow, slow

Slow, fast, fast, slow

Slow, fast, fast, slow, slow

Loud, soft, soft, loud, loud

Soft, soft, loud, soft, loud

Slow, fast, slow, fast, slow, slow

Fast, fast, slow, slow, fast, fast

Questions

1. Reasoning questions—Function (3-5 years)
   a. Level 1 (3-4 years)

      What do you do with: drums?

      bells?

      horns?

      cymbals?

   b. Level 2 (4-5 years)

      Why do we have: bands?

      drumsticks?

      musical instruments?

2. Reasoning questions—Situational/Adaptive (3-6 years)
   a. Level 1 (3-4½ years)

      What do you do to: play cymbals loudly?

      make a horn sound?

      make a bell sound?

   b. Level 2 (4½-6 years)

      What would you do if:

      you were playing the rhythm sticks too fast?

      you wanted to know when it was your turn to play?

3. Reasoning questions—How (3-6 years)
   Use instruments and experiences.
   a. Level 1—Manner (3-4 years)

      How does a cymbal look?

      How do: triangles feel?

      castanets sound?

      castanets feel?

      kazoos sound?

      flutes sound?

   b. Level 2—Method/Ordered sequence (4-5 years)

      How do you: play in a band?

      blow a horn (cornet)?

   c. Level 3—Degree/Quantity (4-6 years)

      How many instruments do you strike?

      How many instruments do you shake?

      How many instruments do you blow?

   d. Level 4—Cause (4½-5 years)

      How do you play together?

4. Time-based questions (5-6 years)

   When: do you play the cymbal?

   do you play soft music?

   do you march and play at the same time?

Narratives

The Homemade Band

One day Mrs. Abbott told her preschool class, "We need a band. Let's make some musical instruments."

"How?" asked the class.

So Mrs. Abbott showed them how.

She gave one group some old coffee cans and dowel rods. She showed them how to put a round piece of rubber sheet over each end of the can and hold it on with tight rubber bands. They made drums!

Another group filled plastic bottles and wooden match boxes with pebbles, beans, and sand. They made rattles!

The third group folded wax paper over the teeth of a comb and attached it with rubber bands. They made kazoos!

Then the last group made sand blocks with blocks of wood and sandpaper!

When the instruments were made, Mrs. Abbott put on a record and the children played their instruments.

What happy music they made together!

> Where did Mrs. Abbott say the class would get instruments?
> How did they make drums?
> How did they make kazoos?
> When did they play their instruments?

Baby's First Parade

Albert was a little baby whose favorite toy was his drum. His big brother, Harvey, played a drum in a band.

One day Harvey said to Mama, "Our band is having a parade Saturday. Why don't you bring Albert to see it and hear us play?"

"What a good idea!" said Mama.

On Saturday, she dressed Baby Albert warmly and gave him his little drum and drumstick. They drove downtown, parked their car, and waited.

Soon they could hear the sounds of horns and drums. Baby Albert smiled and began to hit his drum happily.

There they came! The band marched by the car, playing loudly.

Albert saw his brother. "Ha'ey! Ha'ey!" he shouted.

"Yes, there goes Harvey!" said Mama.

"Ha'ey d'um! *Me* d'um!" Albert smiled and tried to play his drum like his brother.

Mama smiled and hugged him. "Yes, *you're* a good drummer, too!"

> Why do you think Albert loved the drum?
> Where did Harvey ask Mama to bring the baby?
> How did Albert act when he saw his brother?
> How do you think Mama felt about what the baby did?

Going to the Symphony

Uncle Louis and Aunt Gina were taking Sandra and Linda to hear the symphony. They were so excited! They were going to *really* dress up!

When they came into the big concert hall, the children were amazed.

"There are so many instruments!" said Linda.

"There are so many sounds!" said Sandra, as the orchestra tuned up.

"Wait until you hear them play!" said Aunt Gina.

Soon the orchestra leader came in. He bowed to the audience, turned, and lifted his arms to the orchestra. The orchestra began to play.

They played music so sad, the children almost cried. They played music so happy, they wanted to laugh. It was a wonderful night!

After the symphony was over, Uncle Louis asked, "What did you think?"

"I think music is the most wonderful thing in the world!" said Linda.

"I want to learn to play the violin!" said Sandra.

Uncle Louis laughed. "I think they liked it!" he said to Aunt Gina.

> Where were Linda and Sandra going?
> How did they feel about the concert hall?
> How did the music make them feel?
> Do *you* like music?

TOTAL: Teacher Organized Training for the Acquisition of Language (1983, 1986)
by Beth Witt and Jeanne Boose

Here's a comprehensive language curriculum with lessons and activities for every day of the school year—summer, too. *TOTAL* contains 15 teaching units that train and reinforce a 250-word vocabulary (both verbally and in sign language). This basic, functional core vocabulary is stressed again and again through games, songs, art activities, 175 teaching pictures, 175 full-color teaching photographs, coloring pictures and worksheets, 15 storybooks. Plus, TOTAL Summertime Activities and TOTAL Lesson Plans. Help your preschool and language-delayed children learn the communication skills they need.

Catalog No. 4659-Y $399

GREAT BEGINNINGS FOR EARLY LANGUAGE LEARNING:
Nouns 1
Nouns 2
Concepts
Associations
Verbs
Prepositions

with Language Activity Booklets by Linda Levine (1988)

Great Beginnings is ideal for speech-language clinicians and teachers who need specialized materials for language and speech delayed and developmentally delayed children who are acquiring basic language skills. The complete kit includes a manual featuring a complete description of all the materials in each set, instructional objectives, and important information about early language development for paraprofessionals or offering a quick review for speech-language professionals. Color photographs, pictures, and manipulatives help you use play therapy as well as traditional drill activities to stimulate language acquisition.

Nouns 1 and *Nouns 2* each include 40 color photographs that are sure to appeal to youngsters. Nouns 1 features food and animals, Nouns 2 includes toys and body parts. Each set includes 40 full-color photo cards and activity booklet.

Nouns 1, Catalog No. 2221-Y $24.95
Nouns 2, Catalog No. 2222-Y $24.95

Concepts features 57 color photographs plus more than 35 manipulatives to introduce and reinforce concepts such as colors, singular and plural, big and little, same and different, categorization, prepositions, and associations.

Catalog No. 2223-Y $75

Associations shows 20 nouns in color photographs, two color illustrations, and two black-and-white drawings. Each picture depicts the noun in a slightly different way.

Catalog No. 2225-Y $39.95

Verbs includes 15 actions presented two times—once by a boy and once by a girl. Thirty color photographs introduce pronoun use and teach early verb vocabulary.

Catalog No. 2226-Y $29.95

Prepositions introduces eight early developing prepositions—*in, out, on, off, under, in front of, in back of (behind),* and *next to (beside)*—with 24 color photographs.

Catalog No. 2227-Y $24.95

Order the entire GREAT BEGINNINGS FOR EARLY LANGUAGE LEARNING kit and save! You'll get the set of manipulatives, plus a special instructional manual and storage box.

Catalog No. 2220-Y $199

Communication Skill Builders ®

3830 E. Bellevue/P.O. Box 42050
Tucson, Arizona 85733
(602) 323-7500